W9-AJM-135

MeL

Jewelry Fix-ups

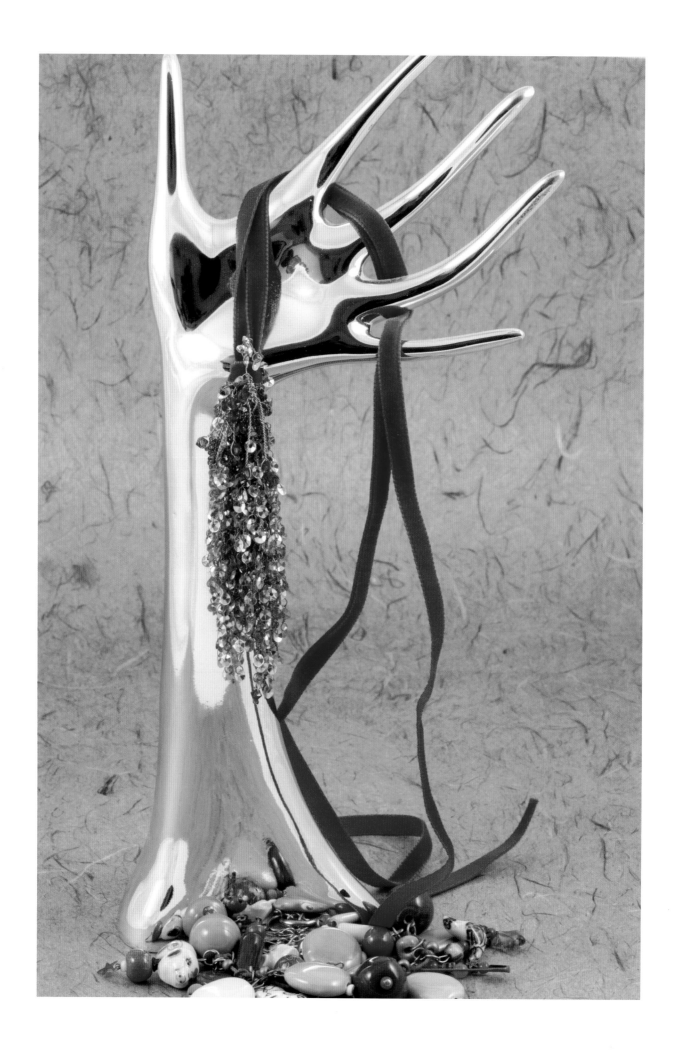

Jewelry Fix-ups

How to clean, repair and restore your jewelry

David McLoughlin

PUBLISHING
www.FoxChapelPublishing.com

For my Mum and Dad

Conceived, edited, and designed by Fil Rouge Press Ltd, 110 Seddon House, Barbican, London EC2Y 8BX

© 2011 by Fil Rouge Press Ltd

Jewelry Fix-Ups is an original work, first published in the United States in 2011 by Fox Chapel Publishing, East Petersburg, PA, and simultaneously in the United Kingdom as *Jewellery Solutions* by A&C Black Publishers Ltd.

ISBN 978-1-56523-563-2

Publisher's Cataloging-in-Publication Data

McLoughlin, David, 1960-
Jewelry fix-ups : how to care for, repair and restore your jewelry /
David McLoughlin. -- East Petersburg, PA : Fox Chapel Publishing,
c2011.
p. ; cm.
ISBN: 978-1-56523-563-2 (U.S.)
"Simultaneously published in the UK as 'Jewellery solutions' by
A&C Black Publishers Ltd."--T.p. verso.
Includes index.
1. Jewelry--Repairing. 2. Costume jewelry--Repairing.
3. Costume jewelry--History. I. Title. II. Title: Jewellery solutions.
TS740 .M35 2011
739.27/028--dc22 1103

To learn more about the other great books from Fox Chapel Publishing, or to find a retailer near you,
call toll-free 800-457-9112 or visit us at *www.FoxChapelPublishing.com*.

Note to Authors: We are always looking for talented authors to write new books.
Please send a brief letter describing your idea to
Acquisition Editor, 1970 Broad Street, East Petersburg, PA 17520.

Printed in China
First printing: March 2011

Fil Rouge Press Publisher Judith More
Project Editor Jennifer Latham
Designer David Jones

Contents

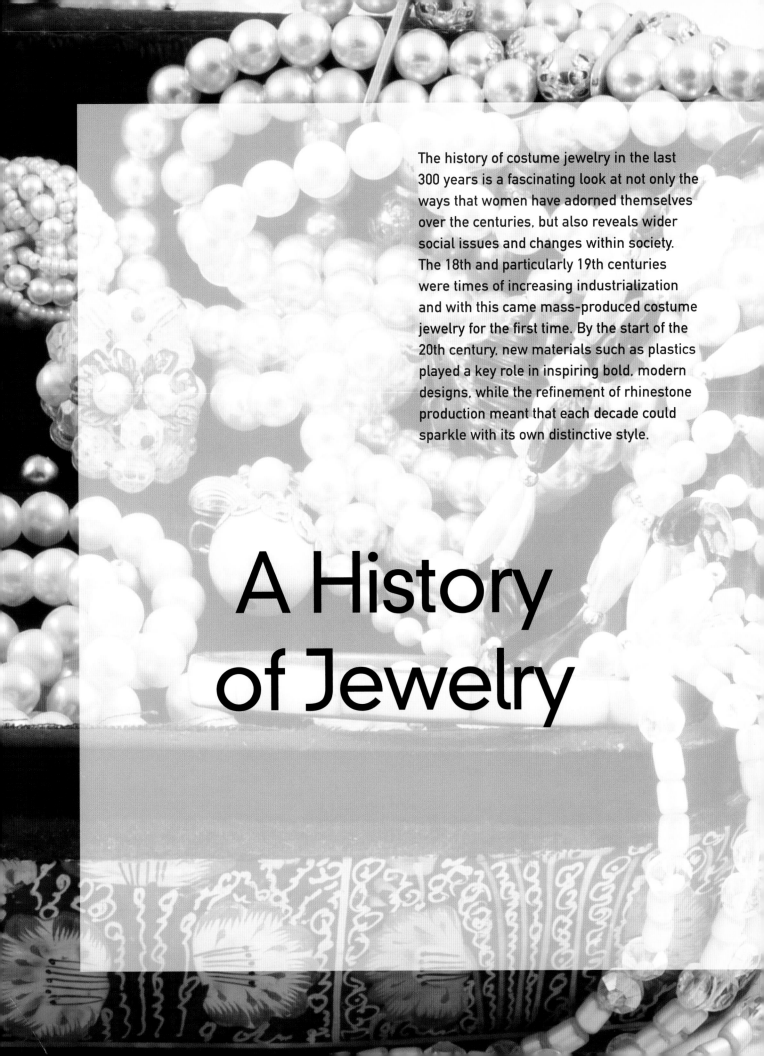

The history of costume jewelry in the last 300 years is a fascinating look at not only the ways that women have adorned themselves over the centuries, but also reveals wider social issues and changes within society. The 18th and particularly 19th centuries were times of increasing industrialization and with this came mass-produced costume jewelry for the first time. By the start of the 20th century, new materials such as plastics played a key role in inspiring bold, modern designs, while the refinement of rhinestone production meant that each decade could sparkle with its own distinctive style.

A History of Jewelry

18th- and 19th-century jewelry

You are unlikely to own fine jewelry from the 18th century as such pieces were often broken up in the 19th century for resetting into more fashionable styles, so that those that survive are rare and expensive. However, 19th-century jewelry in precious metals and stones is more widely found, particularly in the form of more modest pieces such as lockets and rings. Costume jewelry from both the 18th and 19th centuries was influenced by the neo-classical, ancient Egyptian-, Medieval-, and Renaissance-revival styles used for fine jewelry in the 18th century.

Silver filigree cross with amethyst and seed pearls, early 19th century

18th-century manufacture

The Industrial Revolution led to the manufacture of costume jewelry in quantity for the first time. Cut steel and pinchbeck (imitation gold made from copper and zinc) came into use as substitutes for more expensive precious metals, glass "paste" stones were widely used to simulate fashionable diamonds, and cameos were made from porcelain in imitation of classical/ancient shell or lapidiary versions.

Pieces featuring more affordable semi-precious stones, such as garnets, and memorial jewelry in black enamel and gold, sometimes with hair incorporated, can also be found. Ribbon bow motifs were widely used in designs for earrings and necklaces.

19th-century developments

Huge changes all around the world during the 19th century had a profound effect on the type and amount of jewelry made. Exploitation of natural materials found in the colonies, paired with the Industrial Revolution in Europe and America, led to jewelry using everything from new materials such as gutta percha, a by-product of the rubber industry, to diamonds from mines in Southern Africa discovered in 1867. In an era when hunting was fashionable, jewelry was also made from animal materials such as ivory and tortoiseshell that are now banned.

19th-century fashion

The Grand Tour, where the comfortably off traveled through Italy and Greece to view architecture and art, along with well-publicized archeological excavations, led to historical revival styles, including classical, Etruscan, and Renaissance designs. Trade relations with Japan opened up in the 1860s, and Japanese design influence brought in everything from fan and dragon motifs to enamel and inlay techniques. Increased trade with India also influenced designs.

Sentimental jewelry was in favor, with motifs such as love birds and clasped hands, hair jewelry, and hidden messages spelt out in stones. In the second half of the century, photography arrived and lockets became almost ubiquitous for everyday wear as it became possible to have a picture of your loved one inside, not just a lock of hair. The fashion for mourning jewelry was at its peak, and included pieces made from jet and early plastics.

Fashionable forms for pins or brooches included floral motifs and insects, while cameos continued to be popular. Filigree work, chasing, and engraving made the most of thin sheets of precious gold. Inexpensive stones such as amethyst, peridot, garnet, topaz, and citrine were set in both quality gold mounts and in less expensive pinchbeck. Jewelry made with coral and turquoise was also very popular.

1. Cameos that echoed ancient Greek and Roman motifs were popular in the 18th and 19th centuries. Coral cameo pin set in silver surround, late 18th century.

2. Mass-produced costume jewelry became widely available by the mid 19th century, using inexpensive materials. Cranberry glass and faux pearl necklace, late 19th century.

3. Thin metal work was often embellished with raised motifs; the delicate, refined design on these gold earrings is typical of the 18th century. Gold earrings, late 18th century.

4. The widowed British queen Victoria wore mourning jewelry for the rest of her life, sparking a long fashion in this type of jewelry. Mourning pin with lock of hair, 19th century.

5. Early plastics quickly found their way into jewelry; here, combined with a popular 19th-century motif, the elegant hand. Vulcanite bangle, late 19th century.

6. Lockets had their heyday in the 19th century. The finest examples were made from gold and lavishly embellished. Gold locket with fleur-de-lys motif set with seed pearls, 19th century.

20th-century jewelry

During the course of the 20th century traditional styles were revived and new designs and materials introduced. Both mass-manufactured and artisan pieces became more widely available and women had an expanding wardrobe of pieces—from the plastic beads picked up in a supermarket or drugstore to the graduation set of pearls or diamond wedding ring that were gifts to mark rites of passage. Innovative design could be found at many levels of the market, and today Venetian or Czech glass beads, costume pins from manufacturers such as Trifari, Hobe, and Eisenberg, and Bakelite bangles are all highly collectable.

Trifari rhinestone owl pin, 1950s

Art Nouveau

Originating in France at the turn of the 19th and 20th centuries, the Art Nouveau movement brought organic forms and materials to the fore in jewelry design. Sinuous shapes, stylized motifs from nature, and the use of non-precious materials such as glass, horn, and enamel are hallmarks of the style. The movement lasted only a decade or so, and the artisan jewelry produced at the start was eclipsed by later mass-produced copies. French and Czech work is particularly sought-after.

Popular motifs for pins included dragonflies, lilies, and languorous female heads entwined in long, flowing hair. Oval sash pins were a new variation on the pin, and were used to fasten the fashionable waist sash at the hip, or pinned to a hat.

Jugenstil

The northern European equivalent of Art Nouveau, Jugenstil designs were more abstract, and paved the way for the Bauhaus and Art Deco styles that followed. Companies such as Theodore Fahrner in Germany employed artists as designers for their high-end costume jewelry pieces, made in silver, enamel, and marcasite.

SEE ALSO:

Pins:
William Kerr silver flower pin, page 58
Plique-à-jour pin, page 138

1

KEY DESIGNERS & MANUFACTURERS

Frederic Boucheron, France (1830–1902)
Child and Child, UK, 1880–1916
Theodor Fahrner, Germany, 1883–1979
Charles Horner of Halifax, UK, 1857–1984
Chaumet, France, 1780–present day
Georg Jensen, Denmark, 1904–present day
Georges Fouquet, France (1862–1957)
Peter Carl Fabergé, Russia (1846–1920)
Emile Gallé, France (1846–1904)
William B. Kerr & Co, US, 1855–1906
René Lalique, France (1860–1945)
Liberty & Co, UK, 1875–present day
Murrle Bennett & Co, UK, 1896–1914
Louis Comfort Tiffany, US (1848–1933)
Philipe Wolfers, Belgium (1858–1929)
Henry Wilson, UK (1864–1934)

1. Theodore Fahrner's company in Germany produced jewelry influenced by the Art Nouveau and Arts and Crafts movements, and continued to make jewelry into the Art Deco period. Gold-tone necklace with filigree flowers, c.1930s.

2. The natural world and its creatures was a constant source of inspiration for Art Nouveau jewelers—everything from the dragonfly to snakes—and this included the humble snail, here given elegant form in a series of silver plaques. Sterling silver necklace with snail on leaf motif, c.1900s.

3. Inspired by the work of the Czech artist Alfonse Mucha, whose work was embraced by the Art Nouveau movement, nymphs and mermaids were a recurring theme. Silver pin of girl's head with flowers, 1900s.

4. Designed by Harald Nielsen for the Danish jeweler Georg Jensen, these Moonlight grape earrings are quintessential Art Nouveau. Harald Nielsen/Georg Jensen silver earrings, 1900s.

5. Jewelry drew on unusual motifs, such as marsh plants, the forms of which are echoed in this gold-tone bracelet. Gold-tone bracelet with rhinestones, c.1900s.

6. Art Nouveau jewelers preferred to use inexpensive materials such as brass, copper, glass, and semi-precious stones. Silver lily-of-the-valley capped pendant with green agate drop, c.1900s.

Arts and Crafts

At the heart of the Arts and Crafts movement was the artist and writer William Morris (1834–1896). Morris was dismayed by the shoddy mass-produced goods that were being manufactured in the mid 19th century, and what he saw as tasteless, ostentatious design. He wanted to bring back craftsmanship and good, simple design to the decorative arts. Morris looked back to Medieval times and the Renaissance, when the craftsman was valued for his skill and creativity. The Arts and Crafts influence was to affect not only the applied arts in Britain, but also in Europe and North America during the late 19th century and early 20th century.

Earrings with Ruskin cabochon ceramic stones, 1900s

Key figures

The English designer Charles Robert Ashbee (1863–1942) was an important figure in the Arts and Crafts movement who set up his Guild and School of Handicraft in 1888. Craftsmen at the Guild produced jewelry and items in metalwork, as well as furniture. Many such guilds were to open in the period, both in the UK and North America.

Liberty & Co of London and Tiffany in New York are associated with the Art Nouveau movement, but they also commissioned Arts and Crafts artists to produce jewelry for them. One of the most noted designers at Liberty's was Archibald Knox, who designed a range of products, including jewelry with a Celtic theme that was to prove very successful for the company.

Arts and Crafts materials and themes

The Arts and Crafts movement coincided with the Aesthetic and Artistic dress movements in the late 19th century, when women in artistic and intellectual circles favored long, flowing robes in rich velvets and silks, rather than the restricting garments most women wore at the time. Such clothes called for statement necklaces that distinguish the Arts and Crafts period.

Arts and Crafts jewelers liked to work with plain materials such as pewter and dull silver, and they preferred cabochon stones (stones that have been rounded and smoothed, and are often elliptical in shape) rather than faceted ones. Semi-precious stones were also preferred over precious ones, especially translucent stones such as opal, moonstone, amethyst, and carnelian. Mother of pearl and blister pearls were also in vogue. Ceramic "faux" stones were popular, notably those produced by William Howson Taylor at his Ruskin Pottery (see page 141). Many of them were produced in the blues and turquoises that distinguish Arts and Crafts jewelry. Enamel was also popular, used by Knox and other designers.

Motifs were taken from nature to produce stylized flowers and leaves, as well as animals and birds—owls and peacocks were favorites. Key colors were sea colors in a wide range of blues and greens. Jewelry inspired by the Renaissance and its colors was made in sumptuous deep pinks and reds.

SEE ALSO:

Necklaces:
Arts and Crafts hammered silver pendant with citrine, page 111
Arts and Crafts enamel pendant, page 139
Bernard Instone enamel necklace with mother-of-pearl pendant, page 139
Pins:
Charles Horner silver pin with amethyst, page 41
Rings:
Arts and Crafts silver ring with flowers and leaves and onyx stone, page 115

KEY DESIGNERS & MANUFACTURERS
Carence Crafters, US, c.1901–1915
Nelson Ethelred Dawson, UK (1859–1941)
Sybil Dunlop, UK (1889–1968)
Guild and School of Handicraft, UK, 1888–1905
Theodor Fahrner, Germany, 1883–1979
Arthur and Georgia Gaskin, UK (1862–1928 and 1866–1934)
Charles Horner of Halifax, UK, 1857–1984
George Hunt, UK (1892–1960)
Georg Jensen, Denmark, 1904–present day
Bernard Instone, UK (1891–1987)
Archibald Knox, UK (1864–1933)
Liberty & Co, UK, 1875–present day
Henry George Murphy, UK (1884–1939)
Dorrie Nossiter, UK (1893–1977)
Louis Comfort Tiffany, US (1848–1933)

1. This pin epitomizes much that distinguishes Arts and Crafts design—dulled silver, semi-precious stones in blues and greens, and an early Renaissance-inspired design. Sybil Dunlop silver pin with semi-precious stones, c.1920s.

2. Moonstones and chalcedony were often used in Arts and Crafts jewelry: The stylized leaves in silver that edge the settings for the stones are a signature Arts and Crafts treatment. Silver ring with moonstone and chalcedony, 1900s.

3. Enamel was very popular in Arts and Crafts jewelry, here used to give a pin a Medieval stained-glass effect. Silver enamel pin, 1910s.

1

2

3

Art Deco

A reaction to the organic forms of Art Nouveau (see pages 10–11), Art Deco was named after the influential 1925 exhibition in Paris— the Exposition Internationale des Arts Décoratifs et Industriels Moderne. Streamlined, geometric, and modern, the Art Deco spirit was embraced by designers in the decorative arts, industrial design, and architecture from the end of the 1920s until the early 1940s. Designers of Art Deco jewelry not only looked to the machine age for inspiration, but also turned to the past, with ancient civilizations from Egypt to the Aztec providing a rich vein of exotic motifs.

Silver-tone dress clip with Lucite and rhinestones, late 1920s

KEY DESIGNERS & MANUFACTURERS

Amco, US, c.1919–1970s
Jakob Bengel, Germany, 1873–1939
Castlecliff, US, 1918–1977
Ciner Co, US, 1892–present day
Coco Chanel, France (1883–1971)
Coro, US, c.1900–1979
Miriam Haskell, US, 1926–present day
Theodor Fahrner, Germany, 1883–1979
Georg Jensen, Denmark, 1904–present day
René Lalique, France, 1885–present day
D. Lisner & Co, US, 1904–c.1985
Mazer Brothers, US, c.1923–1981
Napier Co, US, 1875–1999
Richelieu, US, 1911–present day
Schiaparelli, US, c.1930–1973
Trifari, US, 1918–present day

Key figures

Noted industrial designers created jewelry in their favorite materials. For example, the German firm of Jakob Bengel employed designers such as William Wagenfeld to design Bauhaus-inspired jewelry in chrome and Galalith (see page 136). French designer Jean Després created machined geometric pieces that nod to his industrial design training, and Swiss designer Jean Dunand produced hammered metal pieces in geometric shapes.

Fashion designers stepped in too. Both Coco Chanel and Elsa Schiaparelli began producing costume jewelry made from non-precious materials, making this type of jewelry acceptable to wealthy couture customers and starting a product line that today's fashion stars still include in their repertoire. Their designs influenced lesser manufacturers—Coco-style long ropes of imitation pearl beads were popular with 1920s flappers, and Schiaparelli's dramatic, bold rhinestone dress clips were widely copied.

1. "Tut mania" followed the discovery of the young pharaoh's tomb, and ancient Egyptian-revival jewelry was all the rage. Silver lotus flower pin, 1920s.

2. The Art Deco architecture of geometrics and stepped forms also inspired jewelry design. Silver-tone dangle earrings with rhinestones, 1920s.

3. New materials such as Bakelite (see pages 134–5) epitomized the modern age. Silver-tone swordfish pin of green Bakelite and rhinestones, 1930s.

Luxury materials included dramatic combinations of platinum or white gold with richly colored stones such as emeralds, rubies, onyx, and jade, while less expensive designs used the latest chrome and colorful plastics.

Styles and influences

Art Deco is closely associated with the Jazz Age, cocktail bars, and the early years of Hollywood. The newly fashionable short dresses, bared arms, and bobbed hair were a foil for long necklaces, dress clips, bangles, dangle earrings, and cocktail rings. The style was to wear them all together in one glorious, bejeweled ensemble.

In addition to the characteristic geometric shapes associated with the Art Deco style, other strong influences can be seen. Events such as the excavations of King Tutankhamun's tomb in 1923 led to designs influenced by the style of ancient Egypt, including sphinx and scarab motifs. And the revolution underway in transport led to pins in the shape of streamlined automobiles, ocean liners, yachts, and airplanes.

4. Armlets were hugely popular, especially when they hinted at the exotic and dangerous. Gold-tone snake armlet with rhinestone eye, 1920s.

5. Jewelry motifs celebrated the new, sporty woman of the 1920s, who golfed, played tennis, and swam. Silver swimmer pin with rhinestones, 1920s.

6. Long sautoirs (see page 31) of brightly colored beads gave the flapper girl her distinctive look. Necklace of green beads in early iridescent plastic, 1920s.

1

2

3

4

5

6

Retro

From showy designer cocktail pieces in precious and semi-precious materials to inexpensive plastic beads, the 1940s and 1950s were important decades in the manufacture of jewelry. During the early 1940s, US companies were the main producers of costume jewelry, since production in Europe had shut down for the duration of World War II. Companies in the US experimented with new materials to replace those unavailable as a result of the war. Following the end of the war, production restarted in Europe, and by the 1950s costume jewelry was a major part of every Western woman's wardrobe.

Trifari gold-tone pin with rhinestones and faux seed pearls, 1940s

KEY DESIGNERS & MANUFACTURERS

Amco, US, c.1919–1970s
Jakob Bengel, Germany, 1873–1939
Bogoff, US, c.1940–1960
Marcel Boucher, US, 1937–1971
Hattie Carnegie, US, c.1918–1970s
Castlecliff, US, 1918–1977
Ciner Co, US, 1892–present day
Coco Chanel, France (1883–1971)
Coro, US, c.1900–1979
Eisenberg Co, US, c.1935–present day
Miriam Haskell, US, 1926–present day
Hobé Cie Ltd, US, c.1927–present day
Georg Jensen, Denmark, 1904–present day
D. Lisner & Co, US, c.1904–1985
Mazer Brothers, US, c.1923–1981
Monet, US, 1927–present day
Napier Co, US, 1875–1999
Pell Jewellery Co, US, 1941–present day
Richelieu, US, 1911–present day
Schiaparelli, US, c.1930–1973
Trifari, US, 1918–present day

SEE ALSO:

Necklaces:
Napier gold-tone collar, page 28
Trifari negligée necklace, page 32
Rivière red glass necklace, page 32
Bracelets:
Rhinestone line bracelet, page 43
Gold-tone expansion bracelet, page 42
Pins:
Silver-tone chatelaine pin, page 38
Gold-tone fringe pin, page 40
Rings:
Cocktail ring with faux topaz, page 46

Necklaces enhanced day and evening dresses, brooches or pins were extremely decorative, bold and stylized and widely worn, large colorful rings adorned cocktail party-goer's hands, and charm bracelets enjoyed a heyday. Multi-stranded necklaces, often in faux pearls, were widely worn.

Key figures

Alfred Phillipe at Trifari introduced many innovative designs, from the crown brooch or pin to the Lucite jelly belly stone, while Miriam Haskell pioneered the use of natural materials such as shells in her beachwear collection. Designers such as Christian Dior, Coco Chanel, and Elsa Schiaparelli and companies such as Coro and Eisenberg were also pre-eminent at this time. Figural pieces ranged from animals,

such as horses or big cats, to theatrical imagery such as ballerinas and clowns. Other imagery included artist's palettes, flower baskets, ribbons, and bows. Celebrities such as the Duchess of Windsor, who wore eye-catching pieces like the Cartier tiger brooch, set trends that were copied in less expensive ranges.

New materials

New molded plastics such as Lucite and acrylic were developed, replacing Bakelite. And innovative techniques, such as machine stamping metals and the iridescent aurora borealis finish (see page 119) used on Swarovski crystals, transformed the look of base materials. While in precious jewelry Van Cleef popularized the invisible setting for gemstones in rings.

1. Charm bracelets were very popular from the 1930s to the 1960s. Silver charm bracelet with rhinestones, 1930s.

2. Large, theatrical jewelry was very popular in the 1940s and 1950s. Eisenberg rhinestone pin, 1940s.

3. Fruit-themed jewelry was inspired by the filmstar Carmen Miranda. Glass fruit necklace with faux pearls, late 1940s.

4. The costume jewelry house Hobé produced pieces that rivaled fine jewelry. Gold-tone horse pin with rhinestones, 1940s.

5. The jewelry designer Miriam Haskell is associated with elegant, and highly collectible, designs. Miriam Haskell gold-tone and white bead demi-parure set, 1950s.

6. The Italian designer Elsa Schiaparelli was noted for her flamboyant, highly decorative jewelry in the 1940s. Schiaparelli silver-tone earrings with rhinestones, 1940s.

7. Jazz music was very popular in the 1930s and 1940s, and its influence can be seen in jewelry. Silver-tone demi-parure set of jazz players with chalcedony stones, 1930s.

Globetrotter

From the early 20th century to today, jewelry influenced by the native styles of different countries and by ancient cultures has been popular. Designers looked around the world for inspiration, and authentic pieces were exported to distant cities and sold in specialist stores. Everything from a tribal necklace from Africa, to a Native American woven beaded choker, or an armful of Indian bangles, has added an exotic touch to Western fashions. This trend introduced materials such as clay or seed beads, shells, feathers, leather thongs, and wooden bangles into mainstream costume jewelry.

Taxco silver and green agate pin, 1950s

South American influences

One of the first widely known ethnic jewelry lines is the hand-crafted silver from Taxco in Mexico. In 1929 a visiting American architecture professor called William Spratling (1900–1967) revived the declining silver industry in the town with designs based on pre-Columbian culture. He trained local craftsmen in silver- and goldsmithing. They were later joined by jewelers from outside, and developed a thriving industry that exported pieces worldwide. During World War II in particular, when metal supplies in the US became scarce, Taxco produced significant quantities of jewelry for US stores.

Taxco jewelry was made in 925 silver, and may be set with turquoise, jade, or other stones. Jewelry production continues in Taxco today, although the stylish vintage designs from the 1930s and 1940s are the most sought-after with collectors and jewelry-lovers.

Celtic inspiration

Many fine pieces from Scottish silversmiths, produced in every era from Victorian times to the end of the 20th century, reflected Celtic themes and used local metals and stones such as agate. These pieces influenced the mass-produced costume jewelry by the Scottish firm Miracle (1946–present day), which was popular from the 1950s through to the 1970s. Ancient Celtic motifs were incorporated into cloak or scarf pins or brooches, while crucifixes were also popular.

African style

Glass trade beads made in European centers such as Venice and Bohemia were traded in Africa from as early as the 15th century, and were particularly popular in the 19th century. During the 1960s this trade was reversed and necklaces, bracelets, and earrings made in Africa from these beads were exported back to Europe and America to feed the hippie fashion for ethnic jewelry.

Other popular African jewelry included Ethiopian crosses, and beadwork pieces from Zulu and other tribal cultures. Distinctive materials included coconut shell and cowrie shells (which were a form of currency in some parts of Africa).

Indian influences

India has a centuries-old tradition of goldsmithing, with jewelry holding a particular place in traditional wedding ceremonies. In the West, Indian influence can be seen in everything from elaborately designed chandelier earrings in filigree metalwork to the fashion for items such as ankle bracelets.

Native American style

Woven beadwork and beadwork on a leather base were traditions employed from ancient times. In the 1960s and 1970s they became fashionable with hippies, along with the silver and turquoise jewelry made by the Navajo tribe.

SEE ALSO:

Necklaces:
  Necklace with blue ceramic and cast silver beads, page 92
  Seed necklace, page 147
  Chinese carved nut necklace, page 147
Bracelets:
  Gold-tone snake armlet, page 45
  Silver bracelet with blue marbled faux stone, page 66
  Mother-of-pearl expansion bracelet, page 96

Native American jewelry became fashionable in the 1960s, and pieces from that period are now much sought-after. Native American silver ring with coral and turquoise, 1970s.

1. Hippie fashion favored authentic ethnic styles, setting a trend for this type of jewelry in the 1960s and 1970s. African necklace of brass and seed beads, 1970s.

2. Margot of Taxco was known particularly for her beautiful enamelwork. Margot of Taxco silver snakehead earrings with enamel, 1930s.

3. Native American beadwork jewelry was originally sold as tourist pieces, but is now highly prized for its beautiful and intricate work. Bracelet of glass beads, 1970s.

1

2

3

Modern pop

In the 1960s the influence of popular music and the revolution in mass-market fashion affected jewelry styles too. Costume jewelry reflected the bold Pop Art styles, with graphic shapes in colorful plastics, including the new acrylics, Plexiglass, and vinyl. Advances in plastics technology resulted in new designs such as lightweight giant plastic pearls, while invisible nylon thread replaced silk or cotton to string beads. Designers embraced materials such as paper and textiles for their more transient nature, and transparent plastics and industrial hardware were used for a "space-age" look.

Brass pendant with glass "stone," 1970s

Influences

In fine jewelry, artist jewelers made less formal work for wealthy clients, experimenting with abstraction and innovative techniques, and creating one-off jewelry that was wearable art. Specialist galleries opened in key cities to cater to this market, while in the more commercial field, artists designed collections for jewelry manufacturers.

At one end of the spectrum were the hippie and counter-culture movements that found their expression in Globetrotter-style jewelry (see pages 18–19), at the other was the clean, cool space-age look developed by designers such as Courrèges, Cardin, and Ungaro. Geometrics were key, in designs made from clear or white plastics and metals such as aluminum and silver. The Swinging Sixties girl just wanted to have fun and wore giant golf-ball earrings and huge multi-colored plastic bangles the size of large donuts. The daisy motif was everywhere—Mary Quant's signature motif, which she introduced at the beginning of the 1960s—from daisy earrings to enormous flower pendants.

Modernism

Sleek modernism arrived in the 1970s, with pieces by designers such as Astrid Fog's heart pendant for the Danish design company Georg Jensen, which is still in production today. Hoop earrings, Russian bands for rings and bangles, and puzzle rings were popular. Silver and stainless steel were fashionable, with platinum and white gold finding favor at the top end of the market. Like the Art Deco era, opals, onyx, jade, and diamonds were in vogue, and Art Deco and Bauhaus modernist influences abounded.

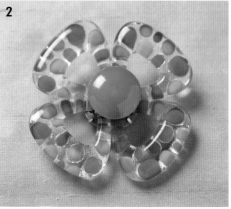

SEE ALSO:

Earrings:
Brass chandelier earrings with Austrian red glass, page 34

Pins:
Gold-tone tremblant butterfly pin with rhinestones, page 38

Rings:
Sterling silver ring with tiger's eye, page 113
Silver ring with turquoise, page 114

KEY DESIGNERS & MANUFACTURERS

Amco, US, c.1919–1970s
Bogoff, US, c.1940–1960
Marcel Boucher, US, 1937–1971
Hattie Carnegie, US, c.1918–1970s
Castlecliff, US, 1918–1977
Ciner Co, US, 1892–present day
Coro, US, c.1900–c.1979
Eisenberg Co, US, c.1935 -present day
Miriam Haskell, US, 1926–present day
Hobé Cie Ltd, US, c.1927–present day
D. Lisner & Co, US, c.1904–1985
Monet, US, 1927–present day
Napier Co, US, 1875–1999
Pell Jewelry Co, US, 1941–present day
Richelieu, US, 1911–present day
Schiaparelli, US, c.1930–1973
Trifari, US, 1918–present day

1. Loud, huge earrings were a signature look in the 1960s. Danish red plastic door knocker earrings, 1960s.

2. The daisy motif was very popular in the 1960s, and pieces ranged from delicate representations of the flower to pop plastic versions in acid colors. Plastic daisy-style pin, 1960s.

3. Raw rock wrapped in crushed silver brought modern jewelry up to date. Scandinavian silver pendant with amethyst, 1960s.

4. Bright colors, clean lines, and geometric shapes were hip and modern. Plastic round-square bracelet, c1960s.

5. Art Nouveau design was revisited in the 1960s, and flowing motifs inspired by nature and organic forms appeared on everything from Biba dresses to jewelry. Stainless steel cuff with etched flowers and leaves, c.1960s.

4

5

Disco glitz

The 1970s saw the birth of the disco scene, memorably encapsulated in the film Saturday Night Fever. During the late 1970s the price of precious metals was soaring, and costume jewelry became more widely worn. The style epitomized by iconic New York nightclub Studio 54, which opened in 1977, heralded a fashion for glitzy jewelry that continued into the 1980s. The 1970s saw influences from the jazzier end of Art Deco, with geometric motifs and rhinestones, while in the 1980s oversize panther brooches had an echo of the cocktail-hour jewels of the 1940s.

Biba elephant's head pin made of horn, brass, pewter, and rhinestone, 1970s

Influences

The 1970s opened to a world recession that had set a subdued tone—ostentatious costume jewelry of the 1960s was replaced by Globetrotter-style jewelry (see pages 18–19), focusing on natural materials; Native American silver and turquoise jewelry was particularly popular. At the end of the 1970s, the exhibition of artefacts found in King Tutankhamun's tomb traveled the world, including London and New York, and triggered a demand for Egyptian-themed jewelry. One of the key designers of the decade was the Italian jewelry designer Elsa Peretti, whose fluid, organic designs for Tiffany were an instant hit.

New materials

At the fine jewelry end, new materials introduced in the 1970s included titanium, which could be colored using a special anodizing technique. The emerging disco scene saw bangles and necklaces of fluorescent plastic that glowed in the disco lights.

In the late 1970s cubic zircona synthetic stones, a substitute for diamonds, became available and laser engraving arrived, bringing imitations of expensive hand-engraved gemstone pieces to the wider market.

The arrival of bling

The 1980s saw the arrival of "bling;" faux pearls, gold-tone chains, and diamanté were worn in the day, earrings were oversize and pins flamboyant. Logo jewelry from brands such as Chanel and Dior were popular, and costume jewelry designers such as Kenneth Jay Lane catered for celebrity clients. Celebrity influence was important—from Madonna's giant crucifix necklace to Princess Diana's chunky pearl chokers and sapphire engagement ring. Butler and Wilson in London started producing fashion jewelry that catered for the 1980s appetite for glitz and glamor.

1

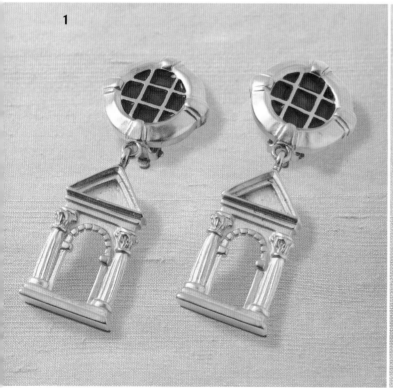

2

KEY DESIGNERS & MANUFACTURERS

Butler and Wilson, UK, 1960s–present day
Castlecliff, US, 1918–1977
Ciner Co, US, 1892–present day
Karl Lagerfeld for Chanel, France, 1983–
   present day
Christian Dior, France, 1946–present day
Coro, US, c.1900–1979
Eisenberg Co, US, c.1935–present day
Kenneth Jay Lane, Inc, US, 1963–present day
Elsa Peretti for Tiffany, US, 1974–present day
Hobé Cie Ltd, US, c.1927–present day
D. Lisner, US, c.1904–1985
Monet, US, 1927–present day
Robert Lee Morris, US, 1977–present day
Napier Co, US, 1875–1999
Swarovski, Austria,1895–present day
Trifari, US, 1918–present day

SEE ALSO:

Necklaces:
   Sterling silver torque with Lucite and
      insect pendant, page 30
   Erikson Beamon bib of silver and
      hematite, page 29
Earrings:
   Silver-tone creole earrings, page 34
Bracelets:
   American cuff of painted papier mâché,
      page 42
   Steel hinge bracelet with clear
      rhinestone, page 42

1. Karl Lagerfeld classical-themed earrings that sum up the 1980s—large clip-on earrings with heavy drops in the shape of a Corinthian doorway. Karl Lagerfeld gold-tone earrings, c.1980s.

2. Dubbed the "king of costume jewelry," Kenneth Jay Lane produced some of the most memorable pieces of the 1980s and 1990s. Gold-tone frog bracelet, c.1990s.

3. Oversize, ostentatious jewelry was everywhere in the 1980s. Kenneth Jay Lane gold-tone and rhinestone earrings, c.1980s.

4. Jewelry also looked back to earlier decades; this tiger bracelet is reminiscent of the one bought by the Duchess of Windsor in 1956. Gold-tone tiger bracelet, c.1980s.

3

4

The design of necklaces, earrings, pins, bracelets, and rings have always followed changes in fashion and they come in many different styles. Discover the fascinating history behind the jewelry you may have in your own collection, and gather lots of care and repair advice and tips. Advice is given on the types of jewelry repairs that anyone can do at home, and when it's time to call in the professionals. Guidelines for storing and cleaning your jewelry will help to keep your pieces in top condition. Learn all about the equipment and tools you need to clean and repair your own jewelry—you're ready to get started!

Jewel Box

Amateur or pro?

Jewelry, particularly vintage costume jewelry, will need cleaning and repairing from time to time. Vintage costume jewelry in particular can have missing clasps or fastener pins. Everyday problems include jump rings (see page 76) that have come apart, stones that have become loose or are missing, or pierced earring wires that are bent. These are all jobs that are well within the grasp of the amateur. You need only a few tools to get started (see pages 52–5), an understanding of the basic techniques, and the do's and don'ts when it comes to cleaning metals, stones, and other materials.

Painted horn pin, 1920s

Care and repair

Throughout, you will find guidelines for the most effective and safest ways to clean a wide range of materials. You may find some of the advice is different to that found on the Internet. For example, some sites suggest using toothpaste or baking soda for some cleaning jobs. I never recommend these, since they are abrasives and can scratch some metals and stones.

The following three chapters show you a range of simple repairs that anyone can tackle, from putting a new clasp on a bracelet, to attaching a new fastener pin to a pin. The final chapter in the book, Jewel School (pages 150–181), shows more advanced projects. You should consider these only once you are confident with the smaller, simpler repair jobs.

Time to call in a professional

However, there are some repairs that require professional skills. Cameos are usually made from either stone, such as lava or onyx, or animal materials such as coral or shell. Because of their delicately carved surfaces, cameo repairs should only be undertaken by an expert.

Chipped or cracked enamel also needs specialist knowledge, tools, and techniques—and some types of enamel damage cannot be repaired.

Vintage plastics, too, can be difficult for an amateur to repair because the material can be very brittle. If the piece has plastic sickness (see page 136), it will not be possible to repair it. Materials such as horn, bone, and coral should also be given to an expert to repair.

With very fine or valuable jewelry, such as the micro-mosaic pin shown opposite, it is always best to take such items to a jeweler for repair. Even if the mosaic itself doesn't need to be repaired, any work done on the piece runs the risk of damaging it, and is best left in the hands of a professional.

Professional cleaning

You can bring your jewelry to a high polish, but a jeweler has mechanical polishing equipment that will bring a super shine to your jewelry. If you have pieces of jewelry with precious stones (see pages 108–109), it is worth having them professionally cleaned occasionally.

Opposite: This 19th-century micro-mosaic pin is made up from intricate parts. Such pieces are best left to the professionals for repair.

Cameos are often made from coral, shell, or bone. These are best left to specialists for repair. 19th-century shell cameo.

Vintage plastics are often brittle and easily broken; I don't recommend home repairs on these. Bakelite bangle, 1930s.

Chipped or cracked enamel jewelry needs to be repaired by an expert. Arts and Crafts enamel pin, 1920s.

Gold pin set with micro-mosaics of birds and flowers, 19th century

Sandor necklace, 1940s

Necklace styles

Arguably, the single piece of jewelry with the most power to impress, as they are worn close to the face, necklaces are an essential part of every woman's wardrobe. Styles range from discreet and delicate to statement designs that will create the maximum impact.

On these pages you will find information that will help you recognize and care for a wide range of popular vintage and modern necklace types. For information on chains, see page 77, and for advice on beads see pages 92–3.

Silver choker of grey freshwater pearls, 1990s

Napier gold-tone collar, 1950s

CHOKER

A single band or linked strands of beads that sit closely high up around the neck itself, in the manner of a dog collar. They are often made from pearls, following the influence of the British Queen Alexandra in the early years of the 20th century. You will also find chokers made from ribbon with a pin-style jewel or cameo attached at the center.

Typical faults: A broken clasp, due to the tension it is held under. To repair a clasp, see pages 78, 81. You may find a jewel or cameo that has survived after the ribbon has gone. This will have double metal loops on the back as part of the jewel base, allowing you to attach the jewel to the ribbon.

Tips: If you put on weight and cannot fasten the choker, purchase an extension chain (see page 76). Do not put your choker on until after you apply perfume as this can damage pearls and some other stones.

COLLAR

A close-fitting necklace that sits just above the collarbone, and is often made from gold or silver. This timeless style can be seen in the wall paintings of ancient Egypt. Collars that include a series of drop ornaments are sometimes referred to as fringe necklaces.

Typical faults: Damage to the coatings on non-precious metal versions. This is very difficult to repair. Seek specialist advice.

Tips: The type of damage described in faults can be caused by contact with harder metals or stones in the jewelry box. To prevent this happening, make sure that you store each piece separately, see pages 48–50.

BIB

So-called because they resemble a bib, these sizeable necklaces comprise several stepped strands or rows of beads, chains, metal, or plastic palettes or rhinestones. They can have a mesh of chainmail appearance—this style of bib was common in the 1930s. Bibs were particularly popular in the Art Deco era, and they have also recently enjoyed a revival. Modern types often have a fabric or leather base with beads or stones attached, and may be tied with a ribbon at the back, as an alternative to a conventional clasp.

Typical faults: Broken links. To make a new link, see pages 162–3.

Tips: Do not wear a necklace with a broken link, even if you think it is not noticeable, since this will put extra strain on the rest of the necklace and cause further damage.

FESTOON

An intricate necklace style comprising swagged interlinked chains and dangling pendants or drops. Precious gem-set versions were worn with ballgowns in the 18th and 19th centuries. Later, exquisitely detailed Arts and Crafts and Art Nouveau examples incorporated enamel and pearls, while 1940s retro versions featured rhinestone or glass drops.

Typical faults: Broken links or chain. To make a new link, see pages 162–3. To repair a damaged chain, see page 80.

Tips: Do not wear a festoon necklace that has a broken link or chain, even if you think the damage is not noticeable, since this will put extra strain on the rest of the necklace and cause further problems.

LARIAT

A very long rope necklace that doesn't meet at the ends and has no clasp, a lariat fastens by knotting or looping the free ends at the front. Popular in the Art Deco era, these 1920s versions were often made from tiny glass seed beads around a rope-like core.

Typical faults: A loose thread on a section of beading, perhaps with missing beads.

Erikson Beamon bib of silver and hematite, 1980s

Festoon of silver and amazonite, 1900s

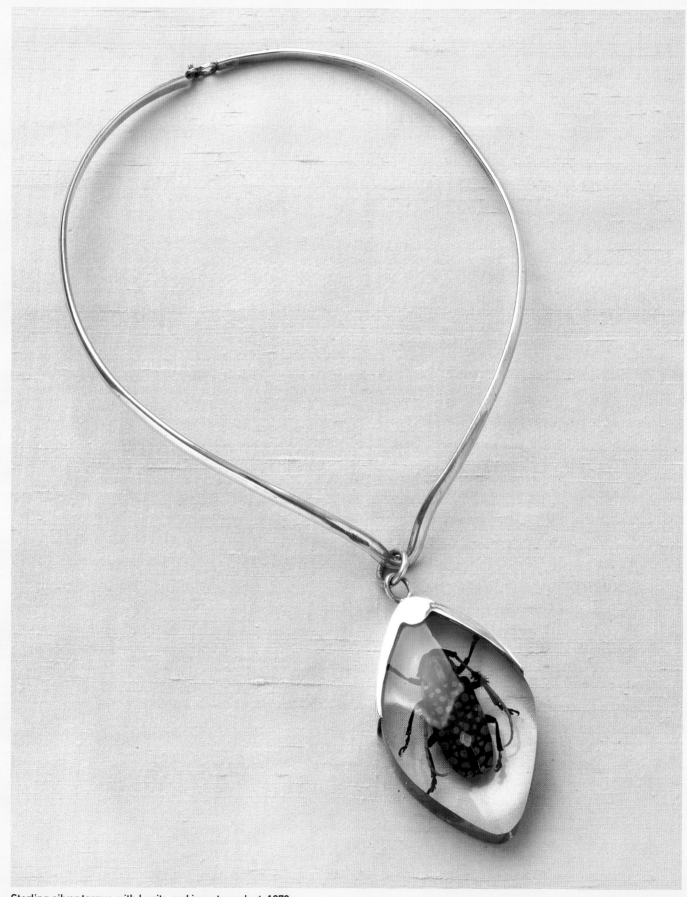

Sterling silver torque with Lucite and insect pendant, 1970s

Tips: Secure any loose thread to prevent bead loss. Avoid wearing a beaded lariat with anything that might catch in the weave and loosen a thread.

LAVALIERE

A pendant or pendants suspended on a chain, typically with a drop below the pendant. Said to be named after the Duchess de la Vallière, a mistress of King Louis XIV of France, the style has been popular since the 17th century and often features baroque pearl drops.

Typical faults: Missing drop of a pair.

Tips: Where the missing drop cannot be matched, you could consider removing the other drop (store it safely in case you find a match in the future) in order to balance the necklace.

LOCKET

A pendant that opens to reveal a hollow space for storing a photograph, lock of hair, or other memento of a loved one. Made from base metal, silver, or gold, the locket can be plain or engraved, inset with stones or other materials. Usually oval in shape, you may also find round or heart-shaped versions. The design dates back to the 18th century and is a perennially popular item, often presented as a love gift either to a newborn or to a lover.

Typical faults: A dent to the metal; for repair see page 157. Missing glass to the interior; replace with a piece of clear stiff plastic. Hinge problems or a jammed catch; for repair see page 156.

Tips: If you buy a vintage locket and replace the picture or hair inside with something meaningful for you, retain the original memento in a labeled bag in case you want to resell the locket in the future.

NEGLIGÉE

An asymmetric pair of pendant drops of differing sizes, joined by a small plaque and then suspended from a fine chain. Popular at the beginning of the 20th century, costume jewelry examples are found in base metal and Czech glass, while fine examples range from silver set with semi-precious stones, such as amethyst, to platinum and topaz versions.

Typical faults: Missing drop.

Tips: To avoid damage, make sure that you store the necklace so that the two pendants cannot knock together by wrapping each pendant in white acid-free tissue paper.

RIVIÈRE

A necklace composed of individually set stones, often glass or rhinestone, that are either graduated or of the same size and set in a row. Originally used for the finest jewelry to show off evenly matched, high-quality stones, in the early 20th century the style began to be used for semi-precious stones such as garnets, as well as for rhinestones.

Typical faults: Dirt between the settings on closely set rows of rhinestones. For cleaning advice see pages 126–7.

Tips: Store rivière necklaces carefully to avoid the stones rubbing against each other and damaging a soft metal setting such as gold or gold-plate. A necklace box is ideal (see pages 49 and 50).

SAUTOIR

A very long bead or chain rope necklace that falls below the waist and typically finishes in a tassel or pendant. They were particularly popular in the 1920s flapper era.

Typical faults: Missing beads from a tassel tail.

Tips: To avoid tangling during storage, particularly with fine seed bead versions, wrap the length in tissue, then coil it carefully to store.

Glass bead lariat, 1920s

Gold engraved locket, 19th century

Rivière necklace of gold-tone metal and Austrian glass, 1940s

Trifari negligée necklace of gold-tone metal and glass, 1940s

Art Deco pendant of silver and faux jade, 1920s

TORQUE

A curved rigid metal shape that is one of the earliest necklace designs. Torques have been found in Iron Age excavations and were popular with the Vikings. The Scandinavian connection continues, with jewelers such as Georg Jensen producing modernist silver torques.

Typical faults: Scratches from poor storage.

Tips: Modernist silver torques look at their best when highly polished, so keep a silver polishing cloth in a separate bag in the box that you store your torque in.

TORSADE

Parallel multi-strands of small, usually glass, beads that can be twisted or left loose. Popular in the 1920s, they enjoyed a renaissance in the 1950s, when they were often produced in pastel, ice cream colors. In later versions the tiny beads are simply threaded, while in early ones the beads are individually locked in so that if a strand breaks you only lose one bead.

Typical faults: Broken strands of beads.

Tips: When twisting the strands, take care to do this very gently and be extremely careful not to over-twist to avoid breakage.

Y NECKLACE

Forming a Y shape with a long dangle that is often composed of multiple beads, these necklaces are made in a wide variety of materials, including pearls and glass, and are perennially popular.

Typical faults: Broken dangle.

Tips: Check carefully to make sure that the dangle is intact and has not lost any parts from its length.

PENDANT

The word pendant is derived from the Latin word "*pendere*," which means to hang. This type of necklace consists of a medallion or shaped jewel suspended from a chain. The pendant part can be anything from a brooch or pin style jewel-set oval to figurative motifs such as animals, birds, figures, and stars. Pendants also encompass styles such as lockets (see page 31), crucifixes, and medallions.

Typical faults: Missing chain. Damaged pendant loop.

Tips: If you are concerned about value when purchasing a vintage pendant, check that the chain is original to the piece.

PARURE

Traditionally, the term parure described a set of fine jewelry consisting of a tiara, necklace, pendant (that could be turned into a pin or brooch), earrings, and a bracelet. Often made of precious metals and stones, these were popular in the 19th century for evening wear, and were designed to be worn together. By the 20th century, parures had been pared down to a necklace as the centerpiece with matching earrings, bracelet, and pin or brooch. Partial sets with a necklace and one or two of the other items are known as a demi-parure. Parures and demi-parures enjoyed a renaissance in the 1940s and 1950s, with designers such as Miriam Haskell and manufacturers such as Trifari producing enchanting costume jewelry parures.

Typical faults: Parures were originally supplied in custom-designed boxes with shaped compartments to protect and separate the individual pieces. Where these have been damaged or lost, the items may suffer scratches and knocks from being jumbled together. It is very common to come across parures that have lost one or more items.

Tips: Store the pieces in individual bags inside a larger bag or pouch to reduce the risk of damage and to make sure that the pieces remain as a set.

Torsade of blue glass beads, 1920s

Silver Y necklace with pink glass beads, 1920s

Chandelier clip-on earrings of Austrian glass and brass, 1960s

Earring styles

More than any other type of jewelry, earrings have a special place in a woman's jewel box. Earrings frame the face, and can add shimmering brightness, color, and even drama to a look.

Styles range from the neat button or stud, to eye-catching chandelier and dangle styles that are guaranteed to get noticed.

On these pages you will find information that will help you recognize and care for a wide range of popular vintage and modern earring types. For information on findings, see pages 82–3.

Button clip-on earrings of yellow glass, 1950s

Silver-tone creole earrings with rhinestones, 1970s

BUTTON

Also known as disc earrings, button types have no moving parts, and lie flat against the earlobe. They have been made from metal, semi-precious stones, silver, gold, and glass. They were popular as clip-ons during the 1950s and 1960s, when many were made from the plastic compound Lucite. Colors included shimmering pearl, green, and yellow. Typically button earrings are slightly domed and sit snugly against the ear.

Typical faults: Flaws in or damage to the stone or to the clip.

Tips: You can repair damaged clips quite easily. See page 84.

CHANDELIER

So-called because they look like chandeliers, these earrings include some exquisite designs. They are often multi-layered and branched, mimicking the shape of a chandelier. Dressier styles have precious or semi-precious gemstones which, dangling from a filigree setting, sparkle and catch the light as they move. Diamond chandelier earrings have been consistently popular, but they have also been made of citrine, garnet, glass, sequins, plastic beads, or even feathers. Art Deco chandeliers incorporated diamonds and emeralds in striking angular designs.

Typical faults: Some of the stones, or even a whole section may be missing.

Tips: To replace a stone see pages 121–2, 171. Avoid heavier varieties that can pull on the lobes.

CLUSTER

Clip-on earrings consisting of a cluster of stones or other ornaments grouped in one setting. Styles have included sparkling diamanté clusters, popular in the 1960s, and clusters of tiny china flowers arranged on a single setting, which were worn in the 1930s. Jewelers have also produced lavish earrings, in which the cluster acts as a holder for a detachable drop, usually a single large gemstone.

Typical faults: Broken clip; damage to the cluster.

Tips: To repair a clip, see page 84.

CREOLE

A type of hoop, these are oval or three-quarter moon-shaped earrings worn in pierced ears. They were popular with the Victorians and again during the Art Nouveau period, particularly for day wear. Modern versions are made in gold and silver and are either plain, patterned, or inlaid with colored stones. Some versions may be hinged.

Typical faults: Damage to hinge or fastening.

Tips: Bent posts can be straightened with pliers.

DANGLE

Earrings that dangle from the bottom of the earlobe; also referred to as drop or pendant earrings. They are usually attached to the ear by thin wires that go through a piercing and are connected by a simple hook at the back. A popular style was the girandole. This first appeared in the 17th century and consisted of a surmount, usually shaped as a ribbon bow, from which three pear-shaped drops were suspended. Early designs were very heavy. The Art Deco period produced some striking dangle earrings with geometrical designs.

Typical faults: Missing drop or stones; damaged fitting. To replace stones see pages 121–2, 171.

Tips: Keep a box of earring drops or stones for possible repair.

DOME

Earrings consisting of a single highly polished curved or dome-like stone without any facets, such as a pearl, often surrounded by a ring of small precious or semi-precious gemstones or rhinestones. A claw setting holds stones in place. These are clip-on earrings. The dressier forms were used for evening wear; simpler styles

Gold-tone plastic dome earrings with rhinestones, 1950s

Danish red plastic door knocker earrings, 1960s

Gold-tone huggy earrings with white glass beads, 1950s

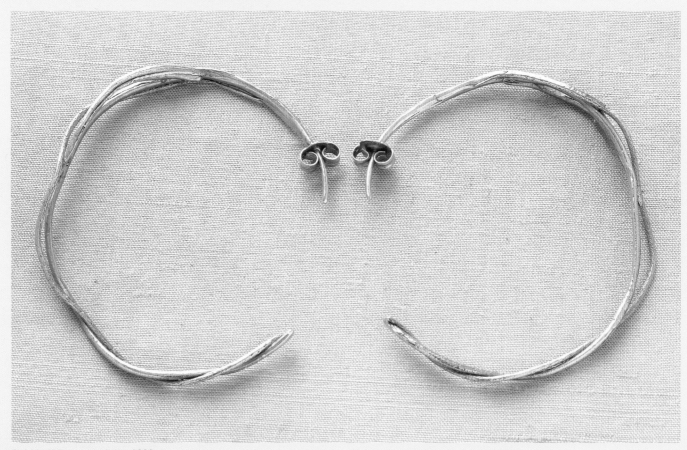

Gold half-hoop earrings, 1990s

were suitable for daytime. During the 1930s, many domed earrings were large and solid designer pieces.

Typical faults: Damaged or cracked stones. To replace a stone, see pages 121–2, 171.

Tips: If you find these uncomfortable to wear, try sticking self-adhesive ear cushions to the clip, see page 84. You will also find advice on page 84 on adjusting the fit of the clip.

DOOR KNOCKER

As their name suggests, these are hinged earrings that sway backward and forward, rather like a door knocker. There are clip-on and pierced styles. They are often made from plastic in bright, primary colors, or in different forms of metal. Popular versions during the 1970s and 1980s included clip-on gold-plated circular door knockers, swinging from a knot and even swinging from a gold-plated lion's head, so mimicking an old-fashioned door knocker. Glitzy and dramatic, door knockers are associated with "bling" and hip-hop.

Typical faults: Broken hinges, damaged rivets. To replace a rivet, see page 158.

Tips: Because they are often on the heavy side, door knockers can be slightly uncomfortable to wear, so make sure you can take them off easily.

HALF HOOP

So-called because these earrings consist of an incomplete hoop. Some versions are screwed onto the earlobe or attached with a clip. Styles vary considerably, from plain silver half hoops through to more ornate semi circles made up of stones attached to a metal base. In the 1970s stylish half hoops were made of yellow gold, set with diamonds. Modern styles tend to be designed for pierced ears.

Typical faults: Damaged clip. To repair a clip, see page 84.

Tips: Avoid wearing with high-collared clothes or scarves in case these catch in the semi-circle.

HOOP

Round or slightly oval earrings that are worn in pierced ears. The hoop is a thin tube, and may be made of gold, silver, or other metals. Hoops vary in size from tiny through to huge circles that brush the shoulder. They may be fastened with a hook, or by sliding one end into the other. Hoop earrings date back to antiquity and were probably the first earrings of all.

Typical faults: Hoops may bend out of shape, or break. They can be reshaped with pliers.

Tips: Thread a small ornament such as a bead, gemstone, or lucky charm to your hoop earrings.

HUGGY

Also known as huggies, these earrings are so called because they fit snugly into, or "hug," the ear. They come in numerous different shapes and sizes, ranging from small thick hoops through to rectangles and hearts. Styles are available with pierced and non-pierced fixings.

Typical faults: Missing stones, cracked, or damaged setting.

Tips: Unlike hoops or half hoops, huggies are less likely to catch on clothing.

STUD

A simple style for pierced ears. Each earring consists of one single ornament, such as a gemstone, pearl, or diamond, attached to a straight post, which is held in place with a butterfly fixing behind the ear. Traditionally, diamond studs have been classic evening wear for women, particularly for formal events. Modern studs come in various sizes and styles—round, square, decorative, and shaped—and are made from all sorts of materials from gemstones to plastics.

Typical faults: Lost butterfly fixing. Replacements are easily available.

Tips: To avoid losing studs, keep them in a special box separate from other earrings.

Art Deco silver-tone dangle earrings with rhinestones, 1920s

French sterling silver stud earrings with blue enamel, 1960s

Gold-tone tremblant butterfly pin with rhinestones, 1960s

Pin styles

Once an essential accessory to hold garments together, pins are now used exclusively as decorative finishing touches to outfits. They work particularly well worn with dresses, jackets, and coats, but may also be used to adorn hats and scarves. Pins are very versatile items of jewelry, and can brighten a simple ensemble, make a statement, or express your individuality.

On these pages you will find information that will help you recognize and care for a wide range of popular vintage and modern pin types. For information on fittings, see pages 86–7.

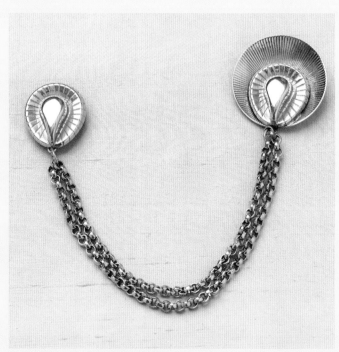

Silver-tone chatelaine pin, 1940s

Crescent pin with pink paste stones, 18th century

PIN/BAR

An oblong brooch style that developed from the earliest safety-pin-like Roman "fibulae." The pin or bar can be used to fasten clothing. Usually in metal set with either a single central stone, a central stone and two smaller ones either side, or an entire bar set with small stones. It may also have an ornament suspended from the bar.

Typical faults: Missing stones. To repair a damaged clasp, see pages 88–9.

Tips: It is easy to forget these modest brooches when you remove clothing; make sure you remove them before you put the garment in the washing machine.

CHATELAINE

A linked pair of pins tethered together by chains, these dramatic designs are worn either side of a neckline with the chains crossing the cleavage. Popular in the early 20th century, they often featured novelty themes such as a pair of birds or a lady and dog.

Typical faults: Broken chain; to repair see page 80.

Tips: Wrap in tissue, placing first the pin, then the chains, then the second pin all on separate layers to avoid tangling during storage.

ANNULAR OR RING

A circular style with a central hole that reveals the pin when it is not in use. When the brooch or pin is worn, you see only the fabric to which it is pinned. A pennanular pin is similar to an annular one, but has a gap in the ring for the fastener pin to pass through. Common in Medieval times, they enjoyed a revival in the Arts and Crafts period. More elaborate garland variations were produced in the 19th century and the 1950s, featuring a circle of stones, or even leaves and flowers fashioned from metal and stones.

Typical faults: Bent or broken pin, see page 88.

Tips: To remove fiber strands trapped in the pin mechanism use pointed tweezers.

DISCOID

The most common pin style today and popular through the centuries, discoid pins are round or oval in shape, with a large central stone framed by smaller stones or metal scrollwork.

Typical faults: Missing stones; to replace them, see pages 121–2.

Tips: Take care when cleaning the metal frame and make sure that the solution you use won't harm the stones.

FIGURAL/REPRESENTATIONAL

Pins in the shape of animals, birds, insects, butterflies, flowers, and leaves have been popular since the 18th century. Also common are symbols of luck and love in different cultures—from horseshoes to cats, hearts to Cupid's arrow. Novelty brooches appeared in the 19th and 20th centuries, representing folk figures such as chimney sweeps or the man in the moon, and later popular characters from film or television.

Typical faults: Because these were fun pieces, they were not always treated with care, so missing stones or broken fastener pins are common. To replace a fastener pin, see page 88.

Tips: A figural theme such as butterflies is the perfect start for a new costume jewelry collector.

CRESCENT

Pins in a crescent shape have been popular since the 18th century. They are found in everything from precious stones and metals to base metal and glass rhinestone.

Typical faults: Missing stones, see pages 121–2.

Tips: Crescent pins are a flattering style for pinning to hats and scarves.

Gold-tone discoid pin with faux amethyst, 1950s

Dress clip of Lucite and rhinestones, 1920s

Gold-tone fringe pin with rhinestones and faux pearl, 1940s

Silver duette pin with marcasites, 1940s

PENDANT PIN
These dual-purpose pins come with a pendant fitting as well as a clasp on the back, so they can also be hung from a chain and worn as a necklace (see page 108). They were very popular in the 19th century, though later examples can be found.

Typical faults: Most pendant pins have lost their original chain.

Tips: If you are looking for a new chain for the pin, then take it with you on your hunt so that you can make sure it will fit through the loop. These can vary widely in size.

TREMBLANT
These quivering pins have moveable parts, usually flower petals or insect wings, and were popular in the early to mid 19th century. They saw a revival in the 1940s and 1950s, with Coro, Trifari, and Schreiner, for example, producing some fine pieces. Made in a variety of metals, they are often set with tiny stones so that they sparkle as they move.

Typical faults: Broken spring mechanism.

Tips: Moveable parts are easy to catch in clothing, so take care when wearing pieces.

FRINGE
A round or oval pin with a fringe falling from the bottom of the disc. Popular in the Art Deco era, they are often found in all-over rhinestones or chain fringes with dangling stones at the tips.

Typical faults: Missing strand of fringe.

Tips: Store carefully so the fringe doesn't tangle and stones damage each other.

MOURNING PIN
Although the mourning pin (see page 9) is associated with the mid to late 19th century, this type of pin was popular from the 17th century onward. Early versions were fairly simple gold pins with a glass front or back in which to hold a memento of the deceased such as a lock of hair. Nineteenth-century versions combined gold and black in ornate surrounds. A variation on the mourning pin was the memento mori pin ("Remember your mortality") decorated with suitably sombre motifs, such as skeletons.

Typical faults: The contents may be missing; hair may be attacked by various insects.

Tips: If the glass is broken, you can buy clear sheet plastic and cut it to size as a replacement.

DRESS CLIP
Instead of a fastener pin on the reverse, this type of pin has a hinged clip that hooks over and into clothing and was popular from the 1920s to the 1950s. A variation is the fur clip, which has a double set of clips, or prongs. Because they were an innovation, they are often found in materials such as Bakelite and other plastics, pressed glass, and aluminum. Many dress clips were designed as a pair to be worn either side of a neckline.

Typical faults: Loosened hinge on the clip; see page 84. Bent prongs.

Tips: If you are going to wear the clip, take care not to damage delicate fabrics with the prongs as they are less forgiving than a pin.

DUETTE CLIP
A pair of dress clips set into a frame so they can also be worn as a pin. Often found in rhinestone or marcasite, they date from the 1920s through to the 1950s.

Typical faults: One of the pair may be missing.

Tips: If you take off the pin frame to wear the duette as clips, make sure that you store the frame carefully so it doesn't get lost.

Charles Horner sterling silver bar pin with amethyst, 1910s

Gold-tone poodle pin with jelly belly and rhinestones, 1950s

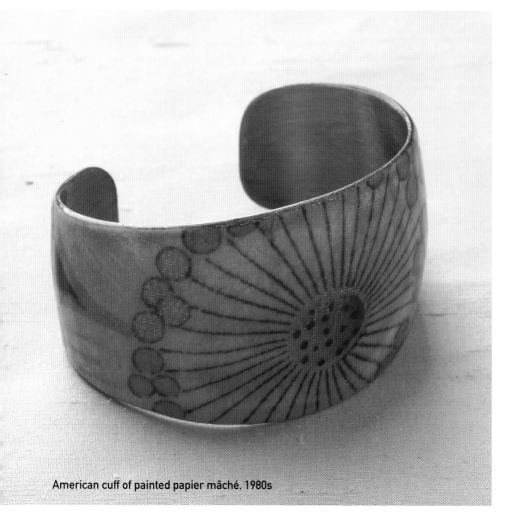

American cuff of painted papier mâché, 1980s

Bracelet styles

One of the pleasures of wearing a bracelet is that it moves with the wearer, bringing motion as well as decoration to the arm. Bracelets can also create sound—from the delicate clinking of lots of thin metal bangles, to the heavy rattle of a well-stocked charm bracelet. And there are many styles to choose from—ranging from the ancient cuff to the modern tennis bracelet.

On these pages you will find information that will help you recognize and care for a wide range of popular vintage and modern bracelet types. For information on clasps, see pages 74–6.

Gold-tone expansion bracelet with pink plastic plaques, 1950s

Steel hinge bracelet with clear rhinestone, 1980s

CUFF

The wrist equivalent of a torque (see page 30), a cuff is a wide, flat solid bangle with a gap at the back for access. The term is also sometimes used to describe a very wide hinged bracelet that fastens. Made from metal or plastic, they can be plain or highly decorated—designs can range from classical motifs engraved on gold or gold-tone metal to Art Nouveau florals in enamel on copper or pop art swirls on composition plastic.

In 1937 Coco Chanel collaborated with the Sicilian designer Fulco Verdura (1895–1978) to produce a range of jewelry which included a cuff embellished with a gemstone-studded Maltese cross. Chanel wore these frequently herself, one on each wrist, and set a trend for cuffs that has continued to this day. Vintage silver cuffs with embellished metalwork or set with turquoise, coral, or other semi-precious stones from Taxco in the 1940s and 1950s are also fine examples.

Typical faults: Not usually adjustable, so fit can be an issue. Can get bent out of shape if made from softer metals.

Tips: Because these bracelets are rigid it is awkward to use a computer while wearing one. If you take off your cuff to type, remember to put it back on at the end of the day.

EXPANSION BRACELET

Interconnected links allow this style of bracelet to expand to be fitted over the wrist, then contract to stay in place during wear. Popular in the Victorian and Art Deco eras, the decorative front of the links can be plain or set with stones. Inexpensive vintage expansion bracelets were threaded with elastic thread.

Typical faults: Don't force the mechanism; open it gently as damage can be difficult to fix. Dirt can accumulate in the links that open and close; remove regularly with a Q-tip and the appropriate cleaner for the bracelet material.

Tips: Take care to avoid trapping delicate sleeve material in the bracelet mechanism.

HINGED BRACELET

A rigid bracelet, rather like a cuff but with no gap. Instead, there is a hinge at the back that opens the circle like a clamshell to fit the bracelet onto the wrist.

Typical faults: Wear or damage to the hinge.

Tips: Though these bracelets can close with a satisfying snap if you pull back hard on the hinge, it is best not to overstretch the mechanism or you may damage it.

LINE BRACELET

Stones of the same size are set in a single, flexible line. Whether an antique diamond-set example or a modern rhinestone version, they are usually fastened with a snap lock clasp. The line bracelet was renamed the tennis bracelet after Chris Everett wore a diamond one to the US open tennis tournament in 1987. The bracelet broke and play was halted briefly; the incident set a trend for the newly dubbed tennis bracelet.

Typical faults: Broken links; to repair see page 80.

Tips: Store the bracelet flat to help prevent damage to the links.

CHARM BRACELET

Bracelets decorated with charms attached by jump rings into each link of a chain base were first widely available in the 19th century; Britain's Queen Victoria was known for her love of charm bracelets. They became hugely popular in the US in the 1930s when themed bracelets were all the rage—bracelet collections ranged through everything from "sweethearts" to "city girl." Servicemen returning home to Europe at the end of World War II brought trinket charms for loved ones, resparking the popularity of charm bracelets. They continued to be in high

Sterling silver line bracelet with red and clear rhinestones, 1920s

Sterling silver charm bracelet, 1950s

demand in the 1950s and 1960s. Many girls and women during those decades collected charms to represent important events in their lives, and these vintage bracelets often feature travel charms and figures, some of them with moving parts. Charm bracelets have recently become popular again.

Typical faults: Charms can catch in loose or openweave clothing and tug open the jump ring that holds them in place. To replace a charm, see page 79.

Tips: Charms will rub against each other when the bracelet is worn, so if you are adding charms place delicate charms with care to avoid damaging them.

ARMLET
A bracelet that is designed to be worn on the upper arm. Although armlets have a long and ancient history in many parts of the world, they were not a feature of Western jewelry until the Art Deco period (see pages 14–15). The discovery of Tutankhamun's tomb in 1922 saw a flood of Egyptian-revival jewelry, amongst them the armlet, and in particular the coiled snake armlet. Made from base or precious metal or resin, they were set with large rhinestones to represent eyes.

Typical faults: On snake armlets, lost stone eyes. To replace a missing stone, see pages 121–2.

Tips: Some armlets are articulated or expansion-type bracelets; these need to be stored carefully to avoid damage.

LINK BRACELET
Chains or linked plaques are a common method of bracelet construction from earliest times, and these designs vary widely in size and appearance. All types of metals are used for chains and plaques and they can be plain, set with stones, enameled, or made from a wide variety of materials. One notable example is the cameo-link bracelet, with cameos made from stone or shell (see pages 148–9), which was popular from the early 19th century onward. Cameos became popular again in the 1930s, and cameo bracelets are a feature of the period. Another is the link bracelet made with Scottish agate, which was popular in the late 19th century.

Typical faults: Damaged links or fastenings; to replace a link, see pages 162–3; to replace a clasp, see page 78.

Tips: Store link bracelets flat if at all possible to ensure the links and plaques don't get damaged.

BANGLE
A solid or hollow tubular bracelet, like a giant ring, bangles have been produced in every era. You will find them in every material, from gold to glass, ivory to inexpensive plastic. Bangles came into their own in the 1920s with the new fashion for bare arms. Thin metal bangles were worn in multiples, sometimes as many as 20 or more at a time. Others were made of plastic, often carved and painted to imitate ivory. The advent of Bakelite in the 1930s brought brightly colored bangles that are now highly collectible.

Typical faults: Thin metal bangles are easily bent.

Tips: Don't store thin bangles together with chains, since they become easily entangled.

TRIPLE BRACELET
Similar to an oversize Russian wedding ring, this variation on a bangle is basically interlinked bangles, which are usually identical, but can be of complementary sizes or finishes.

Typical faults: Triple bracelets are often made of plain metal, so need to be kept scratch-free to keep them looking good.

Tips: Keep silver bracelets tarnish-free in a plastic zip-lock bag with a sachet of silica gel.

Gold-tone snake armlet with rhinestone eye, late 1920s

Bangle of carved Bakelite, 1930s

Gold cigar ring with sapphires, 1960s

Ring styles

Worldwide, rings are probably the most commonly worn piece of jewelry. They adorn fingers, toes, and many other parts of the body as well. Rings have an ancient history: spectacular gold rings were found in the tomb of Tutankhamun that date back some 3,500 years. Unlike other forms of jewelry, rings have had many functions. They have been used as seals to stamp important documents, to carry poison, and as a sign of social status. In the form of betrothal and mourning rings, they have also been used to mark important rites of passage. And of course, created in different styles, shapes, and materials, they are also purely decorative fashion items.

Silver cocktail ring with faux topaz, 1930s

Gold eternity ring with garnets, 1950s

Gold signet ring with jasper (bloodstone), 19th century

Brass stack rings with glass beads, 1990s

BOMBÉ

Rings with dome-shaped settings, so-called after the word "bombé," which means "curving or bulging outward." During the 1940s and 1950s bombé rings enjoyed considerable popularity, and usually consisted of one large stone, such as a pearl, set in a gold surround.

Typical faults: Scratches on the stone; distortion of the shank (bottom and lower sides of the ring) from wear and tear.

Tips: A good jeweler will be able to replace or alter a shank to fit.

CIGAR BAND

Popular during the 1950s and 1960s, these thick, band-style rings take their name from the paper cigar band that encircles a cigar. Designs vary. Some are just plain bands; others may be engraved with intricate designs. Others may have precious or semi-precious stones set into a wide band or filigree work.

Typical faults: Missing stones; band distorted or misshapen; dulled base.

Tips: For cleaning advice and to bring the shine back to your rings see pages 64, 67, and 124.

COCKTAIL

Dramatic, overlarge, and flamboyant, cocktail rings made their debut during the 1920s, it is said, because during Prohibition, daring women wanted everyone to know that they drank illegal cocktails. Early designs contained precious and semi-precious stones; these gave way to imitation stones during the 1940s and 1950s when cocktail rings were particularly popular.

Typical faults: Damage to stone or setting. To reset a stone, see page 120.

Tips: Authentic vintage examples can be expensive.

ETERNITY

A thin band of gold or silver, set with precious stones, of the same cut and size. The stones are set in a row around the ring, using either a claw or channel setting (see right). As the name suggests, eternity rings symbolize eternal love—a ring has no beginning and no end.

Typical faults: Loose or missing stones; a jeweler may be able to improve settings or find replacements. See also page 120.

Tips: Although this type of ring is worn on a daily basis, do not wear an eternity ring when using household cleaners; they will damage stones.

SIGNET

Also known as seal rings, these carry a coat of arms, family crest, monogram, or other insignia, and were originally used to sign or seal important documents. By the 1700s there was little need for them as a seal, but they continued to be made for decorative purposes. Since the 1900s, signet rings tend to comprise a large bezel (ring top) that is engraved.

Typical faults: Dirt or damage to the ring. See pages 64, 67, and 124 for advice on cleaning.

Tips: Store rings carefully to avoid damage.

SOLITAIRE

As the name suggests, these rings consist of a single (solitary) stone set in a simple gold or silver setting. They are often used as engagement rings. The stone itself is most typically a diamond, but rubies, sapphires, and emeralds are also used, and during different periods some exquisite styles have been created.

Typical faults: Loose or missing stone. A jeweler will be able to repair the setting. See also page 120.

Tips: Store diamond rings separately. Diamonds will scratch diamonds and other jewelry.

STACK

Stack rings are rings that are specifically designed to be stacked above each other. They may have a curved band, to enable two or three rings to be piled on top, or have an integral three-dimensional design, which resembles three coils. Designs vary from simple stackable gold or silver bands through to heavier coils incorporating precious or semi-precious stones, glass, beads, and other materials.

Typical faults: Broken or damaged coils, missing stone in one of the rings.

Tips: Apply perfume or oil before putting on silver rings because perfume damages silver.

RING SETTINGS

The method a jeweler uses to secure a stone into a ring is called its setting. Each type of setting affects the way the gemstone is seen.

Channel setting: Round or baguette-shaped stones are placed side by side in a grooved channel, edged with a rim. The stones must be small and of the same size; the rim and cut of the stone keep the stones in place.

Claw setting: Four to six metal prongs or claws hold the stone in place. Light enters underneath the stone, displaying its brilliance to best effect. The six-claw setting was introduced by Tiffany & Co. in 1886.

Grain setting: Four very small claws hold the stone in place at four equally spaced points. This setting produces a square-shaped, sloping indentation in the metal, making the stone look square rather than round.

Invisible setting: Developed in France, this design involves placing small grooves into each gemstone's girdle and slipping them into a metal framework below the surface. The gemstones sit side-by-side and no metal can be seen, creating a solid surface of gems.

Pavé setting: In this setting, small gemstones—usually diamonds—are set very close together as if they were brick paving. The gemstones cover the entire surface, almost entirely hiding the metal beneath them.

Rubover setting: Also known as a bezel setting, this places the stone inside a metal band cut to fit exactly around the stone's edge. It is a very old setting, frequently used for diamond rings because it helps to protect the stone from damage.

Enamel and seed pearl earrings, 1900s

Caring for jewelry

Storing your jewelry properly and keeping it clean and dust free preserves its beauty and ensures that it maintains its value. In particular, jewelry made from delicate or special materials such as leather, insects, or hair must be stored correctly to prevent damage. Advice is given throughout the book on caring for different materials. However, looking after your jewelry doesn't stop at the storage box. How you treat your jewelry when you are wearing it can also affect its condition. This is particularly important with vintage costume items, which were not always designed to be long-lasting and may be fragile.

STORING JEWELRY

How you store your jewelry can make a big difference to its condition; and there are many practical and decorative storage options available.

- Most jewelry benefits from being stored in dark, cool conditions. Some stones—notably amethyst, aquamarine, rose and smoky quartz, and citrine—will fade over time if exposed to sunlight and should not be left out when not being worn.

- Don't keep your jewelry out in a jumbled pile. This is a surefire way to scratch, chip, or even break items. Diamonds, the hardest gemstone, can damage other jewelry. Rhinestone pieces stored together can result in scratches. Keep items in their own individual compartments in a jewelry box, cloth bag, or plastic zip-lock bag (however, see the point below). You will also find it is much easier to locate individual items if each of them has a home. If you use tissue paper, make sure that it is acid-free, and only ever use white tissue paper—colored papers may transfer their color to delicate stones.

- Some materials should not be stored in plastic zip-lock bags. Pearls, for example, need air to circulate around them. The same applies to jewelry made from leather and fur. Foil-backed rhinestones should not be stored in plastic bags because of the risk of moisture forming and damaging the stones (see pages 126-7).

A traditional leather jewelry box offers a safe place to keep your collection, with specially designed compartments for storing different types of jewelry.

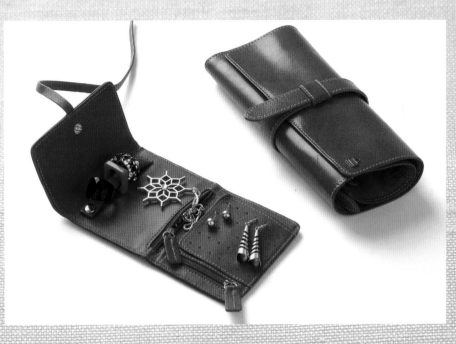

Jewelry bags are often made from breathable velvet or silk, so are suitable for storing most types of jewelry. If you own many of these, you may want to pin small labels to the bags to identify the contents.

Jewelry rolls—made from leather or fabric—are designed to store your jewelry safely while traveling. They keep everything together in one place, reducing the risk of losing an item, and have numerous compartments to keep items separate and scratch-free.

Clear plastic boxes with compartments are a decorative way to store and display your jewelry collection and keep it dust free.

VINTAGE JEWELRY BOXES

In recent years, collecting vintage jewelry boxes has become increasingly popular. Some are beautiful objects in themselves, and often come with luxurious velvet or silk linings; in addition, the value of any piece is increased if it comes with its original box.

Gold and jade ring in its original box from Amsterdam, the Netherlands, 1920s

- Keep silver in plastic zip-lock bags with a sachet of silica gel. This will help to prevent the silver from tarnishing.

- Fine necklaces, such as those made from saltwater pearls, should be stored in a specially designed necklace box. This maintains the shape of the necklace, and prevents beads from rubbing against each other and causing surface damage. Boxes designed to hold rings and bracelets are also advisable if they are particularly valuable items.

- Jewelry stands and display boxes designed to hold necklaces, bracelets, and rings are an attractive way to store and display jewelry.

This painted Art Deco necklace box, a collector's item in itself, keeps its glass bead necklace in perfect condition.

CARE AND REPAIR

Cleaning and repair guidelines for particular materials are given throughout the book. However, bear the following in mind:

- Always check a jewelry item before cleaning it to make sure that there are no loose stones, no lifted claws in stone settings (see page 120), or chips or cracks. If you discover a problem, repair the piece before cleaning or wearing it, or take it to a jeweler for repair. Never put off a repair.

- Before undertaking a repair yourself, read the guidelines on page 26. If the item is precious to you, take it to a jeweler for repair.

- If you are not sure what your jewelry is made from, the following cleaning approach is safe for most jewelry. First lightly brush the item with a jeweler's brush or a soft-bristled toothbrush (see page 53) to remove any stubborn particles of dirt. Use a gentle, sweeping movement, do not scrub at the piece. If a stone falls out, this is not the fault of the brush. The stone was either already loose in its setting or the glue has decayed. Use a slightly damp, soft, lint-free cloth (a cloth that does not have any raised fibers, or nap) to wipe over the piece. Dry with a clean, soft cloth and leave out to dry thoroughly before putting away.

- When cleaning jewelry with stones in water, always wash items in a small bowl and rinse under a running faucet with the drain hole closed. Mishaps do happen, and stones do fall out sometimes.

OUT AND ABOUT

Jewelry is designed to be worn and enjoyed, but there are things you can do to preserve the life of your jewelry and keep it in good condition.

- Check that clasps are working and that claws, jump rings, and so on are not damaged. If they are, they can catch on skin and clothing; there is also a risk that stones will fall out or chains will come undone.

- Always apply lotions and perfume before putting on jewelry. If you plan to wear fresh- or saltwater pearls or delicate gemstones (see pages 94 and 125) avoid perfume in the décolleté area. The chemicals in perfumes can discolor and even corrode the surface of these stones. You may want to wipe your

Jewelry stands in the shape of a hand have been popular since the 1920s. This modern version is suitable for holding necklaces, bracelets, and rings.

Dedicated bracelet stands are shorter than those designed for necklaces; check before you buy a stand that you know which type you are purchasing. As stands expose jewelry to light and dust, they are best reserved for less valuable pieces.

pearls or delicate stones with a damp, soft, lint-free cloth after wearing them. Allow the stones to dry before putting them away.

• Remove rings and bracelets before doing housework or washing up. The chemicals in cleaning products can harm some stones and glues. Plastics (see pages 134–7), and animal and plant materials (see pages 142–5 and 146–7) are also vulnerable to damage if exposed to chemicals. Delicate gemstones (see page 125), glued stones, and foil-backed rhinestones (see pages 126–7) should never be submerged in water.

• Always remove jewelry before showering, taking a bath, or swimming in chlorinated or other treated water. As with perfume, the

chemicals used to treat pool and hot tub water may discolor or otherwise harm stones and metals. Glues, particularly early glues, may be weakened when exposed to water. Foil-backed rhinestones and bead necklaces strung with natural thread (see page 105) should never be submerged in water.

• Leave your jewelry behind when you go to the beach. Sand is a highly abrasive material and it can scratch the surfaces of gemstones. Some gemstones are vulnerable to heat and bright light and will permanently change color if repeatedly exposed to harsh sun. Some plastics, particularly early plastics, may not stand up well to heat. The salt in seawater is another type of corrosive that can affect the condition of stones and metals.

• Remove jewelry before gardening, playing a sport, or engaging in any activity where your jewelry can be pulled, knocked, or scratched. I would advise not to wear rings—apart from a simple band—bracelets, or long dangle earrings when repairing jewelry.

• Remove rings and bracelets when preparing food. Foods contain chemicals and colorants that may harm some types of stones and metals. Foods that contain sulfur, such as eggs, onions, and leeks, will tarnish silver (see page 64).

• Remove jewelry, apart from simple rings, before you go to bed. Lying on earring fixings, for example, can damage them quite easily, or earrings can come out and go astray.

Basic toolkit

For the projects that follow, the tools covered in this section will enable you to keep your jewelry clean and polished, mend clasps, fix broken chains, re-attach fastenings to pins, and glue stones back in their settings. There is nothing more satisfying than repairing your own jewelry—especially repairs of costume jewelry, which some jewelers will not take on—and most of the repairs in this section should be well within anyone's grasp.

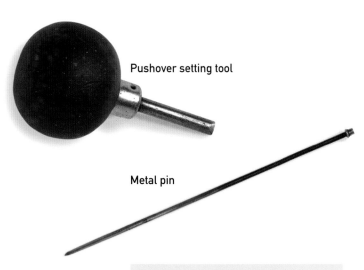

Pushover setting tool

Metal pin

The basic cleaning and repair toolkit

A basic cleaning and repair toolkit should include a jeweler's loupe (see opposite); the cleaning tools shown opposite; a penknife, tweezers, and duckbill pliers for opening and closing jump rings and necklace links—you will need two pairs of pliers for these jobs—all shown on page 54, and the glue shown on page 55. You can add more tools to your toolbox as and when you need them. Keep your tools together in a toolbox, and keep them clean; apply a 3-in-1 oil to oil metal parts from time to time.

Practice makes perfect

Before you attempt to repair a special piece from your jewelry box, practice using your tools first. Experiment with the best way to hold them; explore how each tool behaves when you use it for the job it was designed for—whether bending or twisting wire, prising out a stone, or pressing metal parts together. Try your skills on items that you don't mind getting damaged if things go wrong. You may even want to consider buying some inexpensive items from a thrift store to practice on. Follow the pictures and instructions carefully in the step-by-step repair projects. Take each repair job slowly. Don't rush them.

A note of caution: costume jewelry was, and often still is, made of cheap metals that fatigue easily—that is, there is structural damage to the metal. The first time you will know about it is when, during a repair, the metal breaks. This is not your fault, but a hazard of working with this type of jewelry.

MAKING YOUR OWN TOOLS

As you become more adept at jewelry repair, I encourage you to adapt or make your own pieces of equipment. I have done this over the years, and many jewelers have their own homemade favorites. Two tools that I have made and that I use again and again are a metal pin adapted from an old steel hat pin and a pushover setting tool made with a nail driven into an old wooden handle (see above). The pin can be used for anything from removing dirt between stone settings to applying solder. The pushover tool is used for pressing into metal (for more information, see page 152). Although you can buy ready-made pushover setting tools, my homemade version does the job perfectly and suits me best.

WORKING SAFELY

- Do not use the kitchen table as a work surface if there is any risk that cleaning chemicals will come into contact with food preparation surfaces.
- Rinse off cleaning chemicals in a sink that is not used for food preparation or for washing dishes.
- Always read the manufacturer's instructions before using a product, and follow their safety guidelines.
- Always wear protective gloves when advised.
- You may want to wear an apron when polishing and cleaning to protect your clothes.
- Dispose of cleaning chemicals safely. Check the manufacturer's guidelines.
- If there is any risk of flying objects or fragments, wear protective eyewear. This is particularly important if you are removing small stones, or cutting small bits of wire.
- If there are small children in the home, do not leave tools out where they can reach them. Put your tools away in a secure place when you have finished the repair.

Duckbill pliers (see page 54)

CLEANING TOOLS

The following items make up your basic cleaning kit. You will also need a pair of protective gloves—thin latex or vinyl gloves are ideal. A long pin is useful for removing ingrained dirt between settings (see opposite).

1 Jeweler's brush: The long-handled jeweler's brush is perfect for cleaning jewelry. Use it with long, gentle sweeping movements, not a scrubbing action.

2 Soft-bristled toothbrush: A soft-bristled toothbrush, such as a children's toothbrush, is a suitable replacement for a jeweler's brush.

3 Soft, lint-free cloth: A cloth without a nap. The cloth glides over jewelry, ensuring that claws and other sharp edges do not pick up lint.

4 Q-tips: Handy for numerous cleaning jobs where a delicate touch is required.

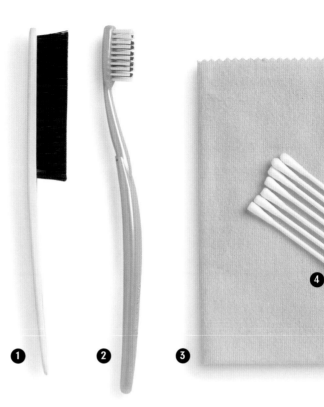

MAGNIFIERS

Magnified lenses are essential for examining jewelry, either to look for hallmarks and other signs of provenance, or to check for flaws and faults.

1 Loupes: Jeweler's lenses are known as loupes. They come in two basic styles—those that come with a separate cover (left), and those that have a self-attached cover (right). When buying a loupe, choose one that has x 10 magnification (objects are magnified 10 times their actual size.). There is a knack to using a loupe—hold the loupe about 1½ –2 in (4–5 cm) away from your eye, and the item you are examining about the same distance again.

2 Optivisor: A headband magnifier; I wear one all the time for my work. Again, I recommend x 10 magnification. The optivisor enables you to see fine detail while leaving your hands free.

READY-MADE CLEANING PRODUCTS

There is a wide range of proprietary cleaning products available for jewelry. Always follow the manufacturer's guidelines when using proprietary cleaners; they may contain hazardous chemicals. Always wear protective gloves when working with cleaning chemicals.

Jeweler's polishing cloth: Made from a soft, lint-free fabric, a jeweler's polishing cloth is chemical-free, so the cloth can be used to buff any type of metal and stone. It is washable and can be used repeatedly. Note that some cloths sold as jeweler's polishing cloths do contain chemical products, so check which type you are buying.

Jeweler's silver polishing cloth: A lint-free cloth impregnated with chemicals for removing tarnish and polishing silver. The cloth should not be washed, and should be discarded when it is black. After polishing with an impregnated cloth, wipe your jewelry with a damp, soft, lint-free cloth to remove any residual product.

Liquid, paste, or cream polish: Different solutions are available for cleaning silver and brass and copper. These should be reserved for heavily tarnished items. The solution is applied to the metal, and left to dry. Once dry, polish off with a clean cloth. Rinse the item with water to remove any residual product, then dry.

Silver dip: A liquid cleaning product designed to remove tarnish from silver. As this contains hazardous chemicals, only use very occasionally for intricate pieces of silver that cannot be cleaned in any other way (see page 65). After use, rinse the item well, then dry.

Jeweler's gold polishing cloth: A lint-free cloth impregnated with chemicals for removing tarnish and polishing gold.

Pearl cleaning kit: These kits usually consist of tissues infused with a gentle cleaning product plus a microfiber cloth (see page 104). Such kits can usually be used to clean delicate stones too.

BASIC TOOLS

The following four tools are useful for taking on simple repairs, together with a few pairs of pliers (see below).

1 Small, fine penknife: Ideal for removing stones, scraping, and many other small jobs.

2 Shears: Used to cut through metal; the long handles and short blades enable you to apply the maximum amount of pressure to cut through thick metal or wire.

3 Diamond tweezers: Sharp pointed tweezers designed to pick up small stones. The best way to pick up a stone with tweezers is to approach it sideways, not from above—slide the tweezers horizontally to the bench and pick the stone up by its sides.

4 Spring-loaded tweezers: When opened, they remain in position, making them invaluable for holding items steady while you work on another part.

PLIERS

Hand tools used for gripping, turning and bending, or compressing; some pliers are also designed for cutting. To get the most from your pliers, keep them clean and oil the joints regularly with 3-in-1 oil.

1 Side snips: Used for cutting metal. The long handles and short blades give you the necessary leverage to cut through thick sheet metal and wire.

2 Round-nosed pliers: Used for turning small curved shapes and jump rings.

3 Needle-nosed pliers: Also called long-nosed pliers. Used for fine repair work: They are designed to reach small areas and they can make fine joins.

4 Parallel pliers: These close in a parallel action, reducing the risk of marking or indenting metal.

5 Half-round pliers: Used for bending wider wires without leaving a mark.

6 Duckbill pliers: Used to bend wire, and open and close jump rings.

7 Crimping pliers: Specialist pliers designed to close crimping beads (see pages 98–9). They have two notches in the blades, one for flattening the crimp bead and the other for rounding it.

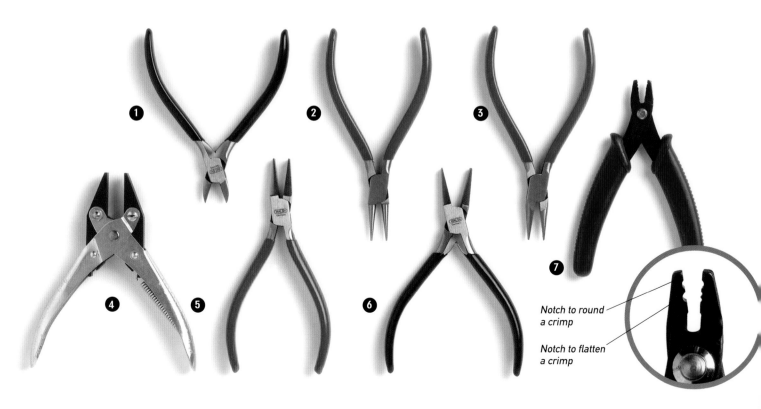

Notch to round a crimp

Notch to flatten a crimp

BEADING THREADS

These come in a wide range of materials. If you are restringing a necklace, try to match the type of thread and thickness to the original.

1 Natural silk thread: Silk thread is traditionally used to string pearls and small stones. It comes in a wide range of colors. While silk thread may not be as durable as synthetic threads (see below), is prone to fraying, and will stretch, it is the easiest thread to work with if you are knotting a necklace (see pages 100–103). It comes in either in a 6-ft (2-m) length with beading needle attached, or in reels for stringing longer necklaces. Silk thread comes in different thicknesses—typically, thin is 0.5 mm, medium is 0.7 mm, and thick is 0.9 mm. You can also buy nylon thread that looks very similar to silk, but doesn't fray or stretch.

2 Elasticated beading cord: A stretchy cord, it comes in a clear form as well as in a wide range of bright colors. Used for restringing stretchy bracelets (see pages 96–7).

3 Beading wire: Very strong thread, consisting of very thin strands of steel covered in nylon. There are different grades—the higher the number of steel strands in the wire, the more flexible it is. Typically, beading wire comes in 7-, 19-, and 49-strand wire. It also comes in different diameters, from 0.13–0.14 mm for small beads, to 0.16–0.18 mm for larger, heavier beads. Suitable only for unknotted necklaces.

In addition, there are a number of other types of threads on the market.
Nylon beading thread: Strong thread very similar to fishing line; it is sometimes referred to as illusion cord or monofilament. Suitable for unknotted necklaces.

Waxed cotton thread: Strong cotton cord that has been lightly waxed to make threading easier. Suitable for unknotted necklaces.

Suede thread: Cord made from suede. It is used for thong-type necklaces, and comes in a range of colors.

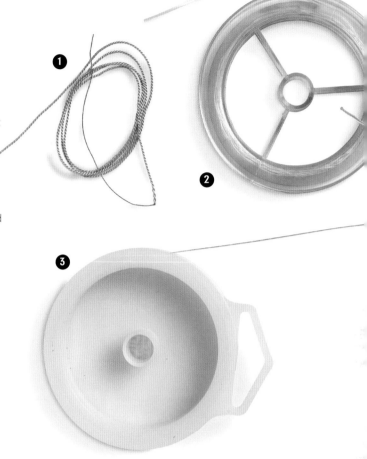

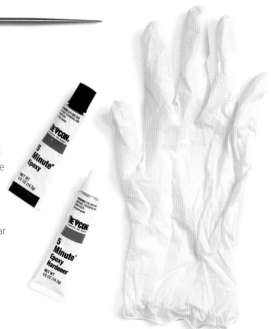

STONE SORTING TRAYS

Trays designed for sorting beads and stones. They come in a range of designs and lengths. They are usually rectangular in shape and consist of at least two sections—a wide section for holding the loose beads while they are being sorted, and another section of grooved rows for laying out the beads into the design of the necklace or bracelet. Some trays also have a section with holes to receive different-sized beads so the beads can be grouped into the different sizes.

SCRIBER

A probing and scraping tool, useful for scratching away dried glue from stone settings, checking for loose stones, and marking metal.

GLUES

When gluing stones (see pages 121–3), I prefer to use a two-part epoxy resin glue. You have to mix the two glues together—usually in equal amounts—but their advantage is that while very strong, they don't dry straight away, which means once applied you have time to move the stone or stones if you need to. Once dried, this type of glue will hold stones securely. Always follow the manufacturer's instructions when working with glues of this kind, and always wear protective gloves.

Metal is an essential component of jewelry. Learn about the different types of metals used in costume jewelry—from silver to pinchbeck, and pewter to chrome. Find out how to care for a wide range of metals, and discover the different ways you can bring back the shine to your jewelry, whether intricate silver filigree pieces, brass, or copper, or an item that has developed verdigris. If you have a piece of silver jewelry that has lost its patina and look, find out how you can restore it. Finally, discover more about new cleaning technology with an ultrasonic cleaner that will give your jewelry a super clean.

Bring Back the Shine

Metals

It is no exaggeration to say that the discovery of metals changed the course of human history. The invention of bronze for making tools took us out of the Stone Age, and metals have been an integral part of our technological progress. Many of the metalworking techniques were developed by metalsmiths in the ancient world to produce decorative items, including jewelry. The so-called precious metals (gold, silver, palladium, and platinum) have always been prized as they are resistant to corrosion. They are used in making the finest jewelry, often mixed with other metals in an alloy to improve their strength and durability. Other metals, the so-called base metals, are also used to make less expensive jewelry—not only in their pure form, but as ingredients in alloys or as a base for plating with a precious metal. To find out about the Mohs scale, see page 115.

William Kerr silver flower pin, 1900s

GOLD

Gold (chemical symbol Au) is the most treasured of the precious metals, both for its appearance and its rarity—only about 165,00 tons of gold have ever been mined. It is a dense, soft, and malleable metal, with a bright yellow luster, making it an ideal material for jewelry making, and its reputation for "incorruptibility" (it is one of the noble metals that do not corrode in moist air, and pure gold does not tarnish) gives it an added attraction.

Gold is found in the form of nuggets and small pieces in veins in rocks and deposited in streams, and is mined in many places throughout the world. When used in jewelry, it is almost always strengthened by mixing it with other metals, such as silver, copper, or palladium.

The purity of the gold is described by a system of karats, with pure gold being 24 karats (24k): 18k gold is 18 parts gold (75%) to 6 parts (25%) other metal. Gold in jewelry is typically 22k, 18k, 15k, 14k, 10k, or 9k and is marked with a hallmark stating the purity of the metal. While most alloys of gold, especially the purer ones, aim to retain its natural yellow color by mixture with varying proportions of copper and silver, there are other varieties used for jewelry. Rose gold, for example, is made with a high proportion of copper (25% or even more), and white gold can be made with the addition of silver, palladium, or zinc (nickel was also used until recent laws prevented the practice). Items made from other metals can also be plated with gold, gilded with gold leaf (extremely thin sheets of gold or gold alloy), or decorated with gold inlays. Gold is comparatively soft, even in

Rhodium-plated dress clip-cum-pin with rhinestones, 1940s

Reverse of the rhodium-plated pin showing its shiny finish

alloys; pure gold has a hardness of about 2.5 on the Mohs scale. It is used in all forms of jewelry, from the traditional wedding band to ornate chains, necklaces, and bracelets, and is often used as the setting for precious stones.

Problems: Pure gold is very soft, and high karat gold is liable to scratching and denting if its surface is carelessly handled. Gold alloys are more durable, but some can be brittle. Gold plate can wear away from its base and require replating.

Cleaning and care: See page 67.

SILVER

The most common of the precious metals, silver (chemical symbol Ag) is soft and malleable (pure silver has a hardness of about 2.7 on the Mohs scale), and has a distinctive white luster. Although not as rare as gold, and so not as highly valued, it has also been used for coinage throughout history, and has gained value as a material in the photographic and electronic industries. Like gold, it is one of the noble metals that do not corrode in moist air, and it also has antimicrobial properties that make it particularly suitable for items of jewelry such as earrings and

1

2

3

4

5

(1) Rose-gold pin with diamond, 19th century; (2) White-gold solitaire ring with diamond, 1990s; (3) Yellow-gold ring with coral, 1950s; (4) Modern platinum band; (5) Modern palladium band; (6) Cut-steel arrow pin, 18th century

6

Aluminum airplane propellor pin, 1914

Brass pin of pilot Amy Johnson beside her airplane, 1930s

studs (although prolonged skin contact with silver alloys can sometimes cause tarnishing).

It is found naturally as "native silver," but most silver used commercially is derived as a by-product from the refining of other metals such as gold, copper, lead, and zinc. It is found in various degrees of purity, and to improve its durability, silver is generally alloyed with other metals for jewelry making.

Traditionally, fine jewelry is made from sterling silver—92.5% silver and 7.5% copper which is hallmarked as 925 to indicate the number of parts per thousand of its silver content. Other degrees of purity, such as Britannia silver (95.8% silver) and even lower are also used, but are more prone to tarnishing. Argentium sterling silver (92.5% silver, but alloyed with germanium as well as copper) was developed in the 1990s to overcome the problem of tarnishing.

Because of its superior shine and color, silver is also used to plate other base metals, and some fine items of sterling silver are plated with very pure (99% or more) silver to give it a shiny finish. Like gold, silver is easy to work, so is well suited to all kinds of jewelry making, from simple rings to complex chains and brooches.

Problems: A fairly soft metal, silver can scratch and dent with careless handling. Silver and silver alloys can also become dull over time, and many silver alloys tarnish easily. Silver plate can wear away from its base and require replating.

Cleaning and care: See pages 64–5.

PLATINUM

Platinum (chemical symbol Pt) is a very rare precious metal, prized for its gray-white luster. Because of its rarity, and recent demand for use in catalytic converters, it is only found in the finest jewelry today, where it is valued more than gold for its durability. Like gold, it is usually used in jewelry in alloy form, typically 90–95% platinum. Rhodium, another precious metal of the platinum group, is sometimes used to plate white gold, platinum, and metals used to make costume jewelry to prevent tarnishing and give a more shiny finish.

Problems: Loses its shine over time and develops a hazy patina.

Cleaning and care: See page 67.

PALLADIUM

Discovered by William Hyde Wollaston in 1803, palladium (chemical symbol Pd) is a very rare precious metal of the platinum group, with a silvery-white luster. It was first used in jewelry in the 1930s, and is gaining popularity as an alternative for gold or platinum wedding bands as it is cheaper than platinum. However, palladium is often used in white gold alloys, and sometimes as a plating on other metals.

Problems: See Platinum, above.

Cleaning and care: See page 67.

COPPER

One of the first metals to be discovered by man, copper (chemical symbol Cu) occurs naturally in an uncompounded form, making it easy to extract and process. The bright blue-green ore is found throughout the world, and produces a metal that is soft (3 on the Mohs scale) and malleable, with a deep reddish-orange color which can be polished to a high shine.

Copper jewelry was often credited with mystical and medicinal properties, and its popularity continued through to the Art Deco period for pendants, bracelets, beads, and necklaces.

Because it is also ductile (capable of being drawn to make wire), copper wire has also been used for centuries for stringing beads. Its use in jewelry was slowly superseded by copper alloys such as brass (see opposite), but it grew in importance as an ingredient in gold and silver alloys, and its green oxide is used as a colorant in glass and enamels. Copper has also found many commercial uses, from musical instrument-making to plumbing and architecture, and as an ingredient in coinage.

Problems: Copper oxidizes easily in moist air and develops a green coating known as verdigris, which spoils the finish of jewelry and can stain the skin. Like the precious metals, its softness makes it prone to scratches and dents, and large pieces can become misshapen.

Cleaning and care: To clean copper, see page 68; to remove verdigris, see pages 70–1.

STEEL

An alloy mainly of iron, and between 0.2% and 2.1% carbon, steel has been known about since the 3rd century BC, but only occasionally used in jewelry making until fairly recently, mainly because of its tendency to rust. The exception was the cut steel jewelry popular from the 16th to the 19th centuries. The bright metal was cut with sharp, well-defined edges to catch the light in the same way as cut gemstones.

Mass production of steel began in England in the 19th century, at much the same time as the development of stainless steel—an alloy of steel with more than 11% chromium. Stainless steel, sometimes known as inox (from the French "inoxydable"), does not corrode or stain as easily as ordinary steel, and can be polished to a more lasting luster.

Through the 20th century, it has found favor as a decorative as well as structural material in architecture and furniture design, and is slowly becoming more common in jewelry. Its strength and hardness also makes it ideal for use as a base for plating with other metals, particularly chrome (see page 62). Stainless steel offers a cheap alternative for gold and silver studs and earrings.

Problems: Although stainless steel is more resistant to corrosion and staining than iron or ordinary steel, it is not entirely stain-proof, and can discolor in moist air. Plating on steel can wear away or flake. It can scratch.

Cleaning and care: Never wet cut steel jewelry. Clean with a dry jeweler's brush, then polish with a jeweler's polishing cloth. Clean stainless steel with water and mild liquid detergent using a soft, lint-free cloth. Do not use any abrasives on steel. Rinse, dry, and polish with a soft, lint-free cloth.

BRASS

An alloy of copper and zinc in various proportions, brass has proved popular with jewelry makers. Its gold color is attractive, and it is more durable than pure copper. Ancient Egyptians and Romans used it for decorative items, coinage, and jewelry, and it continued as an important metal in African and Middle Eastern jewelry making. In Europe, however, it was increasingly regarded as an inferior substitute for precious metals, and after the Industrial Revolution was used more in industry than jewelry except for cheaper items. However, it slowly made a come-back with the growth of the costume jewelry industry in the 20th

Copper butterfly pin with pink glass body and red glass eyes, 1920s

Pewter pin with leaf and flower motifs, 1950s

Chrome-plated anchor pin with Bakelite life ring, 1920s

Gold-tone astronaut pendant and chain, 1960s

century. It is used today for pendants, chains, rings, and earrings, especially those with an "ethnic" flavor.

Problems: Unplated brass items can oxidize, especially in contact with skin, and leave a green stain.

Cleaning and care: See page 68.

PINCHBECK

Like brass, pinchbeck is an alloy of copper and zinc but in different proportions; there is more copper than zinc in pinchbeck. It is thought that a London clockmaker called Christopher Pinchbeck (1670–1732) invented pinchbeck as a substitute for gold, and it was a very popular metal for jewelry in the 18th century. Pinchbeck continued to be made into the 19th century, but with the advent of new methods to cover base metals with gold, it fell out of favor.

Problems: Like brass, pinchbeck can tarnish; pieces in poor condition may be flaking or show signs of oxidization.

Cleaning and care: See Brass, above.

CHROME

Chromium is a hard (8.5 on the Mohs scale), shiny, gray-white metal (chemical symbol Cr) which can be polished to a brilliant shine. Its hardness makes it unsuitable for many jewelry uses, but it is an important ingredient in several metal alloys and ideal as a coating on other metals, both for protection against corrosion and as a decorative finish.

Chromium plating, sometimes simply known as chrome, was developed in the mid 18th century, but only became popular in the 1920s as the process was perfected. Electroplating with chrome, usually onto stainless steel, gives a very shiny, bright finish, leveling off any surface defects or roughness on the base, so was soon adopted by furniture makers and more especially the motor industry, and only later taken up by jewelry makers.

Problems: Chrome resists corrosion extremely well, but plate can flake and peel off if the underlying metal begins to corrode.

Cleaning and care: As for gold, see page 67, but polish with a jeweler's polishing cloth rather than a gold jeweler's polishing cloth.

Pinchbeck locket with etched floral motif, early 19th century.

Silver-tone pin with metallic beads, 1960s

PEWTER

An alloy of around 90% tin with a combination of lead, antimony, bismuth, copper, or silver in various proportions, pewter has been in use for pots, plates, and ornaments for more than 3,000 years. Perhaps because of the dullness of its gray luster, it was only seldom used for jewelry until the 20th century, when there was a vogue for pewter pins and similar items in the 1940s and 1950s. Modern pewter jewelry is very often plated with gold or silver.

Problems: Pewter is prone to tarnishing, and loses its luster easily. It is also quite soft and can be scratched and dented with careless handling.

Cleaning and care: See Chrome, opposite. To remove tarnish from pewter, use a proprietary metal (not silver) polish.

ALUMINUM

A lightweight, dull silver-white element (chemical symbol Al) of the boron group, aluminum was first successfully extracted from bauxite ore, its principal source, in 1825, and has only been produced on a commercial scale in the 20th century. Aluminum is the most abundant metal in the Earth's surface, and iron is the only metal in more use. At the time of its discovery it was considered more precious than gold, but is now relatively inexpensive.

Vintage costume jewelry made of aluminum is rare, although it does not have a very high commercial value. Aluminum has many industrial uses, especially as an ingredient in several alloys, but has only recently been adopted by jewelry makers. Still widely thought of as an "inferior" metal, it has been restricted to costume or "junk" jewelry, particularly with colored finishes produced by anodizing. There is however a growing interest in aluminum among jewelry makers due to the workability of the metal—it is second only to gold for malleability. The buying public likes its extreme lightness, which makes large and chunky items more wearable than similar items in heavier precious metals (not to mention the lower cost!).

Problems: Surface shine dulls very quickly, and it is also prone to scratches and dents.

Cleaning and care: As it is easily scratched, wash aluminum in lukewarm water with a little mild liquid detergent and a soft, lint-free cloth. Rinse and dry with a soft, clean cloth.

TIN

A soft, malleable metal, tin (chemical symbol Sn) is highly resistant to corrosion. Like chrome, it is suitable more as a plating material to protect other metals and give them a shiny finish than for structure, and its importance to jewelry is mainly as an ingredient in alloys and solders. Tin plating was used to protect pressed steel items in the 19th century, and occasionally for inferior steel jewelry, but its main use has been for lining cans and other forms of food packaging.

Problems: Tin plating can wear away from its base.

Cleaning and care: See Chrome, left.

GOLD AND SILVER TONE

Jewelry made with base metals and finished with a gold or silver effect are referred to as gold- or silver-tone metal. There is no real gold or silver used in the coating. This is distinct from gold or silver plating (see pages 58 and 60).

Problems: The gold or silver coating can rub off.

Cleaning and care: See Aluminum, left.

Cleaning metals

All metals need cleaning from time to time. Although gold and platinum only tarnish very slightly, silver, brass, and copper tarnish noticeably over time. Despite the fact that tarnish can be unsightly, it does not harm metals. Vintage jewelry made from metals does not necessarily need cleaning. Many collectors value the warm tone, or patina, on metals that comes with age. Stamped, molded, or etched items will have darker areas in the crevices. Again, these can enhance rather than detract from the beauty of the piece (see Restoring patina, page 66).

Danish sterling silver heart necklace, 1950s

Cleaning smooth, plain silver

Silver tarnish (silver sulfide) appears as a thin, dark-gray layer on the surface of silver. Silver tarnishes when it is exposed to sulfur compounds in the air. These are naturally occurring, but are also created as a by-product of industry. The combination of sulfur and moisture exacerbates the tarnishing process. Certain foods that contain high levels of sulfur, such as eggs and onions, will also tarnish silver. The following instructions are suitable for silver-only items of jewelry. If your piece contains gemstones, see Cleaning gemstones, pages 124–5.

1 If there is ingrained dirt on the item, first use a jeweler's brush to remove it, using gentle, sweeping strokes. If the silver item is very tarnished, use a jeweler's silver polishing cloth or a proprietary silver cleaner in the form of paste, liquid polish, or silver dip (see page 53) and follow the manufacturer's directions. Rinse with clean water to remove any residual cleaner. Dry on a clean towel, then polish with a soft, lint-free cloth. Make sure the item is completely dry before putting it away, preferably in a plastic zip-lock bag.

2 To remove fingerprints or makeup, clean the item in a bowl of soapy, lukewarm, never hot, water—if the item has been lacquered, hot water may remove the lacquer—using a soft jeweler's brush. Rinse in clean water, dry with a clean towel, then give it a final polish with a soft, lint-free cloth.

Jeweler's silver polishing cloth see Tools, page 53

Jeweler's brush see Tools, page 53

CLEANING SILVER DON'TS
- Don't use brass or chrome cleaners on silver. These cleaners contain chemicals that are too harsh for silver jewelry.
- Never use baking soda or toothpaste to clean your silver. These are abrasive products and they can scratch the surface of the silver.
- Take care not to expose your silver to cardboard, paper (acid-free tissue paper is fine), or protein-based materials such as chamois leather, silk, wool, felt, or baize. These contain traces of hydrogen sulfide and will speed up the tarnishing process.
- Avoid wearing rubber gloves to clean your silver; they also contain traces of hydrogen sulfide. Gloves made from plastic are fine to use.

CLEANING SILVER DO'S
- Clean your silver-plate items as above, but expose them to as little proprietary silver cleaning products as possible. When removing tarnish, you also remove minute amounts of silver every time you clean it, and over time areas of the base metal may become exposed.
- Use an ultrasonic cleaner (see page 69) for silver-only items. Many gemstones cannot be cleaned in an ultrasonic cleaner.
- Take your item to a professional jeweler for a super clean. They have specialist equipment that removes tarnish and restores a high shine.
- Use silica-gel packs and store them with your silver jewelry. The silica absorbs humidity in the air, reducing the risk of tarnish.

Cleaning intricate silver

To remove tarnish on intricate silver jewelry, silver dip is a good option. However, the dip will also remove traces of silver every time you use it, so avoid using silver dip too often, and try to keep your silver as tarnish-free as possible (see box opposite). Although the dip will remove tarnish, it does not polish the silver, so you will need to polish it with a jeweler's silver polishing cloth afterward.

Silver filigree bracelet, 1940s

1

1 Wear protective gloves when using silver dip, but not those made from rubber (see box opposite). If you have a spare piece of silver wire handy, shape it into an S-hook to hold the item so that you can easily lower it in and take it out of the dip with minimal contact.

2 It's a good idea to place the dip container on newspaper so that the solution doesn't come into contact with surfaces. Follow the manufacturer's recommendations carefully, but as a general guide don't leave the item in the dip for longer than a minute or so. Bear in mind that the dip will dissolve the tarnish but it won't polish the silver, so don't expect the item to look polished when you remove it from the solution.

3 Remove the item from the dip and rinse it thoroughly under running water. Dry it with a soft, lint-free cloth. Polish the item with a jeweler's silver polishing cloth, then wipe it with a damp, soft, lint-free cloth to remove any residual cleaning solution. Dry with a soft, lint-free cloth.

2

Protective gloves see Tools, page 53

Silver dip see Tools, page 53

Soft, lint-free cloth

Jeweler's silver polishing cloth see Tools, page 53

Restoring the patina on silver

Old silver jewelry that has been stamped (a type of embossing using a stamp or punch) may develop an attractive dark patina in the recesses that highlights the intricately embossed design. This bracelet has had a repair at some point in time, and one of the chain medallions has lost its patina. You can use commercial products to oxidize silver to darken the surface, but household bleach will usually do the job just as well.

Stamped silver bracelet with blue marbled faux stone, 1940s

1 The repaired medallion to the right of the central stone on this bracelet is far too shiny and stands out from the other medallions that have retained their patina. In order to restore the patina to a piece like this, you need to oxidize the silver. However, the following method is not suitable for delicate stones (see the box on page 125). Use a Q-tip dipped in the water-bleach solution instead (see Step 2).

2 Wear protective gloves, but not those made from rubber (see page 64). Add 1 part bleach to 10 parts water in a small bowl. Place the affected area of the item into the bleach solution (if you are working with a smaller item of jewelry, use tweezers to place it into the solution). If the silver doesn't start to darken after a minute or so, add a little more bleach.

3 As soon as the silver has darkened sufficiently—usually after no more than a minute and a half—remove the item from the solution and rinse it under a running faucet (with smaller items, make sure that the drain hole is covered first). Discard the solution. Dry with paper towel. Lightly polish the restored section with a jeweler's silver polishing cloth to bring out the shine in the raised areas of the design. Finally, wipe with a damp, soft, lint-free cloth to remove any residual product, then dry.

Protective gloves see Tools, page 53

Small bowl and household bleach

Paper towel and a soft, lint-free cloth

Jeweler's silver polishing cloth see Tools, page 53

Cleaning gold

Jewelry made from a high percentage of gold (usually 14 karat and above) tarnishes much more slowly than silver, so will not need cleaning as often. The oils in your skin, lotions, and soap can all dull the surface of your gold jewelry. Although there are a number of proprietary products on the market for cleaning gold, soapy water and a soft-bristled toothbrush or jeweler's brush will do the job just as well at a fraction of the cost. Lower-karat alloys may tarnish more quickly, and can be cleaned in the same way as silver (see pages 64–5).

Modern distressed gold ring with a small central diamond

1 Add a little mild liquid detergent to a bowl of lukewarm water. Stir it gently. If the dirt on the item is very ingrained, leave it to soak in the soapy water for 5–10 minutes. Using a soft-bristled toothbrush (don't use hard bristles, since they may scratch the gold) or a jeweler's brush, lightly scrub the piece until all the dirt is removed.

2 Make sure that the drain hole is covered, then rinse the item under a running faucet. Dry it with a soft, lint-free cloth or paper towel, then polish it with a jeweler's gold polishing cloth. Finally, wipe it with a damp, soft, lint-free cloth to remove any residual product, then dry.

Small bowl and mild liquid detergent

Soft-bristled toothbrush or jeweler's brush see Tools, page 53

Soft, lint-free cloths see Tools, page 53

Jeweler's gold polishing cloth see Tools, page 53

CLEANING GOLD DON'TS

- Never use bleach to clean your gold jewelry; if it is made from low-karat gold, chlorine can damage the surface over time.
- Don't boil it. This is completely unnecessary, and risks damaging your jewelry.
- Never use toothpaste or baking soda to clean your gold jewelry. Gold is easily scratched and these substances are too abrasive.

CLEANING GOLD DO'S

- Store your lower-karat gold jewelry with silica-gel packs; as with silver, exposure to moisture can speed up the tarnishing process in lower-karat gold, and the silica gel will absorb excess moisture. The higher the karat content (14 karat and above) the slower your gold will tarnish.
- Use an ultrasonic cleaner (see page 69), as long as the piece is a gold-only item. (Note: Many gemstones are delicate and should not be cleaned in an ultrasonic cleaner.)
- Take any lower-karat items that have become tarnished to a professional jeweler for specialist cleaning. If your gold jewelry is very scratched, a professional jeweler can also polish damaged items to remove unsightly scratches.

CLEANING GOLD-PLATED JEWELRY

Gold-plated jewelry is very delicate and requires special handling. Gold-plate rubs off easily, so only use a damp soft cloth to clean it lightly. Don't use a soft-bristled toothbrush or a jeweler's brush, which can scratch away the surface over time. Dry with a soft, lint-free cloth, then polish it with a jeweler's gold polishing cloth. Finally, wipe it with a damp, soft, lint-free cloth to remove any residual cleaning product, then dry.

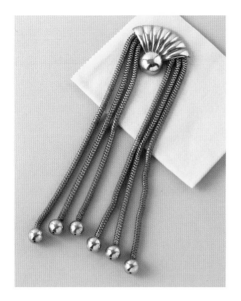

Cleaning brass and copper

Proprietary cleaners are available to clean your brass and copper jewelry, but you can also make homemade solutions that can be just as effective. Undiluted Worcestershire sauce or catsup both contain acids that remove tarnish from brass and copper. A gentler option is to use a solution made with lemon, salt, and water. If your brass or copper jewelry contain gemstones or other materials, such as Bakelite, follow the advice for the relevant material. Finally, it is not essential to clean your brass or copper jewelry—the tarnish won't damage it, and some collectors prefer to leave it with its interesting patina.

Brass dangle pin, 1940s

1

3

1 Brass and copper tarnish quickly and jewelry made from these metals requires frequent cleaning to keep the piece looking good. If the item is dirty as well as tarnished, clean it first in a bowl of lukewarm water to which you've added a little mild liquid detergent. To clean, use a very soft-bristled toothbrush or jeweler's brush and gentle, sweeping strokes.

2 To remove tarnish, take a small bowl and fill it with lukewarm water. Add a squeeze of lemon juice and a teaspoon of salt and stir it to dissolve the salt. Place the item in the solution and leave it there for a minute or two—you will see the tarnish dissolve.

3 Remove the item from the solution and rinse it under a running faucet—make sure the sink hole is covered first. Dry it with a soft, lint-free cloth and leave it to air until it is completely dry. When the item is dry, polish it with a jeweler's polishing cloth.

Soft-bristled toothbrush or jeweler's brush see Tools, page 53

Small bowl

Lemon juice

Salt

Soft, lint-free cloth

Jeweler's polishing cloth see Tools, page 53

Using an ultrasonic cleaner

Domestic ultrasonic cleaners are widely available and inexpensive. The device works by sending high-frequency sound waves into a liquid solution held in the chamber. This causes the water to vibrate, creating tiny bubbles that form and burst at high velocity. These act as mini scourers, dislodging dirt in the smallest of crevices. Ultrasonic cleaners are ideal for cleaning intricate items of jewelry, including elaborate chains. They are not suitable for certain precious and semi-precious stones (see box below).

Silver belcher chain necklace, 19th century

1 Before using your ultrasonic cleaner for the first time read the manufacturer's instructions. These may vary from one machine to another. Fill the chamber with the recommended cleaning solution—many manufacturers recommend warm water only or, as here, a mixture of warm water and mild liquid detergent for more heavily soiled items. Place the item of jewelry to be cleaned in the basket supplied with the unit.

2 Lower the basket into the chamber and put the lid on. (Note: in the photograph the lid has been left off in order to show the action of the ultrasonic sound waves in the liquid solution; this is not recommended for actual use.) Push the control button to the desired setting. Some ultrasonic cleaners have set timers, others allow you to switch them on and off at will. If the unit doesn't have a timer, try three minutes and repeat if necessary.

3 Remove the item from the basket. Scrub gently with a soft-bristled toothbrush or jeweler's brush to remove any remaining particles of dirt. Rinse in clean water, then leave to dry. Polish with a jeweler's polishing cloth if necessary. Note: ultrasonic cleaners may not remove all of the tarnish on silver items. If this is the case, intricate silver items may need to be cleaned in silver dip (see page 65) afterward. Pour away the liquid from the chamber and wipe the ultrasonic cleaner dry.

Ultrasonic cleaner and approved cleaning solution

Jeweler's brush and polishing cloth see Tools, page 53

CHOOSING THE RIGHT MATERIALS FOR ULTRASONIC CLEANING

Many gemstones and other materials are not suitable for ultrasonic cleaning. Check below to see what you should and should not clean using this method. If an item is not on these lists, err on the side of caution and clean by hand. Don't put glued stones in an ultrasonic cleaner.

Suitable for ultrasonic cleaners
Diamond
Garnet
Glass, but not rhinestones
Gold
Platinum
Ruby
Sapphire
Silver

Not suitable for ultrasonic cleaners
Amber
Amethyst
Animal materials (see pages 142–5)
Aquamarine
Cameos
Ceramics (see pages 140–1)
Citrine
Emerald
Enamels (see pages 138–9)
Jade
Lapis lazuli
Malachite
Marcasite
Turquoise
Onyx
Opal
Patinated metals
Pearls
Peridot
Plant materials (see pages 146–7)
Plastics (see pages 134–7)
Quartz
Rhinestones (see pages 116–19)
Tanzanite
Textiles, e.g. silk thread used in necklaces
Topaz
Tourmaline
Zircon

Treating verdigris

Costume jewelry is often made from metals with a high brass or copper content. These metals are particularly prone to verdigris, a chemical reaction caused by exposure to moisture. Sterling silver, platinum, and gold do not succumb to verdigris damage. Visible as a powdery dark green to bluey-green staining, verdigris may damage plating and even make metal brittle. Often found on clasps and chains, unsightly patches can be difficult to remove and will corrode metal jewelry if left unattended. Bear in mind that if the metal has been coated with verdigris for a long time the surface underneath the coating may be damaged. Take care if your piece has stones, especially rhinestones, protecting them from the cleaner if possible, to avoid damage.

1 First, try to brush off as much of the verdigris as you can, using a jeweler's brush. Brush in one direction, using gentle, sweeping strokes. Don't scrub at the piece or you might dislodge stones.

2 Examine the piece for any remaining verdigris. Next, raid your kitchen—acidic materials such as catsup, lemon juice, and white vinegar will remove all but the most stubborn deposits. In a difficult case, you may need to resort to a proprietary cleaner.

3 Apply the produce only to the damaged area—this is where catsup is a good choice as it is less liquid than the alternative products —and leave to work for at least an hour.

4 Using paper towel, gently wipe off your chosen cleaner—in this case catsup. Wipe the necklace again, this time with a damp, soft, lint-free cloth, to remove any remaining traces of the acidic product. Dry on paper towel, then polish with a jeweler's polishing cloth.

Jeweler's brush see Tools, page 53

Catsup

Paper towel

Soft, lint-free cloth

Jeweler's polishing cloth see Tools, page 53

Czech brass necklace with blue glass beads, 1920s

Learn all you need to know about vintage findings—the term jewelers use to categorize all the small components that make up an item of jewelry. These include necklace and bracelet clasps, and earring and pin fastenings. Discover when they were first produced, how they work, and the pros and cons of wearing each type of finding. Also included are invaluable care and repair tips for every type of finding. Discover step-by-step the right technique for replacing clasps and closing links on chains. Find out how to repair faulty clip-on earrings, and put in a new fastener in a pin or replace a rollover catch.

Findings

Clasps and chains

A fastener that can open and close, attaching two things together (for example, two ends of a necklace or bracelet), is known as a clasp. The clasp is a good place to search for marks that indicate the maker and/or the precious metal content. However, don't rely on this—as the working part of any piece, the clasp is a common area of damage and replacement, so you may not be looking at the original. In the following pages you will find everything you need to know about popular styles of clasp, along with detailed information on how to repair damaged clasps or replace them with appropriate substitutes.

Elaborately decorated box clasp on a
Miriam Haskell bead necklace, 1950s

TYPE		HOW IT WORKS	PROS	CONS	DAMAGE
S hook clasp A variation of the hook and eye fastening, S hooks are probably one of the earliest types of clasp used for necklaces. Designs range from simple bent wire to ornately decorated cast metal.		One loop of the S hook is closed around a jump ring, the other left slightly open to hook onto a jump ring at the other end of the necklace or bracelet.	A simple clasp to operate, and a classic design.	The hook on lightweight necklaces can come undone; consider fitting a safety chain—see chain extender on page 76.	Bent S hooks can be reshaped with pliers; broken ones can be replaced with a new clasp—for full instructions, see page 78.
Hook and eye clasp A simple clasp common in early jewelry, although later designs can be ornately decorated. Used with both single- and multi-strand necklaces and bracelets.		A hook attached to one end of the necklace or bracelet is latched onto a loop—the eye—at the other end. The weight of the item helps keep the hook engaged in the eye, so these clasps work best with heavier pieces of jewelry.	Sturdier than tensioned clasps; easier to use than barrel types.	The clasp relies on gravity to keep it secure, so can come undone when loose; consider fitting a safety chain—see chain extender on page 76.	Bent hooks can be reshaped with pliers. Replace worn clasps with new—for full instructions, see page 78.
Toggle clasp Many modern necklaces and bracelets have a toggle closure, also called a bar and ring clasp, based on the traditional watch chain design.		The design consists of two parts—a bar and a circle. Thread the bar through the circle in a vertical direction and turn it to horizontal to lock together.	Doesn't break as easily as tensioned clasps; easier to undo than barrel types.	The closure can work loose through friction.	Replace with a new clasp—for full instructions, see page 78.
Box clasp Though described as a box, these clasps are not always square or rectangular. They are available with either single or multiple attachment rings for single-, double-, or triple-strand necklaces or bracelets. Often used on pearls, this style of clasp dates back to the late 18th century.		A tensioned tab holds two parts of a box structure together. Press the spring lever set in one side of the box and slide the shaped tab out from the other half to open; push the tab back in to close the fastening. Some box clasps come with a safety catch on the side, particularly on more valuable necklaces.	Wide range of design styles available, including barrel- or round-shaped box clasps (see opposite, top left) and types with multi-strand fittings.	The closure tab can lose its tension over time, or even snap off.	If you have a vintage clasp like the one shown here, you may find that the prongs on the lever are bent or even broken; to repair the tab, see pages 178–181.

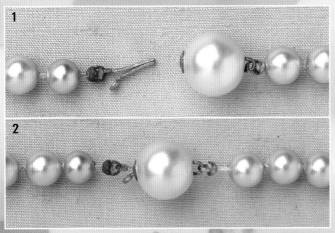

Round "box" clasps (see opposite, below) were widely used on vintage costume jewelry: here the casing is hidden within a pearl; once inserted, the clasp is hidden. Faux pearl necklace, 1950s.

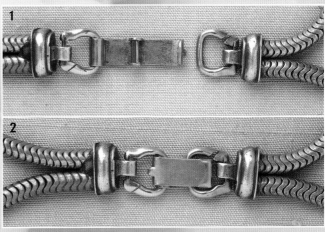

A fold-over clasp (see page 76) on a necklace from the 1940s. When snapped shut, the clasp gives a neat, streamlined appearance. Trifari gold-tone negligée necklace, 1940s (see also page 32).

TYPE		HOW IT WORKS	PROS	CONS	DAMAGE
Barrel or torpedo clasp In the shape of a barrel, these clasps are in two pieces, held together with a screw thread system or, in some modern versions, a pair of magnets (see page 76). The design first appeared in the early 19th century.		The two non-tensioned pieces of the clasp resemble a barrel. They have screw threads inside to screw them together.	Easy to fasten, inexpensive, no protruding lever to irritate the skin.	The screw type can untwist as it slides over your neck or arm, leading to loss of the jewelry.	To free a jammed screw thread use a drop of oil.
Spring or bolt ring clasp This popular clasp design was developed in the late 19th century and is mainly used on inexpensive jewelry, particularly on bracelets and strings of beads.		Two rings and a tensioned mechanism form this design. One ring has a small prong or lever, held on a hidden spring, that you push back to open the ring. Insert the other ring, then release the lever to close the clasp.	A simple clasp with a discreet appearance.	Small versions can be hard to open.	Replace with a new clasp—for full instructions, see page 78.
Fish hook clasp This type of clasp was particularly popular for pearl necklaces, but is found on more inexpensive vintage necklaces too.		The hook-shaped tongue acts as a spring, and locks into place when pushed into the casing. Squeeze and pull out to release.	A durable clasp, suitable for heavy necklaces.	The hook can be pulled out of shape so that it no longer fits securely into the casing.	Misshapen hooks can be reshaped with pliers—for full instructions, see page 81.
Push clasp A variation on the box clasp seen in some vintage necklaces. The comparatively large casing can be heavily decorated and become a feature of the necklace or bracelet.		The spring action of the tongue locks it in place within the casing. To release, squeeze the two side pieces inward and pull out.	Easy to fasten. Suitable for single- and multi-strand necklaces.	Fiddly to undo. The tongue can become distorted and no longer fit securely in the casing.	The tongue can be straightened as for an earring clip, see page 84. Otherwise, replace the clasp—for full instructions, see page 78.

Necklace and bracelet accessories

Jump rings Circles made of wire of different gauges, but left with an opening, used as connectors between links, clasps, and other rings. Once the jump ring is attached, it is squeezed shut, and may be soldered.

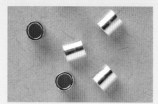

Crimps Small metal beads with comparatively large holes used to secure end loops of stringing onto clasps as an alternative to knotting (see page 98). They are squeezed tight around the thread with crimping pliers.

Crimp covers Cup-shaped covers to conceal crimps or knots at the end of stringing, squeezed gently shut with pliers (see page 99). More elaborate covers incorporate a hook for attaching to a clasp.

Chain extender A short chain for lengthening a necklace. It has a clasp at one end for attaching to the necklace; adjustment can be made by attaching the necklace's clasp to any part of the extension chain. It can also act as a safety chain.

TYPE		HOW IT WORKS	PROS	CONS	DAMAGE
Fold-over clasp Popular in the 1940s and 1950s, especially in mass-produced necklaces and bracelets. Generally left undecorated, but often bearing the maker's mark or hallmark.		The casing opens with a hinge and is folded around a jump ring. When closed, the top of the casing snaps shut.	Unobtrusive and suitable for many styles of necklace or bracelet.	May come open while being worn; when misshapen will not snap securely shut. Consider fitting a safety chain—see chain extender above.	Reshape with pliers, or replace with a new clasp—for full instructions, see page 78.
Lobster claw, or parrot, clasp Essentially a hook and eye fastening with a spring closure. The hook is in the shape of a lobster claw or parrot's beak. Widely used for necklaces and bracelets since the 1980s.		The hook is opened by pressure on the spring-loaded catch, and hooks onto a jump ring.	Very secure, and easily done up.	Can be fiddly to undo. The spring may weaken or break with use.	Difficult to repair: replace with a new clasp—for full instructions, see page 78.
Trigger clasp Similar to a lobster claw clasp, but with a simpler spring closure. Introduced in the 1980s, it is a popular clasp for contemporary necklaces and bracelets.		A jump ring can be simply clipped into the hook by pressing against the spring-loaded arm.	Reasonably secure. Can be done up one-handed, making it particularly suitable for bracelets.	Spring may weaken or break with use.	Difficult to repair: replace with a new clasp—for full instructions, see page 78.
Magnet clasp A modern variation of the barrel clasp, with magnets replacing the screw fitting.		Strong magnets set in each side of the clasp attach when brought together.	Easy to put on and take off.	Not as secure as the screw type of barrel clasp. Magnets may interfere with electronic equipment; not recommended for people with pacemakers.	Difficult to repair: replace with a new clasp—for full instructions, see page 78.

Chains

Created in gold, silver, platinum, and various other metals, there are numerous styles of chains. Essentially all chains are made up of a series of links, rings, or discs and may be worn on their own, or with ornaments attached to them. Sizes vary, but there are standard lengths. Chokers are 14–17 in (35–43 cm) long, and sit high on the neck. A princess necklace is 18–20 in (45–50 cm) long. A matinée necklace is 20–24 in (50–60 cm) in length. An opera necklace is 30–35 in (76–89 cm) long and sits at the breastbone. Longer chains than an opera necklace are known as sautoir or rope chains (see page 31). All chains are delicate and need to be treated with care. For advice on repairing a chain, see page 80.

TYPES OF CHAIN

There are so many different types of chain that some jewelers now use design numbers for their chains, rather than names. Here are some traditional, vintage chains still referred to by name:

BARLEYCORN CHAIN

Sometimes called a wheat chain. The chain consists of pairs of links closely joined together to resemble the head of a barleycorn, or wheat. There are some exquisite designs, consisting of jeweled pendants attached to a barleycorn chain.

BELCHER CHAIN

Similar to a trace chain, which consists of small oval links, a belcher chain has broad links, which may be oval or round. They are linked alternately, horizontally and vertically. Each link is wider than it is thick.

DIAMOND CUT BELCHER CHAIN

Exactly the same as a classic belcher chain (see left), the links in this chain are cut or faceted with a diamond-tipped tool to give the chain greater brilliance. The chain can be worn alone or with a light pendant.

BOX CHAIN

This type of chain is made up of wide, square box-like links, which produce a smooth-looking chain. The effect is of a sturdy but stylish and simple piece of jewelry.

CABLE CHAIN

Also known as a link chain, this is made up of round or oval interlocking links of a uniform size. It is so-named because it resembles a ship's cable. It does not lie flat because the links are connected in opposite directions.

FIGARO CHAIN

A very popular style, this is similar to a curb chain, which is composed of uniform oval-shaped flattened links. The Figaro chain has flattened links but these alternate long and short versions, usually one long to three short.

PRINCE OF WALES CHAIN

Made up of small circular links, twisted into an intricate spiral. The chain can be worn alone or with a medium-sized pendant attached.

ROPE CHAIN

A richly textured chain in which two strands are twisted together, giving the appearance of a rope. The chains are made up of small oval-shaped links, arranged in a spiral design.

SPIGA CHAIN

Made up of small figure-eight links, which form a three-dimensional chain. This gives the chain a slightly square appearance as well as making it look as if it has been plaited.

Repairing clasps and chains

Most repairs to clasps and chains involve jump rings (see page 76). These small circles or ovals of metal are the bedrock of clasps and chains. Once you have mastered how to open and close a jump ring properly, many necklace and chain repairs are within your grasp.

Putting on a clasp

Clasps come in different sizes, and it is important for the look of the finished item to use one that is in proportion with the piece you are repairing. If you still have it, use the existing clasp as a guide to size. Here, the clasp is a spring ring. As a rule of thumb, most spring ring clasps for bracelets are a medium size, either 7 mm or 8 mm. If you are replacing a spring ring clasp on a necklace, the standard size is 6 mm.

Silver filigree bracelet, 1940s

1

Jump ring

Spring ring clasp

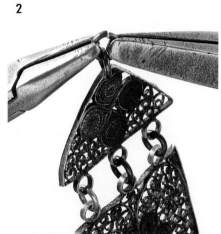

2

3

4

1 Before you start the repair, place the clasp beside the jewelry item where it is to be attached to check that the size is in proportion with the piece. If the attaching jump ring on the item has been soldered, you can buy a clasp with an open jump ring attached and use this to secure it to the piece.

2 Take a pair of duckbill pliers in each hand and place the tips either side of the opening in the jump ring on the piece.

3 Applying gentle pressure, use the pliers to twist the ends of the jump ring apart, moving the ends in opposite directions (north and south). You need to create a gap just big enough to hook the clasp easily into position.

4 Before closing the jump ring, make sure that the catch on the clasp is facing upward so that it is easy to access. Use both pairs of duckbill pliers to close the open jump ring to its original position, again using the gentle twisting motion described in Step 2.

Spring ring clasp see Clasps and Chains, page 75

Two duckbill pliers see Tools, page 54

Adding a charm

Charms are attached to charm bracelets with either open or soldered jump rings. Only use the open jump ring method if all the other charms are attached in the same way. If they have been soldered, then ideally the new jump ring will need to be soldered too (see pages 166–7).

Sterling silver charm bracelet, 1970s

1 Deciding where to put your charm is an important first step. If the charm is large, it may not look very balanced placed beside two small charms. It also needs to be spaced evenly apart from existing charms.

2 Take a pair of duckbill pliers in each hand and use the same technique as in Step 2 opposite to open the jump ring. You need to make the gap just wide enough to hook the charm easily into position. If the charm has a clear front and back, make sure you position the charm so that the front is facing outward when it is attached to the chain.

3 Slip the jump ring with its charm onto the chain. Use both pairs of duckbill pliers to close the open jump ring to its original position, again using the gentle twisting motion described in Step 3 opposite.

JUMP RING TIPS
- Although handling jump rings may look simple, there is technique involved. If you try to open a jump ring using a sideways motion rather than a twisting one, you risk permanently distorting the shape of the ring or even breaking it. Always open and close a jump ring as shown here.
- You can make your own jump ring (see pages 162–3). Make sure that you match the type and gauge of wire to any existing rings; use a degree gauge to measure the wire (see Tools, page 152).
- If a jump ring is soldered, you can cut it off using a jeweler's saw or side snips and resolder it (see page 168). Alternatively, take the item to a jeweler for the repair.

Two duckbill pliers see Tools, page 54

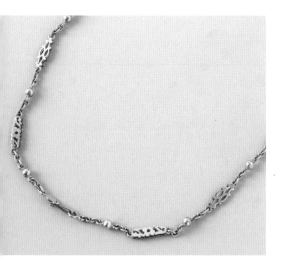

Closing an open link on a chain

An open link on a necklace chain is essentially an unsoldered jump ring (see page 76). They can be round or oval. Open links are often used on inexpensive necklace chains as they are less expensive to produce. Over time, open links can start to pull apart slightly or even come undone. Fortunately, they are very easy to repair.

Gold-tone chain necklace, 1960s

1 If one open link has come undone, it is likely that other open links on the chain are starting to pull apart. Check the necklace chain carefully to see whether any of the other links need adjusting.

2 Take a pair of duckbill pliers in each hand and place the tips either side of the opening in the open link. Applying very gentle pressure, use the pliers to twist the ends of the link in opposite directions, north and south, opening the gap wider (see also Step 3 page 78). You need to make the gap just wide enough to hook the neighboring open link easily back into position.

3 Use both pairs of duckbill pliers to close the open jump ring to its original shape, again using a gentle twisting motion to bring the two ends together.

Two duckbill pliers see Tools, page 54

Adjusting the tongue on a fish hook clasp

Fish hook clasps (see page 75) were popular clasps for costume jewelry from the 1930s to the 1960s. The metal tab, or tongue, on a fish hook clasp is vulnerable to being pulled out of shape, a common problem with this type of fastening. As a result, the tongue no longer springs back into position when inserted into the casing.

Necklace of green and clear glass beads with silver clasp, 1960s

1

1 With wear and tear, the shape of the tongue on this fish hook clasp has been pulled out of shape so that it no longer slips securely into its casing.

2 To repair it, hold the base of the tongue between the forefinger and thumb of one hand. With your other hand, use a pair of duckbill pliers to move the free edge of the tongue back into shape. Use gentle pressure and work slowly. Be careful not to over-adjust the shape.

   After each small adjustment, try closing the clasp—when the tongue slides into the opening easily and you hear a click as it springs into position, the repair is complete (see top).

2

Duckbill pliers see Tools, page 54

Earring findings

An earring finding, or fixing, provides the means with which to attach a decorative ornament to the ear. There are two basic types of earring fixings—those that are fastened through a piercing in the earlobe, and those that attach around the earlobe for non-pierced ears. To a degree, earrings can be dated by their fixings—fixings for pierced ears were used until the end of the 19th century when the screw-on finding was introduced. Clip-on fixings were developed in the mid 1930s and were very popular until the 1960s. In the following pages you will find everything you need to know about popular styles of earring findings, along with information on how to repair damaged fixings.

TYPE		HOW IT WORKS	PROS	CONS	DAMAGE
Hoop finding A circular fixing for pierced ears made from thin wire. Probably the earliest type of earring fixing, examples have been found dating from 1400 BC. Large hoop earrings became very fashionable in the 1970s, and have remained popular to the present day.		One end of the wire circle passes through the hole in the earlobe and is fixed. Many early versions were held in place with a C-catch (see page 86); nowadays, a type of safety clasp may be used, or the hoops may be hollow and the fixing inserted into it.	A comfortable earring to wear for pierced ears. The hoop can be embellished with additional ornaments, making it a very versatile piece of jewelry.	Hollow fixings can be fiddly to secure and can work loose and the earring lost. Very thin wire hoops can be bent.	Bent hoops can be reshaped with pliers.
Hook, or fish hook, finding After the hoop (see above), the hook finding for pierced ears is one of the earliest types of earring findings. Very early forms of hook fixings came in a compressed S-shape with an ornament attached to the front part of the S, with a dangle ornament hanging from the loop part.		The finding is shaped like a fish hook and passes through the hole in the earlobe. The front part is usually reinforced with additional wire and ends with a small circle (jump ring) from which ornaments are hung.	Very easy to put on and comfortable to wear for pierced ears.	The finding relies on gravity to keep it secure, so can be lifted out of the earlobe by hair or clothing. The wire can be bent.	Use a clear plastic bullet (see opposite) to secure the hook. Bent hooks can be reshaped with pliers—for full instructions, see page 85.
Kidney finding Invented in the late 19th century, the kidney finding for pierced ears has been a popular style of earring fixing ever since. This is also sometimes referred to as a plain safety wire.		An inverted U-shaped wire with a loop at the front for attaching ornaments; a bar at the bottom of the finding extends back and ends in a small C-catch shape (see page 86). The wire passes through the hole in the earlobe and hooks into the C-catch.	As comfortable as the hook finding, and with the added security of the C-catch.	Kidney findings can be made of very thin wire, which makes them prone to being bent out of shape.	Bent hooks can be reshaped with pliers—for full instructions, see page 85.
Leverback finding This finding for pierced ears was developed in the late 19th century, and is still used widely. It is also sometimes referred to as a French or Continental wire, possibly because they were associated with jewelry designed in Continental Europe in the 19th and early 20th century.		The earring has a hook (see above) that passes through the hole in the earlobe and is secured at the back by a hinged lever that closes onto the back of the earring hook. Variations include a lever with a hole at the top that passes through the back of the hook (shown).	An elegant design that gives extra security to the finding.	The earring hook can be bent out of shape. Check regularly that the mechanism is working correctly; if it is not, it is easy to lose an earring.	Bent hooks can be reshaped with pliers—for full instructions, see page 85.

1

Antique and vintage hook findings (see opposite) often have a decorative tile feature or a medallion to front the earring. Russian gold earrings with blue enamel, seed pearls, and faux pearl drops, 19th century.

3

Clip-on findings revolutionized earring design, making it possible to create large dome and cluster styles that hug the ear. Gold-tone clip-on earrings with clear rhinestones, 1950s.

2

Screw-on findings first became popular in the 1920s and were still widely used into the 1950s. Gold-tone earrings with faux ruby rhinestones, 1940s.

4

The omega clip-on was introduced in the 1970s and has a clip shaped like the Greek letter omega; some come with a post for pierced ears (shown). Nina Ricci gold-tone and enamel earrings, 1970s.

TYPE		HOW IT WORKS	PROS	CONS	DAMAGE
Screw-on finding These were invented in the late 19th century for non-pierced ears, but were not in widespread use until the 1910s and 1920s. By then, piercing the earlobe had fallen out of favor.		A thread with flat or rounded stops at both ends passes through a barrel screw into the back of the earlobe to hold the earring in place. There is a jump ring at the front on which to hang an ornament.	Pierced ears are not required. Unlike a clip-on earring (see below), the screw is adjustable so you can control the amount of pressure applied to the ear.	Like clip-on earrings, screw-on findings can pinch the earlobe. If not attached tightly enough, the earring can come off.	Clip-on cushion pads (see page 84) can be cut to fit screw-on findings. Screw-ons can be converted to post and clutch findings for pierced ears—for full instructions, see pages 160–1.
Post and clutch finding The original post finding for pierced ears was developed in the late 19th century with a slender screw fitting that passed through the ear onto which a small nut was threaded; the clutch—also referred to as a butterfly—was developed in the 1920s.		The post has a cup on the end to house a stone or a disk on which to fix a larger decorative item (see page 160). The post passes through the hole in the earlobe and the clutch slides onto the post behind the ear to secure the post. Variations include a clutch in the shape of a bullet (shown) that slides onto the post.	Ideal for small, neat earrings that fit closely to the earlobe.	Not suitable for large, heavy earrings, which can drag the finding away from the ear. The post can be bent; because it is so tiny, the clutch is easily lost.	Misshapen posts can be reshaped with pliers. Replacement clutches are widely available from findings stores.
Clip-on finding These were developed in the mid 1930s. The attraction of clip-on earrings was not only that they were suitable for non-pierced ears; they also enabled designs for earrings that covered more of the actual ear. Many earrings from the 1930s, 1940s, and 1950s have clip-on findings.		A hinged clip closes onto the back of the ear to secure the earring. In the 1950s, Miriam Haskell developed the comfort clip, which combines an ear clip with a screw-on finding. Once the clip is closed, you adjust the fit with the screw-on.	Pierced ears are not required. Perfect for large, statement earrings that hug the ear such as dome and cluster earrings (see page 35).	Clip-ons can pinch the ear, making the earrings uncomfortable to wear. The clip can be either too tight or too loose.	The clip can be adjusted—for full instructions, see page 84. Earring comfort pads (see page 84) may help with pinching. To convert clip-ons to post and clutch, see pages 160–1.

Repairing earrings

Earrings come with a wide range of findings (see pages 82–3). If you are a fan of dome or cluster earrings (see page 35), these styles tend to date from the 1930s to the 1950s, when screw-on and clip-on fixings were popular. One of the most common problems with clip-ons is that they can work loose. Fortunately, this is easy to repair. Fine wire findings for pierced ears are prone to getting bent out of shape. The repair technique described opposite can be used for all hooked types of earring findings.

Repairing a loose clip on

Clip-ons for earrings are made up of the hinge, which is secured to the earring, and the earclip, which is the moving part attached to the hinge. The neck of the earclip is placed behind the bar of the hinge and held in place by metal legs inserted into holes in the hinge. The resulting tension gives the necessary pressure when the earclip is closed to keep the earring in place. A clip-on can lose its shape with usage and work loose.

Schriener Swarovski crystal earrings in pale blue and amethyst, 1950s

1

bar
hinge
clip
leg
neck
foot
earclip

2

Inserting the metal legs into the hinge

1 If the earclip is loose but still in place, you may be able to adjust the tension by using a pair of duckbill pliers to force the neck gently toward the bar of the hinge until it is tensioned again. If this doesn't work, remove the earclip from the hinge by squeezing the metal legs together and removing first one foot and then the other from the holes in the hinge. Check that the metal legs and neck are straight and aligned. If they are not, as shown here, use a pair of duckbill pliers to straighten them until they are all in line.

2 Replace the earclip by placing the neck of the earclip on the outside of the bar on the hinge. Use a pair of duckbill pliers to squeeze the metal legs until you can insert the foot of one leg into one of the holes in the hinge. In order to insert the foot of the other leg into the second hole, you will need to apply slightly more pressure. However, if you apply too much pressure, the earclip may become distorted and you will have to start again, as above. This maneuver may take some practice before you get it right.

Duckbill pliers see Tools, page 54

LOOSENING THE TENSION ON A CLIP-ON

Sometimes the problem with clip-ons is that they are too tight and pinch the earlobes. You can loosen them by using a small file to gently prise the neck away from the bar on the hinge. Take it slowly and try the earring on after each small adjustment until you reach the desired tension. You can also remove the earclip from the hinge as above, and move the tongue backward to loosen the tension, but this is more fiddly and likely to result in over-adjustments. To make the earclips more comfortable, you can also buy stick-on cushioned pads to apply to the clip and earring back. These are available from some department stores and specialist findings outlets.

Repairing a bent earring wire

Earrings with leverback findings offer extra security and are widely available. The mechanism—a hinged hollow lever that closes onto the back of the front wire, which is fixed (see page 82)—keeps the earring firmly in place. Although leverbacks are made of toughened wire, over long use they can be pushed out of shape, particularly those with large hook wires, as here. Once the wire is twisted, the lever cannot close properly.

French red resin earrings with brass decoration and set with a marcasite stone, 1960s

1

hook-shaped front wire

hinged hollow lever

2

3

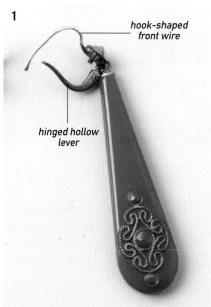

1 The front wire on this leverback earring has been pulled out of shape and the lever cannot close into position. The other earring is still functional and can be used as a template to reshape the damaged wire.

2 Before you start working on the damaged wire, push the lever to the open position. This will enable you to see the wire more clearly as you start to work on it.

3 Using a pair of fine half-round pliers, slowly start to curve the wire back into a hook shape, matching it to the other earring. Move the lever regularly to the closed position and keep adjusting the front wire until the lever can shut properly onto it.

4 The repaired earring is now a match to the other. Note: Despite taking great care, I find sometimes that during a repair the wire breaks, a result of metal fatigue from long usage—costume jewelry findings, which are often made from base metals, are particularly prone to metal fatigue. If this happens, you will need to buy a new pair of leverback findings and replace the fittings on both earrings.

Fine half-round pliers see Tools, page 54

Gold-tone rhinestone pin, 1940s

Pin fastenings

A pin consists of a fastener pin attached to an ornament for fixing to fabric. The ancient Greeks used a safety-pin type of fastener (almost identical to the modern safety-pin) known as a fibula. The Celts favored the annular or penannular pin—an open pin, usually circular. The head of the fastener pin has a ring or tube that attaches to the circle. This basic pin design was used for many centuries, but by the start of the 19th century the flat tube joint (see opposite) was in wide use. Today, the fichu or visor joint is widely used. In the following pages you will find everything you need to know about popular styles of pin fastenings, along with information on how to repair damaged fastenings.

TYPE		HOW IT WORKS	PROS	CONS	DAMAGE
Joints Two typical joints used to fix fastener pins are the fichu joint and visor joint. These started being used widely in the early part of the 20th century, and are common today.		Both joints have two semi-circles of metal attached to a central spine. In the fichu joint, the semi-circles are attached to the length of the spine; the visor joint has circles attached lower down. The semi-circles either have dimples on the inside to which a fastener pin head is fixed (see page 88) or holes through which a rivet is passed (see page 158).	A very simple mechanism—an unriveted fichu or visor joint is easy to mend at home (see page 88).	The fastener pin can work loose from a fichu joint with dimples.	The fastener pin can fall out—for full instructions to replace the fastener pin, see page 88 and 158. The fastener pin can be bent; you can straighten it with pliers.
C-catch C-catches have been used in all periods of pin making. In the 18th century the C is a very simple shape (top image); by the end of the 19th century the C-catch tends to be wider and flatter (bottom image), holding the fastener pin more securely.		A C-shaped piece of metal wire is attached to the end at the back of the pin to catch the fastener pin.	Very simple to fasten and undo.	The fastener pin can work itself loose from the C-catch, and there is a risk the pin can be lost.	The C-catch can come away—for instructions on how to make and attach a new C-catch, see page 173.
Rollover safety catch This type of catch was invented at the beginning of the 20th century, and is now widely used on pins.		This ball-shaped catch has a rotating inner disk which is turned by a lever on top of the catch. This holds the fastener pin securely once the fastener pin has been inserted into the catch. Double safety catches—there are two levers instead of one on the top of the catch—are also available.	Provides extra security to the pin catch. The double safety catch is easier to operate than the single catch.	The single rollover catch can be fiddly to operate.	The rollover catch can break; for full instructions on how to replace a rollover catch, see page 89.
Safety chain Valuable pins sometimes require extra security to the fixing, which a safety chain supplies. Some pins come with a discreet safety chain already attached.		A small, delicate chain with a clasp (a spring-operated clasp is shown) on one end and a secure fastening, usually a safety-pin style, at the other. The clasp attaches to a part of the pin and the fastening is pinned to clothing discreetly behind the pin to hide the safety chain.	Helps to secure a particularly valuable pin.	Depending on the style of the pin it is not always possible to attach a safety chain.	If you have a pin that cannot take a removable safety chain, a jeweler can solder on a permanent chain.

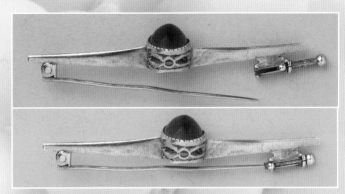

The joint on this pin is a flat tube joint: two tubes sit either side of the fastener pin head, held together with a rivet (see page 158). Carved bogwood pin, 18th century.

The trombone catch was invented in the mid 19th century. The hollow catch pulls back to allow the fastener pin to be positioned in the catch housing; the catch is pushed in to secure it. Silver pin, 19th century.

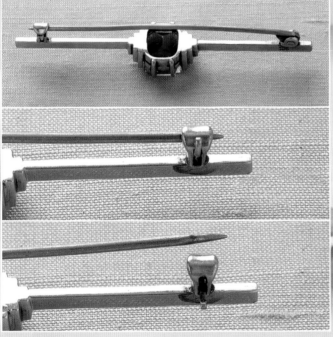

A safety catch that predates the rollover catch, a lever at the back of the C-catch lowers an inner metal guard to hold the fastener pin in position. White-gold pin with tourmaline, 1910s.

Dress clips are a variation on a pin widely worn in the 1920s to 1940s. The catch is hinged and usually has metal teeth that grip onto fabric. Gold-tone dress clip with rhinestones, 1930s.

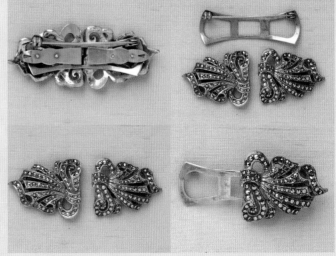

Duette clips were designed as a pin-cum-dress clips. Made of two parts that can undo to form separate clips, the whole is held together with a removable bar frame. Silver and marcasite duette clip, 1940s.

Repairing pin fastenings

In terms of simple repairs to pin findings, the two jobs you are most likely to come across are replacing a missing fastener pin or a faulty rollover catch. Of the two, replacing a missing fastener pin in a joint that doesn't require a rivet is the simpler, and probably the most common repair.

Replacing a missing fastener pin

Many pins or brooches are secured in place with a fastener pin that is held in a joint and fastens into a safety catch or C-catch (see Pin fastenings, page 86). Replacing a missing fastener pin is an easy repair if you can source a ready-made fastener pin and the mechanism doesn't need a rivet (see page 158). Findings stores stock a wide range of ready-made fastener pins, which come in all sizes and metals. Make sure that the replacement fastener pin is the right size for the joint.

Sterling silver rose pin, 1930s

1

Joint with dimples

2

Looped end of the fastener pin in position

1 This type of fastener pin can be set in the joint without a rivet. Other types of fastener pins and joints will need a rivet to secure it, requiring more advanced skills (for more information, see page 158). As a rule, the correct length for a replacement fastener pin is one that sits approximately 2–3 mm beyond the holding catch.

2 Ease the fastener pin into the joint. The looped neck of the fastener pin should be positioned facing downward, as shown. If the fit is too tight, use a small fine penknife to prise the joint apart until the fastener pin falls neatly into place.

3 Use a pair of duckbill pliers to squeeze the sides of the joint gently together, securing the fastener pin in place. Check that the fastener pin is firm and does not move from side to side when you open and close it. Your repair is complete.

3

Fastener pin see Brooch fastenings, page 86

Small penknife see Tools, page 54

Duckbill pliers see Tools, page 54

Replacing a faulty rollover catch

A missing rollover catch mechanism is another common problem with pin fastenings. The rollover catches found in vintage pins are still available today from jewelry findings stores, but if you have lots of spare or damaged pins you may be able to source a suitable replacement catch from among these. Replacing a rollover catch mechanism is not a difficult repair but it can be fiddly.

Gold-tone rhinestone pin, 1950s

1

2

3

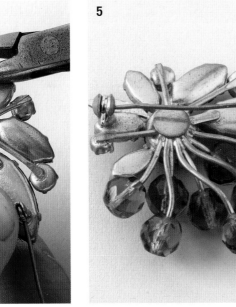

4

5

1 The top pin has lost its rollover catch mechanism, while the bottom one, which is damaged, has an intact mechanism which is an exact match for the top pin.

2 Using a small fine penknife, ease apart the housing for the rollover catch in order to release it .

3 When you have freed the catch, pick it up with a pair of tweezers and check that it fits the housing of the pin to be repaired.

4 Use a pair of round-nosed pliers to squeeze gently together the housing for the rollover catch so that the catch is held securely.

5 Check that the mechanism works by moving the catch back and forward—if the repair has been done correctly, the catch should move smoothly with no play or excess movement in the housing.

Small penknife see Tools, page 54

Tweezers see Tools, page 54

Round-nosed pliers see Tools, page 54

Beads for necklaces are made from a wide range of materials—everything from metal and stones to ceramics and seeds. Discover the many different types of beads available, and the best ways to clean and care for them. Pearls are a precious type of bead, and need special attention. Find out how to clean them safely—natural as well as imitation pearls—and the best way to store them. One of the most common jewelry repairs is restringing a necklace, and here you will learn how to do this, including how to attach a clasp properly. Detailed step-by-step instructions are also given on how to hand knot a necklace.

Beady Basics

Beads

The earliest known examples of jewelry, dating from more than 100,000 years ago, are in the form of strung beads made from sea shells—and it is possible that there were even earlier items made of wood or seeds which have not survived. Beads have been used in almost every culture since, most often strung on cord, thread, wire, or ribbon to make necklaces and bracelets, but also woven to make beaded fabric, and pinned or glued to the surface of cloth or clay. Almost all basic jewelry materials are used for beadmaking (organic, ceramic, stone, metal, glass, and plastics), and come in a huge variety of shapes and sizes. For advice on cleaning bead necklaces, see pages 104–105.

Necklace of metal beads, 1950s

ORGANIC MATERIALS

Beads made from natural materials such as seeds and nuts are still used today in many cultures. Other plant materials, especially carved wood, have also been used in beadmaking, as well as amber and jet. However, the large majority of beads from organic sources are animal in origin—horn, bone, and ivory—together with seashells and coral. The most prized of all is pearl.

Problems, cleaning, and care: For Plants, see pages 146–7; for Animals, see pages 142–5.

STONES AND GEMSTONES

Many semi-precious stones are suitable for beadmaking. These are carved or ground into beads, often by hand, and polished, or in the case of some of the transparent stones faceted to show off their brilliance. In earlier times, amulets made from their beads were thought to have curative or religious powers—the word "bead" is believed to come from the Middle English for "prayer," referring to rosaries or prayer beads.

Problems, cleaning, and care: See pages 124–5.

METALS

Precious metals such as gold and silver have been cast in the form of beads since their first discovery, and all sorts of metals and alloys are used today in beadmaking, since metal can be molded into almost any shape, and is also easily patterned or decorated. Metal beads can also be enameled, often with intricate designs in cloisonné.

Problems, cleaning, and care: See pages 64–71; for care of enamel, see pages 138–9.

Necklace with blue ceramic and cast silver beads, 1960s

Necklace of malachite beads and glass spacer beads, 1950s

GLASS

Well suited to beadmaking, glass can be molded into all shapes and sizes, colored in many different shades, and polished to a high shine. For more information on glass and glass beads, see pages 130–3.

Problems, cleaning, and care: See pages 130–3.

CERAMICS

Simple baked clay was perhaps the first man-made material for beadmaking. In Ancient Egypt and the Indus Valley a technique developed of baking a paste containing quartz or sand until the surface vitrified, known as "Egyptian faience," an early form of glazed ceramic used extensively for beads. Modern ceramic beads can be decorated by painting or applying transfers, and then lacquered or glazed. They are molded into all shapes and sizes before firing, and can be impressed with patterns and designs.

Problems, cleaning, and care: See pages 140–1.

PLASTICS

Older forms of plastic such as Ebonite were popular for beadmaking in Victorian times, and synthetic plastics of the early 20th century such as Bakelite and celluloid were ideal for beads in costume jewelry. Since Word War II, many traditional beadmaking materials have been replaced with plastics, especially acrylic. Modern resins can be molded into all shapes and sizes, and colored to imitate gemstones or coated to simulate metal.

Problems, cleaning, and care: See pages 134–7.

BEAD ACCESSORIES

Apart from stringing materials, many necklaces have two other key features: spacer beads and/or bead caps.

Spacer beads: Small "filler" beads, these are designed to frame the main bead; a different color and material may be used in order to enhance that of the main bead. Filler beads also help to extend the length of the necklace. They come in a range of shapes (see right).

Bead caps: These decorative metal caps are designed to enhance the appearance of beads. They may be used on just one side of the bead or on both sides. They come in a wide range of designs, from a plain metal cap shape to elaborate filigree designs (shown).

Threads: Materials and designs for stringing beads can vary widely, from chains (see below, top) to silk and cotton threads. Strong synthetic threads are also available (see page 55). Natural threads can also be knotted (see bottom); for more information see pages 100–103.

BEAD SHAPES

The classic bead shape is round or oval, but there are many more bead shapes available. Here is a short selection of bead shapes that you may find in vintage necklaces:

1 Seed: A small tubular glass bead; also referred to as a tile, crow, wheel, or pony bead

2 Watermelon: A large oval bead; the bead shown also has ridges, known as a corrugated bead

3 Flattened oval: An-oval shaped bead that has been flattened. A flattened round bead is known as a button bead

4 Barrel, drum: A short, thick tube-like bead

5 Cube: A six-sided square bead; a hexahedron

6 Tube: A circular bead that is long and narrow

7 Disk: A thin, circular bead, similar in shape to a coin

8 Bicone: A bead in the shape of two cones stuck together; these can have rounded or faceted sides

9 Faceted: A bead cut or molded to have a number of flat surfaces

10 Nugget: A bead with an undefined, irregular shape.

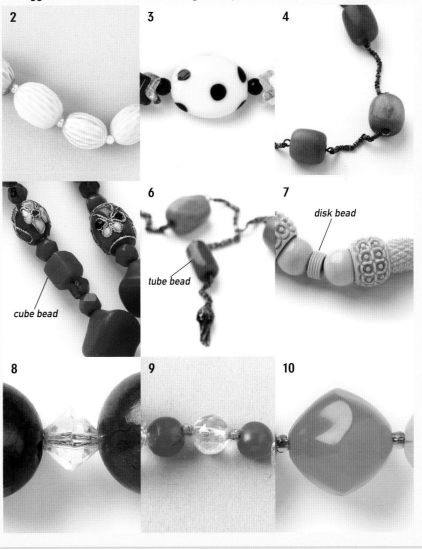

cube bead

tube bead

disk bead

Pearls

The "Queen of gems," the pearl is one of the earliest recorded gems. Ancient Middle Eastern cultures were the first to prize pearls, with the oldest known pearl necklace, found in the sarcophagus of a Persian princess, dating back 2,500 years. Until as recently as the 20th century, the wearing of pearls denoted wealth and status, and some countries forbade the wearing of them by any but nobility. Symbolically, pearls represent purity, and the practice of a bride wearing pearls endures today. Successful pearl culturing in the early 1900s brought them to a mass market, reducing their worth, but these iridescent jewels are still desired, with the most perfect specimens highly valued.

White-gold dome ring with cultured pearl and engraved shoulders, 1920s

SALTWATER PEARLS

Natural saltwater pearls are organic gems produced by oyster mollusks. They form in response to an irritant, such as a parasite or grain of sand, lodging itself in the mollusk. This triggers a defensive process whereby thousands of layers of "nacre" are secreted, enclosing the irritant in a protective coating to form a pearl over several years. Saltwater pearls are usually yellowish white and prized for their near perfect roundness and smoothness and for their superior "luster," or iridescence, which results from the thick layers of nacre. Pearls were especially popular from the 1920s to the 1950s. Today, they are harvested mainly in the Persian gulf, but the yield is tiny. Since thousands of oysters need to be opened to find just one pearl, natural saltwater pearls are rare. Most saltwater pearls sold today are cultured (see below). Genuine pearls have a gritty texture and feel grainy if rubbed over a tooth, unlike a smooth fake pearl. Real pearls are also likely to have variations in their iridescence, visible when held to a bright light, and differences in their shape, and are cool to the touch.

Problems Pearls are softer than other gemstones and so more easily damaged. Their luster can be affected by perfume, body oils, and cosmetics. Do not expose to heat.

Cleaning and care Store pearls on their own, ideally in a lined pouch or their own box. Apply perfume and cosmetics before putting on pearls to avoid dulling their luster. When you take them off, gently wipe them with a damp cloth. Clean them occasionally using a pearl cleaning kit (see page 104), then lay them out to dry. Have them restrung every year or so. Knotting the string

Necklace of freshwater pearls with silver box clasp, 1990s

Necklace of saltwater pearls with gold box clasp, 1950s

between each pearl (see pages 100–103) avoids losing pearls if the string breaks, and stops pearls rubbing against each other.

FRESHWATER PEARLS

These are formed in pearl mussels found in rivers, lakes, and ponds. Natural freshwater pearls are rare as they form in the same chance way as saltwater pearls. Over-fishing and pollution has added to their rarity and today, as with saltwater pearls, the vast majority are cultured (see below). In the 19th and 20th centuries, natural freshwater pearls were harvested from the Mississippi River; they are also found in Europe, including Scotland. They were popular during the Art Nouveau movement, which favored their irregularity of shape over the rounder saltwater pearl. Freshwater pearls come in an

array of colors, including silvery white, white, yellow, lavender, purple, pink, salmon, copper, bronze, green, and blue. The pearl usually takes on the color of the mussel's shell. In contrast to saltwater pearls, whose surface tend to be more mirror-like, freshwater pearls have a softer luster and an inner glow with a satiny surface.

Problems As with saltwater pearls, freshwater pearls are prone to damage. The many colors can make it hard to create matching strands.

Cleaning and care As for saltwater pearls.

CULTURED PEARLS

These are real pearls that form in the same way as natural pearls, but through human intervention, when pearl farmers artificially inject

Necklace of pearl-like plastic beads, 1960s

Necklace of coated glass beads to resemble pearls, 1960s

PEARL SHAPES

Pearls are graded on various aspects, including their luster and surface quality. Pearls also have a range of shapes:

- Round, symmetrical pearls are the classic pearl shape. These are the rarest and most valuable pearls. Saltwater pearls tend to be the most spherical.
- Near-round pearls are slightly elongated rather than round, but are classified as symmetrical.
- Mabe pearls are dome-shaped pearls that form on the inner shell of the mollusk.
- Oval pearls are sometimes referred to as "rice" pearls after crisped rice breakfast cereal; these are lower-quality freshwater pearls.
- Baroque pearls are irregularly shaped pearls.
- Drop pearls are shaped like a teardrop; these are often fashioned into earrings.

Miriam Haskell necklace of gray baroque faux pearls, c.1950s

a foreign object into a mollusk. Attempts over centuries to culture pearls usually produced hemispherical pearls. It wasn't until the early 1900s that the Japanese company Kokichi Mikimoto produced round, commercially viable, pearls. This revolutionized the market, enabling the reliable mass production of spherical pearls. As the availability of cultured pearls grew, they became increasingly popular with the middle classes. Long ropes of Japanese pearls were fashionable evening wear, favored by 1920s "flappers." By the 1950s, shorter strings of cultured pearls were everyday accessories for women in Europe and the US. Nowadays, up to 95 percent of commercial pearls are cultured. Saltwater pearls are cultured by injecting a mother-of-pearl bead nucleus, together with a piece of mantle tissue. The oyster is placed in a cage in sea water, and the natural process of secreting layers of nacre begins.

Freshwater pearls are cultured in a similar fashion, but mantle tissue only is inserted. Multiple pieces of mantle tissue are used in freshwater pearls, so one mollusk can produce from 30 to 40 pearls.

Problems See the entries for saltwater and freshwater pearls.

Cleaning and care As for saltwater and freshwater pearls.

FAKE PEARLS

Artificial, or "faux," pearls are made with a variety of materials, including glass, ceramic, or plastic beads. The beads are coated with substances such as crushed fish scales and lacquer to simulate a reflective shine. The popularity of costume jewelry in the 1930s saw a market for

fake pearls, and designers such as Gabrielle "Coco" Chanel enjoyed combining strings of real and fake pearls. Some high-quality fake pearls, notably the "Majorca" pearl, can be hard to tell apart from the genuine article. Generally though, fake pearls can be identified in several ways. Although they shine, they lack the distinctive glow of real pearls, which comes from the many layers of nacre. Their surface also tends to be too perfect: real pearls usually have a flaw, even if tiny.

Problems The varnish can chip and lose its shine. After cleaning (see below) add a dab of clear nail varnish to chips to prevent further damage.

Cleaning and care Fake pearls can yellow with age. Clean them with mild soap, warm water, and a soft, lint-free cloth.

Restringing beads

Many bead necklaces are strung with thread rather than linked together with metal chain. The skill in simple restringing, where there is no knotting involved, is in attaching the clasps securely (see pages 98–9). If the beads are valuable, they are usually strung with knots between each bead (see pages 100–103). This not only stops beads from knocking against each other and causing damage, but also prevents beads from being lost if the necklace is broken accidentally. Not all knotted necklaces have knots between each bead—sometimes a series of beads is strung and then finished with a single knot before a second series of beads is strung, and so on. Expansion bracelets are also strung, but with elastic. This ensures that they fit the wrist snugly, but are easy to put on and take off. Elastic has a finite shelf life, and earlier expansion bracelets often require restringing.

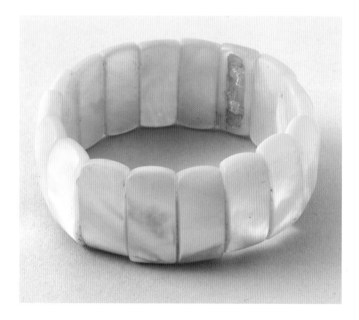

Re-elasticating an expansion bracelet

Elastic was invented in the 1820s, and by the 1920s it was being mass-produced and used in everything from industry to clothing. With metal shortages during and between the two world wars, elastic provided a novel and inexpensive way of making bracelets. It is not unusual to find expansion bracelets from that time made from materials such as bone (see page 142) or from mother of pearl.

Mother-of-pearl expansion bracelet, 1940s

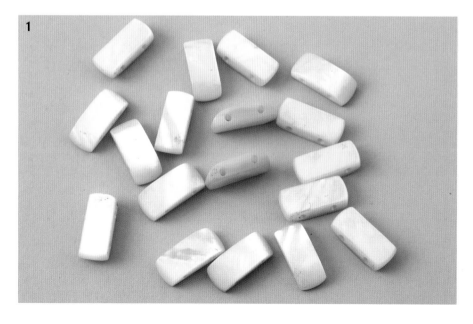

1 The elastic in vintage expansion bracelets is often stretched out and in need of restringing—the more the bracelet has been worn, the more likely that the elastic will have become loose.

Clear elastic thread see Tools, page 55
Bulldog clip
Side snips see Tools, page 54
Clear nail varnish

2

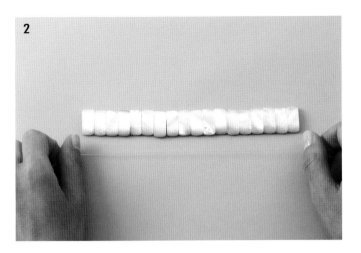

2 Arrange the beads in the order to be restrung. Clear elastic thread is available from findings and bead stores and is ideal for this type of restringing job. Many beads for expansion bracelets have double holes and are strung with two lengths of elastic, as here, to make them more secure and fit comfortably. Cut two lengths of elastic slightly longer than the bracelet, with enough extra length to tie knots at each end.

3

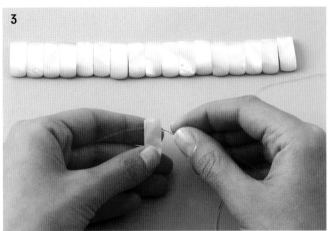

3 Place a bulldog clip or something similar at one end of the first length of elastic to close off the end and stop the beads falling off. Thread on all the beads.

4

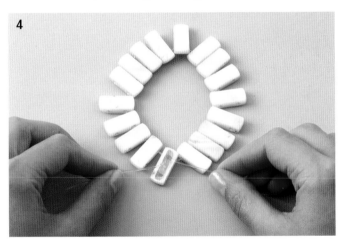

4 When you have completed threading the first length, tie the two ends together in a knot that fits into the recessed area behind the last bead. Not all expansion bracelets have this feature. If this is the case, it should be possible to pull the knot inside the adjoining bead to hide it.

5

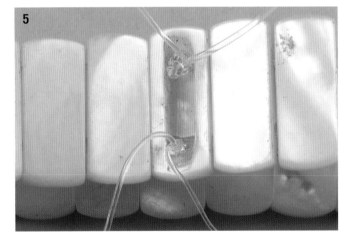

5 String the other length of elastic through the second row of holes and tie the two ends together in a knot. If there is room in the recess, tie a double knot to secure the fastening.

6 Cut off the surplus lengths of elastic. If you want to make sure the knots are extra secure, you can apply a dab of clear nail varnish and leave them to dry (usually within 5–10 minutes).

6

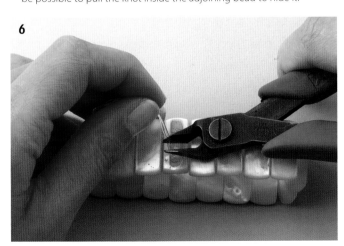

Restringing a bead necklace

Bead necklaces are often strung on a length of thread, such as silk or synthetic beading wire, unknotted, and with a clasp attached to either end. Necklace threads and wires may break, or the clasps pull away, either through wear and tear or if they are accidentally pulled. Even if the thread or wire remains intact, if one or both ends of a clasp are missing, the necklace will have to be restrung. Professional restringing can be expensive, sometimes to more than the value of the actual beads. Simple restringing is relatively easy to do at home, the skill lies in correctly attaching the necklace clasp.

Modern necklace of multi-colored corrugated plastic beads

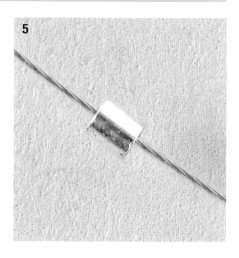

1 If your necklace has a fairly complex design and has lost either one or both clasps but is still threaded, take a photograph of it before you remove the beads. Use the photograph to replicate the design when you are arranging the beads prior to restringing (see Step 4).

2 Before you buy beading thread or wire, check the size of the holes in all the beads. These may vary in size, even in the same bead type. The replacement thread or wire must be able to pass through the smallest bead hole, but the fit should be snug—the bead should not slide easily on the thread or wire. You need a length of thread or wire about 9 in (22 cm) longer than the actual necklace. If the beads are heavy, make sure that you have the right strength of beading wire. Here I have used nylon-coated steel beading wire, which is suitable for a wide range of necklaces.

3 Place the beads in the center of a stone tray—use a folded towel on a flat surface if you don't have a tray. If the beads vary in size, group the various bead sizes together. This makes placing the beads in the final order easier (see Step 4).

4 Arrange the beads in the order to be strung. Work from the center of the necklace outward, i.e. usually from the largest stone or stones— here, a large blue bead. Work your way outward, graduating the beads from medium to small, and finishing with the smallest bead at either end (see also Step 1, page 100). Make sure, too, that the color combinations are correct, and that you are happy with them. Take your time to make sure that you are happy with the design—or you may have to start all over again at a later stage.

5 Before stringing the beads, attach the clasp housing—here a spring box clasp (see page 74)—to one end of the thread. To do this, first place one end of the wire in a crimp.

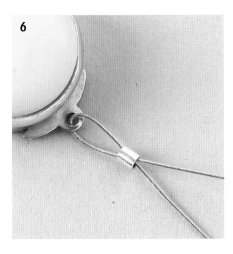

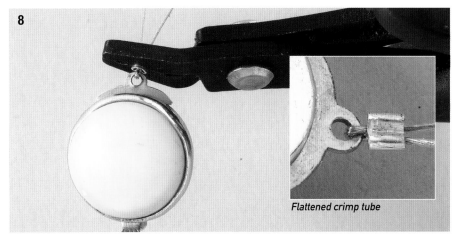

Flattened crimp tube

6 Thread the wire though the hole on the clasp. Double the wire back on itself and back through the crimp to join the first wire, forming a loop.

7 Hold the clasp with one hand and pull the loose end of the wire with a pair of needle-nosed pliers away from the clasp. The crimp tube will pull tight to the clasp.

8 Use a pair of crimping pliers to close the crimp. This two-stage technique may take some practice to get right. First, place the crimp tube in the crescent-shaped notch in your pliers closest to the handles. Squeeze tightly to close. You may need to apply a fair amount of pressure to do this. This flattens the crimp tube (see detail).

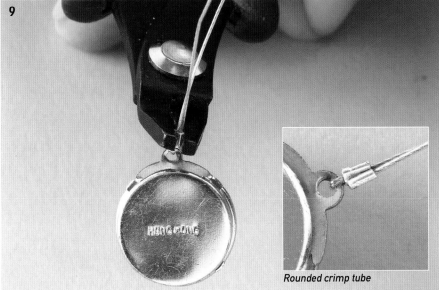

Rounded crimp tube

9 Second, turn the flattened crimp tube on its side and place it in the round notch closest to the tip of the pliers. Squeeze tightly again to form a neat, rounded shape (see detail). Again, you may need to apply firm pressure. Give the loose end of the wire a good tug to check that the crimp is securely in place.

10 Place a crimp cover over the crimp tube and close it using a pair of duckbill pliers.

11 String the beads one by one onto the wire, in the order selected. If you can, thread the end of loose wire through the first two beads, then cut off the excess using a pair of side snips. If the wire will not fit, cut the excess off at the base of the crimp.

12 When you have threaded all the beads, attach the other end of the clasp in the same way as described in Steps 5–10.

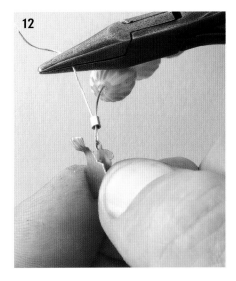

Stone sorting tray see Tools, page 55
Stringing wire see Tools, page 55
Crimp tubes see page 76
Crimping pliers see Tools, page 55
Crimp covers see page 76
Needle-nosed and duckbill pliers see Tools, page 54
Side snips see Tools, page 54

Hand knotting a bead necklace

Necklaces with precious beads—notably pearls, but also necklaces made with high-quality semi-precious stones and crystal beads—are often strung with a knot tied between each bead. This ensures that the beads don't rub or knock against each other, preserving the condition of each stone. A knotted necklace is almost always a sign of a quality piece of jewelry. However, because natural thread—usually silk—is used for knotted necklaces, the thread has a finite life. The technique shown here is a simpler and easier method than the traditional approach taught at jewelry school. Some steps, particularly steps 11–15, may take time to master, but the end result should give you an attractive and securely threaded necklace.

Necklace of crystal glass beads, 1930s

1

1 This is a typical example of a broken necklace that has been knotted. The thread holding the beads is still intact, but the clasps have come away. In order to attach new clasps securely, the whole necklace will need to be undone and reknotted. If the order of the beads is complex, photograph the necklace before you unthread it and use this as reference when arranging the beads in Step 2. When buying new thread, match the type and color to the old thread. Note that the thread needs to fit through the smallest bead three times (see step 16, see page 103).

2 Lay the stones out in a stone sorting tray in the order to be restrung. If you don't have a stone tray, place the beads on a folded towel on a flat surface.

2

Stone sorting tray see Tools, page 55

Silk thread with beading needle attached see Tools, page 55

Necklace clasp and jump ring see Clasps, pages 74–6

Clear nail varnish

Side snips see Tools, page 54

3

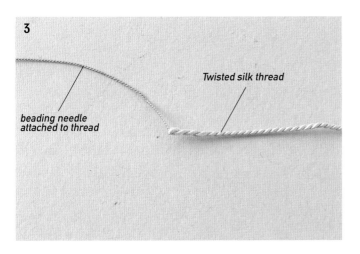

beading needle attached to thread

Twisted silk thread

4

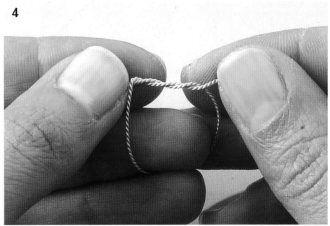

3 Remove all of the silk necklace thread from the packet. You can buy thread in packets in 6-ft (1.8-m) lengths complete with its own beading needle attached, which is suitable for any necklace under 3 ft (90 cm) long. If you are knotting a longer necklace, you will need to buy thread on a reel and a beading needle.

4 If the thread is made from silk, give it a good tug all along its length before you start. Silk thread has some "give" in it, and needs to be stretched prior to working with it. Otherwise, you may find that when you start tying the knots, they will be too loose. Tie a knot at the end of the thread.

5

6

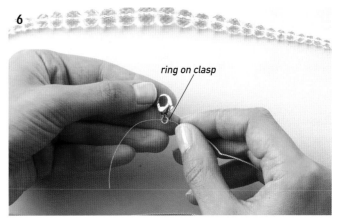

ring on clasp

5 Thread all of the beads onto the silk thread.

6 When you have threaded on all the beads, thread on the clasp. It should have its own ring attached for this purpose.

7 Position the clasp half way along the length of the thread—here, at 3 ft (90 cm). Slide the last bead that you threaded up next to the clasp, and pass the thread through the bead for a second time so that there are two threads coming out of the bead (see Step 10, page 102).

7

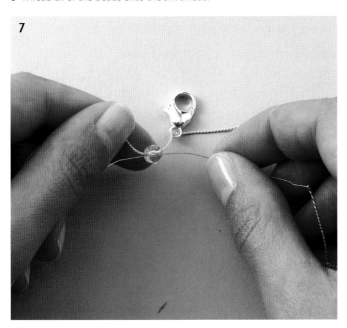

8

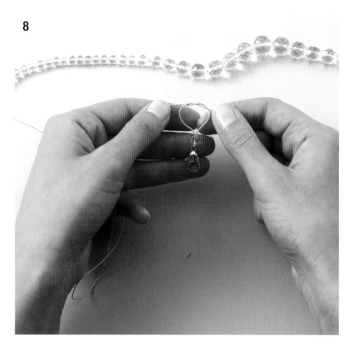

9

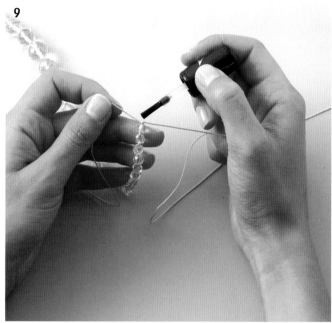

8 Use the two threads to tie a knot behind the bead to secure it in place next to the clasp. Now take the next bead, move it up to the first knot, thread through it for a second time and tie a knot. Continue in this way until all but the last three beads have been knotted.

9 When you have knotted all but the last three beads, place a small dab of clear nail varnish on the last knot and allow it to dry for a few minutes. The varnish helps to secure the knot.

10

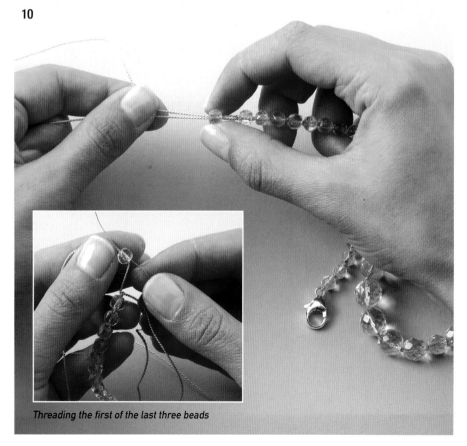

Threading the first of the last three beads

11

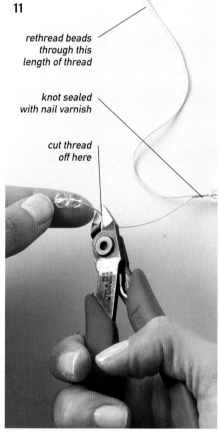

rethread beads through this length of thread

knot sealed with nail varnish

cut thread off here

10 Thread on the first of the last three beads and place it firmly against the varnished knot.

11 Cut the thread that is holding the last two beads, leaving about 3 in (7.5 cm) of thread.

12

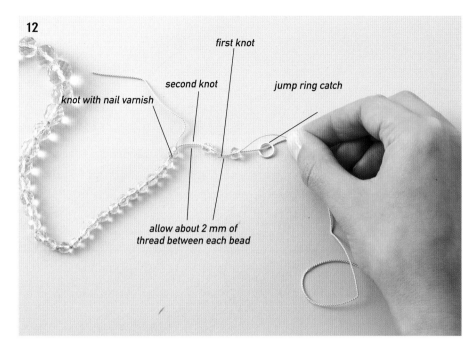

knot with nail varnish

second knot

first knot

jump ring catch

allow about 2 mm of
thread between each bead

12 This is the most difficult part of the process and you may need to practice it a few times before you get it right. The aim is to knot the last two beads. To do this, thread on the last two beads and the jump ring for the clasp. Leave enough thread between the second and third beads to tie a knot between each one—check the width of the other knots, and estimate how much thread you need to allow. Here each knot is about 2 mm wide.

13

13 Thread a second time through the bead closest to the jump ring and tie a knot.

Knot the first bead first

14

15

16

14 Thread through the second bead a second time and tie a knot.

15 Carefully apply a small dab of clear nail varnish on the second knot to secure it. Allow the varnish to dry for a few minutes.

16 Thread through the third bead a third and final time, again give the thread a good tug, then snip off the end as close to the bead as possible. The necklace is complete.

Cleaning beads

Cleaning a bead necklace can take time and patience, depending on the materials it is made from. First establish what type of material the beads are (see pages 92–3). Then check whether the necklace is threaded using a natural fiber or a synthetic one, such as nylon-coated wire. If the thread is synthetic, follow the cleaning guidelines for the particular bead material, even if it involves soapy water. If the necklace is threaded with a natural fiber, you must try to avoid getting the thread wet. Follow the step-by-step guidelines shown opposite. Natural pearls, and beads made from mother of pearl and coral, require delicate handling.

Cleaning natural pearls

The following cleaning approach is suitable for saltwater, freshwater, and cultured pearls. It is also a safe method to use on coral and mother of pearl. You can clean your pearls with plain water (see Step 1 below), but if the pearls are dirty, I recommend using a specialist pearl cleaning solution or kit (see resources). Alternatively, take them to a jeweler for professional cleaning. If you accidentally spray your pearls with perfume or hair spray, both of which contain solvents that can damage the surface of the pearls, wipe them immediately with a slightly damp, soft cloth.

Double row necklace of saltwater pearls with gold clasp, 1950s

1 A typical pearl cleaning kit consists of a sachet holding a wet wipe infused with a very gentle cleaning solution, and a soft, lint-free cloth. Gently wipe the pearls with the wet wipe to remove any surface dirt. For a simple maintenance clean, slightly dampen a soft cloth and gently wipe the pearls.

2 Dry the pearls with the soft, lint-free cloth, then leave them to air until completely dry.

3 When dry, put them away. If you have a saltwater pearl necklace, the best way to store it is in a necklace box (see page 50). Alternatively, wrap the pearls in a natural fiber such as silk (shown top left); any material that is soft and breathable is suitable.

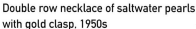

Pearl cleaning kit

Cleaning a necklace strung with natural fiber thread

The aim is to avoid wetting the natural fiber thread; liquid on the thread will weaken it, and make it prone to fraying and breaking. Window cleaning solution is excellent for cleaning glass beads, as here; for beads made from other materials, use the cleaning medium recommended for that particular material.

Necklace of clear glass beads knotted with natural fiber thread, 1980s

1 As you will be coming into contact with cleaning solution, wear protective gloves. Gently brush each glass bead with a jeweler's brush, using a gentle sweeping motion, to remove as much surface dirt as possible.

2 Put a small amount of window cleaning solution into a container. If you prefer, use a 50:50 mixture of water and white vinegar. Take a Q-tip and dip it into the solution, then squeeze it to remove any excess.

3 Wipe each bead with the Q-tip. Avoid coming into contact with the thread.

4 Wipe away any traces of window cleaning solution first with a slightly damp, soft, lint-free cloth, then dry with a soft, lint-free cloth—here a chamois leather. Leave the item to dry completely before putting it away.

Protective gloves see Tools, page 53

Jeweler's brush see Tools, page 53

Window cleaning solution

Glass bowl

Q-tips see Tools, page 53

Soft, lint-free cloths see Tools, page 53

Gemstones bring luminous color and brilliance to jewelry. The visual guide to precious and semi-precious stones will help you to identify the most widely used gemstones in fine jewelry and vintage costume pieces. Rhinestones hold a special place in costume jewelry, and the different types are covered in detail. In the step-by-step sections learn how to secure a stone in its setting, replace missing stones, and source replacement stones from your jewelry box. You will also learn how to clean gemstones and rhinestones safely and bring back their sparkle.

Sparkling Stones

Precious stones

Gemstones have been used in jewelry since prehistoric times, and their loose classification "precious" and "semi-precious" dates back to Ancient Greece, when certain stones were prized for their rarity as much as their quality. Nevertheless, those recognized today as precious stones (diamonds, rubies, sapphires, and emeralds, together with opals and aquamarines) are generally the highest quality, and command the highest prices. For more information on the Mohs scale of hardness, the most commonly used scale for determining the hardness of gemstones, see page 115. For advice on cleaning precious stones, see pages 124–5.

Gold pin and pendant with aquamarine and seed pearls, 19th century

DIAMOND

Formed by the natural compression of pure carbon, this crystallized mineral is the hardest known material, used as a benchmark for hardness and scratch-resistance as number 10 on the Mohs scale. The value of diamonds is rated by: color, cut, clarity, and karat weight. Generally they are expected to be a clear white, but some colored diamonds of pastel shades are also highly valued. The brilliance is also enhanced by the various ways in which diamonds are cut, with multi-faceted cuts emphasizing the fire in larger stones.

Traditionally associated with engagement rings, diamonds are also used in almost every form of jewelry, and have acquired mystical status in many cultures. Imitation diamonds (see Rhinestones, pages 116–19) can be distinguished from the real thing by their lack of hardness and brilliance. Diamonds were originally mined in India and South America, and have recently been mined in Russia, Australia, and China, but the principal source in modern times is Africa, which still produces around two-thirds of the world supply.

Problems: Diamonds are hard but brittle, and can crack or cleave with careless handling. As with all gemstones, the most common problem is stones coming loose from the setting. Dirt and grease can affect the brilliance, luster, and color of diamonds and lead to incorrect grading.

SAPPHIRE

A variety of the mineral corundum, an aluminum oxide, sapphire is a transparent gemstone ranging in color from deep blue (the color usually associated with it—the name comes from the Greek sappheiros, "blue stone") through yellow, green, and purple to pink, which is known as padparadscha. The red variety of the same mineral is ruby (see below). Sapphire is often heat-treated or irradiated to improve the color. It is extremely hard, and its distinctive crystalline structure lends itself to a brilliant or mixed cut that to an expert eye distinguishes it from other stones. Another distinctive feature is its strong dichroism—the way it appears to have two different colors according to the direction it catches the light. Sapphires are mined worldwide, but traditionally the finest examples of blue sapphires are from the Indian subcontinent.

Problems: Heat treating sapphires to improve their color can dull their fire, and the color-enhancing of irradiation fades with time. Stones can crack or cleave like diamonds.

RUBY

A transparent variety of the corundum family of minerals, ruby is similar to sapphire in everything except color, which ranges from dark pink through the classic deep red to purple and brown. Flawless stones are very rare, making good specimens more expensive than similar diamonds, and leading to processes such as filling fractures with lead glass to improve transparency. Synthetic rubies have also been around since the mid-19th century, and are often indistinguishable from the genuine article. Rubies are found throughout the world, but certain countries are famous for particular types: Burma for deep red stones, Thailand for dark reddish-brown, and Sri Lanka for light red.

Problems: See Sapphire, above.

Gold ring with sapphire and diamonds, 1960s

EMERALD

A variety of the mineral beryl, emerald is a transparent green precious stone, highly prized in jewelry making. Fine-quality emeralds are very rare and command prices higher than diamonds. A large proportion of stones have some flaws or cloudiness known as the jardin (meaning "garden" in French) of the emerald. The characteristic green color comes from the presence of traces of the metallic elements chromium and vanadium. Inferior emeralds are often oiled, dyed, and irradiated to improve their appearance, and there are many imitations—although these are easily distinguishable. Emerald is the least hard of the precious stones, and quite fragile. The finest emeralds, with the prized deep bottle-green color, are found in Colombia, but they are also mined in Russia, Southern Africa, and India.

Modern platinum solitaire ring with diamond

Gold snake ring with emerald eye, 1920s

Modern gold pendant with opal and diamonds

Modern white-gold ring with ruby and diamonds

Problems: Emeralds are fragile, and can crack or shatter if carelessly handled. Most emeralds are treated in some way, and should therefore be cleaned with caution (see page 125).

AQUAMARINE

A transparent light blue or blue-green variety of beryl (see also emerald, opposite), aquamarine is similar to emerald in all but color. Sea-green stones were highly prized at one time, but now pure deep blue aquamarine is more valued: Many blue aquamarines found today are in fact green stones that have been heat-treated. Aquamarine is usually faceted when cut, and occasionally cut in cabochons, when it often has a "cat's eye" effect known as chatoyance. It is mined worldwide, but the finest examples have been found in Brazil.

Problems: Aquamarine is slightly brittle. Extremes of temperature can affect the color. Aquamarine can fade if exposed to prolonged sunlight, so store in a cool, dry place when not wearing. Blue topaz (see page 115) can be mistaken for aquamarine.

OPAL

Unique among gemstones, opal is a mineral gel (rather than a crystalline structure) with a high water content—anything from 3 to 20 percent. Opal is relatively soft and usually cut in cabochons, but the finest stones can be faceted, and sometimes treated with oil or wax to enhance the finish and seal the stone. When polished, or dipped into water or oil, it shows a prismatic array of iridescent colors within the milky, translucent stone. This opalescence, as

it is known, is highly prized and distinguishes precious and "fire" opals from the variety simply known as common opal. Imitation opals made from foiled glass may be found in vintage costume jewelry. The main source of fine opals is Australia, but they are still mined in many places worldwide.

Problems: Opals are fragile and crack easily, especially if allowed to dry out; they may also lose their color and "fire" in extremes of temperature. Ultrasonic cleaning can destroy valuable opals. Inexpensive opal jewelry is made by gluing a thin slice of opal onto a dark background, known as a doublet. This is sometimes topped with clear glass or a plastic dome, known as a triplet. Doublet and triplet opals should not be immersed in water. Clean as for softer gemstones, see page 125.

Semi-precious stones

Semi-precious stones are considered less valuable than precious stones (see pages 108-109), but this is not always the case. In earlier times, stones were classified by their rarity; for example, amethyst was considered a precious stone until large deposits were found in Brazil in the 19th century. A more scientific classification is by the species of mineral and its varieties. For example, many are varieties of quartz, the second most abundant mineral in the Earth's crust. Each gemstone has its own characteristics, and can be recognized by color, hardness (measured using the Mohs scale, see page 115), translucency, and crystalline structure, which determines the way it reflects and refracts light and also the shape in which it is cut. For advice on storing jewelry and general care guidelines, see pages 48–51. For advice on cleaning semi-precious stones, see pages 124–5.

Pinchbeck cross with garnets, 18th century

AGATE

A variety of chalcedony (see right) widely used as a gemstone, particularly in 19th-century jewelry. Agate comes in many different colors, from gray, pink, yellow, blue, and reddish brown to black, and often has a variegated pattern, either in bands or cloud- or feather-like shapes. Agate formed of layers of contrasting kinds of quartz, such as onyx, sard, sardonyx, and carnelian, is known as banded agate, or if the bands are in concentric circles as eype agate. Other patterns include cloud agate, feather agate, and moss agate. Agate stones are often dyed and heat-treated to enhance the color and patterning.

Problems: Agate is porous and can absorb moisture and stains.

Necklace of lapis lazuli beads and crystal bicones, 1920s

Necklace of malachite and glass beads, 1950s

AMETHYST

Amethyst is a transparent variety of quartz with a characteristic violet color, ranging in intensity from a pale lavender to a deep purple, the more valued shade, and more rarely green. The name amethyst comes from the Greek for "not drunk," referring to its believed property of warding off intoxication. Synthetic amethysts are difficult to distinguish from real ones, but natural amethysts change color with heat treatment, from a pale yellow (often mistaken for citrine) to reddish brown or even a milky white. Amethysts were popular in the 19th century, and are also a feature of Art Nouveau and Arts and Crafts jewelry.

Problems: Exposure to extremes of temperature may change the color and luster of the stone.

BERYL

A group of translucent and transparent minerals, beryls include emeralds and aquamarine (see pages 108–109). They also include varieties of different colored stones, such as red beryl (the rarest of the group), green beryl, morganite (pink), heliodor (yellow or greenish yellow), maxixe (deep blue), and the colorless goshenite. They are generally used in finer pieces of jewelry.

Problems: Most varieties of beryl are brittle and fragile, and the stone can crack or shatter if carelessly handled.

CARNELIAN

Also known as cornelian or carneole, carnelian is a translucent and porous variety of chalcedony, usually of a flesh-red or reddish-brown color, with a waxy luster. The name is derived from the Latin carnis (for "flesh"), referring to its meaty color. It is hard and tough, so as well as being cut, it can also be carved into beads. The depth of color can be intensified by dyeing and heat treatment, and many carnelians available today are in fact stained and treated agate. Many items of carnelian jewelry can be found dating from the 19th and early 20th centuries.

Arts and Crafts hammered silver pendant with citrine, 1900s

Carved jade earrings, 1960s

Art Deco white-gold pin with tourmaline, 1920s

Gold earrings with moonstones, 19th century

Gold pin with peridot and seed pearls, 19th century

Problems: Carnelian is porous and can absorb moisture and stains.

CHALCEDONY

A group of microcrystalline quartz minerals which includes agate, carnelian, jasper, onyx, and many others. The blue variety of this group is often simply known as chalcedony. Chalcedony is translucent, porous, and ranges in color from milky white through gray and blue. Chalcedony was used in jewelry in the 19th century and early part of the 20th century.

Problems: Because it is porous, all varieties of chalcedony can absorb moisture and stains.

CITRINE

Named for its characteristic yellow color in shades ranging from pale lemon to golden brown, citrine is a variety of quartz found mainly in Brazil. Natural citrine is very rare, and most of the stones sold as citrine are amethyst or smoky quartz that has been heat treated. Because of its rarity, citrine is much prized as a gemstone and is normally cut in facets.

Problems: Citrine is comparatively tough, but can crack with careless handling.

GARNET

Garnet is a group of minerals found in almost every color, but most commonly seen as red or brown gemstones. It is characterized by its granular crystal structure. The group includes stones such as pyrope (deep red), almandine (from red to orange and purple), spessartine (yellow orange), grossular garnets including hessonite and rosolite (colorless), carbuncle

Silver pin with carnelian, 19th century

Gold pin with agate, 19th century

stone (dark red), uvarovite (green), and andradite (including green topazolite and black melanite). Garnets have been widely used as gemstones since Roman times, cut in cabochons, faceted, or sliced and inlaid in gold cloisonné. They were very popular stones in the 19th century.

Problems: Garnets are very brittle and fragile.

JADE
This is a term that is used almost indiscriminately for two distinct minerals, jadeite and nephrite, with similar characteristics. Of the two, jadeite is the harder and more often used as a gemstone in jewelry, while nephrite is used for carving. Both are found in a wide range of colors, but typically in shades of green, and exist in opaque and more highly prized translucent forms. Jade is often cut as cabochons, or carved as beads, but also can be carved to make rings and bracelets. Nephrite has been used for centuries in China and the Far East, where it is considered a precious stone.

Problems: Jade is fragile and quite porous.

JASPER
An opaque variety of chalcedony, jasper is found in several colors, including reds and browns, yellow, green, and more rarely blue. It is often multi-colored in bands or speckles. It can be carved, and so has been used for intaglio seals and cameos, but is usually cut in cabochons or

beads and polished to a high shine, sometimes enhanced and sealed with oil. It is often found in 19th-century jewelry.

Problems: Jasper is porous, and if unsealed can absorb moisture and stains.

LAPIS LAZULI
A rock composed of several different minerals, including calcite, pyrite, and sodalite, lapis lazuli (sometimes known simply as lapis) has been prized for its intense blue color since ancient times. It is relatively soft and dull, but can be polished to a high shine, and is normally cut in cabochons or slices, or carved. As well as its use as a gemstone, it has been used ground into powder as a colorant in paints and cosmetics. The finest lapis lazuli, with a clear deep blue color, is from Afghanistan.

Problems: The surface shine of lapis lazuli can be dulled by water. It is also brittle and chips and scratches easily. Remove before soldering; it cannot be immersed in pickle (see page 155).

MALACHITE
Largely sourced from copper mines, malachite is a mineral made up mainly of copper carbonate, which gives it its characteristic green color. It is soft and opaque, and normally cut in cabochons and set in silver, often sealed with wax or oil to protect and enhance the surface sheen. So-

called "blue malachite" is in fact azurite, a related copper mineral. Ground malachite has also been used as a pigment in paints.

Problems: Malachite is soft and can be easily damaged by careless handling. Unsealed surfaces can lose their sheen.

MARCASITE
In jewelry, marcasite is a misleading name for the mineral pyrite: true marcasite (a similar but much brittler and more fragile material) has not been used as a gemstone since Ancient Greek times. Usually faceted and often set in silver to enhance its natural brilliant sparkle, marcasite is an opaque iron ore with a metallic shine. It is widely used in costume jewelry, and sourced worldwide. Paste and even cut metal is sometimes used as a cheap imitation, and the term "marcasite" is sometimes used loosely to describe cut steel or other faceted white metal. Because it is sometimes cut in a marquise cut, the erroneous spelling "marquisite" is occasionally seen.

Problems: Marcasite is brittle and can crack or chip with careless handling.

MOONSTONE
Light reflected within the translucent bluish-white moonstone gives it its name, an effect known as adularescence after the geological name adularia, the most common type of

Sterling silver ring with tiger's eye. 1960s

Necklace of rose quartz, glass beads, and rhinestones, 1920s

Silver pin with marcasites, 1930s

Silver ring with turquoise and coral, 1960s

moonstone. Other types include oligoclase, labradorite, and albite. Usually thought of as a white stone, with (in the finest examples) a bluish sheen, moonstone can also be found in gray, yellow, and sometimes orange or yellow varieties. Examples can be found in 19th-century jewelry, and it was very popular in Art Nouveau jewelry, almost always cut as a cabochon. Moonstone is not often found in modern jewelry. Sources have been found throughout the world.

Problems: Moonstone can crack or chip with careless handling.

PERIDOT

Also known as chrysolite or misleadingly as "evening emerald," peridot is a transparent green or yellow-green variety of the mineral olivine. Peridot with a deep olive-green color is the most highly prized as a gemstone. It is mostly cut in facets, and is characterized by double refraction (things appear doubled when you look into the stone), which distinguishes it from emerald. Peridot is usually pronounced in the French way, with a silent T. Peridot was used widely in late 19th-century jewelry, and in Art Nouveau pieces. It is mined throughout the world.

Problems: Peridot is relatively soft and brittle, and can crack and chip with careless handling.

QUARTZ

This abundant mineral is the source of a number of semi-precious stones, the most significant being amethyst (see page 110), citrine (see page 111), chalcedony (see page 111), and rose quartz. The latter comes in a range of pink colors, from a very pale pink to a deep rose pink. Rose quartz was used in costume jewelry in the early part of the 20th century; it is less popular today. Quartz is mined throughout the world.

Problems: See Moonstone, above. Rose quartz can fade if exposed to light for long periods.

TANZANITE

A transparent blue-violet variety of the mineral ziosite, tanzanite is similar in appearance to sapphire, but lighter and softer. It takes its name from Tanzania, where it was first discovered in 1967. The more transparent tanzanites are usually faceted, but cloudy stones are also used cut in cabochons. Tanzanite is sometimes heat-treated to intensify the depth of color.

Problems: Tanzanite is soft and easily damaged by careless handling.

TIGER'S EYE

Taking its name from its high degree of chatoyancy (the three-dimensional reflective "cat's eye" effect), tiger's eye is a variety of quartz with a very silky luster, typically in bands of yellow and brown, although sometimes found in green-gray and blue-gray. It is comparatively soft, and polishes to a high shine, so is normally cut in cabochons or carved as beads to emphasize the chatoyancy. The main producer of tiger's eye is Southern Africa.

Problems: Tiger's eye, especially as beads, can easily crack or fracture with careless handling.

TOPAZ

A very hard transparent gemstone ranging in color from pale yellow or even colorless through blues and pinks to brown. Pink topaz is rare and highly prized, and can be simulated by irradiating the more common yellow topaz, and heat treatment can simulate blue topaz. It is invariably cut faceted, often as a pendeloque (pear-shaped brilliant cut). Jewelry using yellow and pink topaz was popular in the early part of the 19th century. It is found throughout the world, but significant mining areas include Brazil and the US.

Problems: Topaz is hard but has strong cleavage and can be easily cracked or broken. Deep-colored stones can fade if exposed to light over long periods.

TURQUOISE

This opaque mineral comes in a range of blue-green colors. It became popular in the mid 19th century with the fashion for Egyptian-revival jewelry. Turquoise saw another surge of popularity with the discovery of Tutankhamun's tomb in the 1920s. In the US, turquoise is associated with Native American jewelry. It was also used in the much-prized Mexican Taxco jewelry in the 1930s and 1940s. It is mined in Sinai; the US also has significant sources of turquoise deposits in the Southwest.

Problems: Turquoise is often treated to enhance its appearance, which can involve waxing and even dyeing the stone. It should, therefore, be cleaned with caution. Turquoise is brittle and can crack or chip with careless handling.

MOHS SCALE OF MINERAL HARDNESS

The German mineralist Frederich Mohs developed a scale of hardness for minerals in 1812, which is still widely used today. Starting at 1—which is talc, for which there is no gemstone equivalent—all the minerals that follow can scratch any minerals in the scale below and other minerals at the same rating. The scale is relative, so for example turquoise at 5–6 is not twice as hard as amber at 2–2.5:

Number	Substance
2–2.5	Amber
3.5–4	Malachite
5–6	Lapis lazuli, turquoise
5.5–6.5	Opal
6	Moonstone, tanzanite
6–7	Jade
6–6.5	Marcasite, moonstone
6.5-7	Agate, carnelian, peridot, tanzanite
6.5-7.5	Garnet
7	Citrine, quartz, amethyst, chalcedony, jasper, tiger's eye, onyx
7–7.5	Tourmaline
7.5–8	Emerald, beryl, aquamarine
8	Topaz
9	Sapphire, ruby
10	Diamond

Modern silver ring with amethyst cabochon

Arts and Crafts silver ring with onyx, 1900s

Modern silver ring with blue topaz

Silver-tone jazz pin and earring set with blue chalcedony stones, 1930s

Rhinestones

The term "rhinestone" is loosely used to describe a number of different simulated diamonds or other gemstones, including those made from rock crystal, glass, and plastic. The name comes originally from the rocks found along the River Rhine in Austria and Germany, which have been used since the 18th century as a substitute for diamonds. Leaded glass, also known as "paste," cut in the same way as gemstones was made popular by Georges-Frédéric Strass—in Europe, rhinestones in general are often referred to as "Strass" as well as diamanté—in the 18th century, and the technique was perfected by Daniel Swarovski. The invention of synthetic plastics in the 20th century provided yet another material for "fake" diamonds, although generally not as brilliant or convincing as true rhinestones or crystal glass.

Silver pendant with clear paste stones, 18th century

TRUE RHINESTONES

A naturally occurring rock crystal found on the bed and banks of the River Rhine in Germany and Austria, rhinestone is a variety of quartz. It is clear, with a crystalline structure and sharp edges, and when cut and polished has the luster and brilliance of diamond, making it an ideal cheaper alternative for jewelry. True rhinestone is in fact a semi-precious gemstone, and as well as its use as a diamond substitute, it found favor as a gemstone in its own right, particularly when the much cheaper cut-glass came into fashion in the 18th century. The word "rhinestone" became used for all kinds of diamond substitutes in the US, although in Europe they are usually known as diamanté or Strass (see page 118). True rhinestone is used in all forms of jewelry, generally in a silver, or silver and gold setting.

Problems: Although comparatively hard, quartz is quite brittle, and can crack or chip. As with other semi-precious stones, true rhinestones can also come loose from their settings.

Cleaning and care: As these are natural stones, not glass or plastic, they have the same characteristics as other semi-precious stones; they should be handled and cleaned as such (see pages 124–5).

PASTE

Glass has been used as a substitute for gemstones since Ancient Egyptian times. The Romans used a technique of grounding glass into a paste,

Pin with early plastic cabochon surrounded with unfoiled rhinestones, 1920s

which was molded into shape and melted, and the process continued to be used until the 18th century. From this, the term "paste" came to be used for all kinds of glass gemstone substitutes. Introducing metals into the glass-making process, especially lead, gives a much clearer and more brilliant glass, well suited to jewelry. This can be molded into traditional gemstone shapes, or cut in the same way as precious stones: Molded glass has a less diamond-like "crystal" feel and look to it, but cut glass has the distinctive well-defined facets with clean edges that give it the sparkle of a gemstone. Paste in the form of

crystal cut glass replaced true rhinestones as an inexpensive alternative to diamonds in the 18th century, and is still the most popular material for simulating gemstones.

Problems: As with all glass jewelry, careless handling and storage can lead to chips and cracks. Because leaded glass is softer than other glass, it is also prone to scratches.

Cleaning and care: All glass rhinestone jewelry is delicate and should be handled with care. For advice on cleaning, see pages 126–7.

Rhinestones through the decades, 1900–1960s. From middle left clockwise: Brass pin with "faux" topaz rhinestones, 1900s; Silver-tone rhinestone dress clip, 1920s; Silver-tone rhinestone necklace, 1920s; Trifari silver-tone bracelet with clear and colored rhinestones, 1930s; Silver cocktail ring with emerald rhinestone, 1940s; Silver-tone rhinestone lizard pin, late 1940s; Warner gold-tone pin with smoky rhinestones, late 1950s; Silver-tone rhinestone chain and disco ball pendant, 1960s.

Antiqued gold-tone dress clip with foiled rhinestones, 1930s

The back shows the distinctive foil backing on the rhinestones

STRASS

The first substitute for true rhinestones was developed by Georges-Frédéric Strass, or Stras (1701–73), a jeweler in Alsace on the River Rhine. He is credited with the invention of cut and polished lead glass "simulated gemstones," as he called them. He backed these hand-cut "gems" with metal foil, and later developed a process of mirror-coating their backs with metallic powder. Strass concentrated almost exclusively on the development of imitation diamonds, which became popular in Europe with the growing middle classes. Today, the word "Strass" is used in Europe to describe cut-glass fake diamonds in the same way as rhinestone is used in the US.

Problems: See Paste, page 116.

Cleaning and care: See pages 126–7.

SWAROVSKI CRYSTAL

The techniques pioneered by Strass led to a huge demand for "simulated gemstones" in the 19th century. Although these were a cheaper material than true gems, they were still cut by hand, until an automated cutting machine was invented by Daniel Swarovski (1862–1956) in 1892. This meant that high-quality cut-glass diamond substitutes could be made even more cheaply in large quantities. Swarovski crystal is considered to be the finest of its type, but there are also manufacturers of fine machine-cut glass gemstones, particularly in the Czech Republic. Swarovski cut glass is sometimes known in the US as Austrian Crystal.

Problems: Foil is likely to peel from the back of stones; the mirror finish may also peel or flake from the back of the stone, and can become scratched if the stone has come loose.

Cleaning and care: See pages 126–7.

FOILED RHINESTONES

Roman jewelers first discovered that an inferior gemstone could be enhanced by gluing metal foil to its back, and also used the technique in order to improve the brilliance of glass paste jewelry. Strass revived the process for his "simulated gemstones" (see left). Foiled "rhinestones" disappeared with improvements in vapor-deposited mercury amalgam coating and silvering in the 19th century, but they are still commonly referred to as foil-backed rhinestones.

Problems: See Swarovski Crystal, left.

Cleaning and care: See pages 126–7.

COLORED RHINESTONES

Cut-glass stones are made as imitations of not only diamonds, but many other gemstones too. By using various metallic additives in the glass-making process, different colors can be achieved—oxides of copper or gold give a red color, manganese gives purple, cobalt blue, and copper or chromium green—mimicking rubies, amethysts, sapphires, and emeralds.

Problems: See Paste, page 116.

Cleaning and care: See pages 126–7.

AURORA BOREALIS RHINESTONES

Cut-glass rhinestones can also be covered with a metallic reflective coating. Swarovski developed a technique in the 1950s to give a multi-colored sheen to the stones which became known as aurora borealis coating, supposedly simulating the effect of the Northern Lights. The coatings reflect and refract light in all colors of the rainbow, against a base color of red, blue, or green. A similar process using deeper greens and reds produces a finish known as "watermelon rhinestone," resembling the iridescent colors of the watermelon tourmaline.

Problems: See Swarovski Crystal, opposite.

Cleaning and care: See pages 126–7.

PLASTIC RHINESTONES

The invention of synthetic plastics in the 20th century made it possible to mass-produce even cheaper substitutes for gemstones. Acrylic in particular was well suited as a substitute for gems because of its clarity. However, plastics do not have the crystalline structure that gives real stones their sparkle, and are molded rather than cut, so do not have such well-defined facets and sharp edges. They are extremely durable when compared with glass, and can be easily colored to mimic many gemstones, but also have the advantage that any mirror backing is an integral part of the stone rather than just a coating.

Problems: Surfaces of plastics such as acrylic are also easily scratched and lose their brilliance.

Cleaning and care: See Lucite, page 137.

SYNTHETIC DIAMOND SUBSTITUTES

Although not usually classified as rhinestones, synthetic diamonds are increasingly being used as substitutes for gemstones in high-quality costume jewelry. Natural minerals such as moissanite and cubic zirconia, which because of their rarity were only discovered in the late 19th century, can now be synthetically produced in a process developed in the 1950s simulating the geological pressures that forms real diamonds. The result is a synthetic gemstone with much of the quality of the naturally formed diamonds.

Problems: See Diamonds, page 108.

Cleaning and care: See Diamonds, page 108.

Gold-tone duette pin and earrings with aurora borealis rhinestones, 1950s

Swarovski crystal clip-on earrings, 1950s

Gold-tone bracelet and earrings with watermelon rhinestones, 1950s

Repairing stone settings

Most stones in costume jewelry are either secured in claw settings (see page 47) or glued in place. Old glues can become unstable, and it is not unusual for glued stones to come away from their settings. Small stones are particularly vulnerable, since they are easily lost once they have fallen out.

Securing a loose stone in a claw setting

Stones in better-quality vintage costume jewelry were often set with claws rather than glued. Claws that have pulled away from their settings should be repaired as soon as you notice the problem. Left unrepaired, the stone may come loose or even be lost.

Arts and Crafts sterling silver ring with faceted glass stone, 1900s

1

The raised claw

1 A raised claw isn't only a danger to the stone, it can also catch on skin and clothing, making it uncomfortable to wear.

DELICATE STONES

- If you rush this type of repair, you can easily break the stone. Use a light touch when using the pushover setting tool and take your time.
- Some stones are very soft and particularly prone to damage. If your claw repair involves any of the following stones, take the item to a professional: Beryl, emerald, lapis lazuli, moonstone, opal, tanzanite, topaz.

2

2 Hold the ring firmly with one hand and use a pushover setting tool to gently and carefully push back the claw to its correct position. If necessary, use a three-square file or a safety-back file to file lightly any sharp edges on the surface of the claw. Check that the other claws are in their proper positions and that they have no sharp edges. Finally, check that the stone is sitting squarely in the setting.

Pushover setting tool see Tools, page 52

Three-square file or safety-back file see Tools, page 154

Replacing a small missing stone

Marcasite, a type of semi-precious stone (see page 112), is widely used in costume jewelry, particularly designs made in silver. Early finer examples were set in grain settings (see page 47), but mass-produced items were more often than not glued in their settings. It is not uncommon for glued stones to fall out, especially in vintage pieces where the glue has deteriorated over time.

Silver earrings with marcasites, faux green stone, and early plastic, 1930s

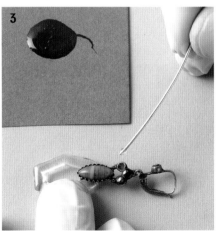

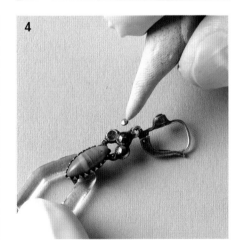

1 Marcasites are still used to make jewelry, and you can buy replacements from any good stone dealers.

2 Before refitting the marcasite, use a pointed sharp tool, such as a penknife or an old fine file, to clean the setting where the stone has fallen out. Make sure that you remove any remains of old glue. The same applies to the stone if you are regluing the original stone.

3 Put on a pair of protective gloves to make up the glue. I prefer to use a two-part epoxy resin glue (see box bottom left). Follow the instructions on the tube to mix the preparation. You need only a tiny amount. Dab the end of a spare piece of wire into the glue and apply a small amount of glue to the setting.

4 As marcasite stones are very small, use a pair of fine tweezers or a piece of poster putty to pick up the stone and transfer it to its setting. To use the poster putty, form it into a cone shape and use the tip of the cone to pick up the stone. Gently nudge the stone off the cone tip with your finger into the setting. Leave the glue to dry, usually about 15–20 minutes. Check the manufacturer's instructions for drying times.

CARE WITH GLUES AND SOLVENTS

I recommend gently scraping the old glue off with a penknife or a scriber (see Tools, pages 54 or 55) rather than using a solvent such as acetate or nail polish remover, since these liquids can damage soft stones such as opal, emerald, and moonstone.

Choose your glue carefully—a slow-drying two-part epoxy resin glue will allow you to fix the stone back securely with enough time to adjust its position so that it sits perfectly. Avoid superglues, since these tend to set instantly. Always follow the manufacturer's instructions and safety of use guidelines.

Small penknife see Tools, page 54

Protective gloves see Tools, page 55

Two-part epoxy resin glue see Tools, page 55

Pair of tweezers see Tools, page 54

Poster putty

Sourcing and refixing a missing stone

It is not always easy to replace a missing stone—here, a rhinestone—but if you have a large collection of costume jewelry you may be able to find a replacement stone from a piece that is beyond repair. When removing rhinestones, always wear eye protection. Sometimes the stone can fly out unexpectedly, which is a potential hazard.

Gilt and white enamel pin with clear rhinestones, 1950s

1 Put on eye protection. To remove a rhinestone, use the blade of a small penknife to pry the stone away gently. If you work very carefully, rest a finger on the rhinestone that you are removing to prevent it suddenly flying out of the setting. Sometimes rhinestones have already been reglued using superglue; these are virtually impossible to remove. If you struggle to remove the stone, stop and try another, which may still have its original glue. Stones set with conventional glues should be easy to remove.

2 Before you reset the stone check that it is in good condition. Sometimes when foil-backed rhinestones (see page 118) are removed, the foil or metal coating is damaged. The stone will look dull, with black marks where the metal backing is missing. This is often referred to as a dead stone. If the stone is damaged, discard it and try another stone. Check that the replacement stone is a good fit for the item being repaired.

3 Glue the stone in place as before (see page 121).

Eye protection

Small penknife see Tools, page 54

Pair of fine tweezers, see Tools, page 54

Two-part epoxy resin glue, see Tools, page 55

Protective gloves, see Tools, page 55

Refixing a large stone

Brooches may come with larger set stones, and these are often glued in position. Old glues will deteriorate over time, and the stone falls off. The type of glue I prefer to work with—two-part epoxy resin glue—is suitable for larger jobs like this, as well as for gluing smaller stones.

Brass butterfly pin with nephrite
jade carved wings, mother-of-pearl
body, and rosin eyes, 1960s

1

2

3

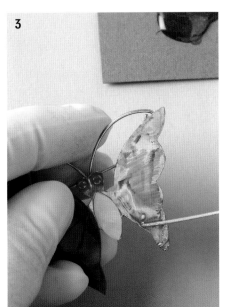

4

1 If one stone has fallen off it is always worth checking to see if the other old glued areas are weak and the stones are loose. If there are signs of this, remove the stone or stones gently and reglue these at the same time.

2 Gently remove the old glue from the setting and from the stone to be refixed. This must be done carefully using a scraping tool, such as a scriber, or a fine penknife, taking care not to damage the pin or the stone.

3 Put on a pair of protective gloves to make up the glue. Use a two-part epoxy resin glue and follow the instructions on the tube to mix the preparation. You need only a small amount. Apply the glue to the area, using the applicator that comes with the glue or a spare piece of fine wire as shown here. Don't take the glue right to the edge of the setting or it will run over the edge of the metal when the stone is positioned in place. Leave about ⅛ in (5 mm) clear around the edge.

4 Position the stone back in its setting and hold it with a pair of tweezers until the glue starts to set, usually within a minute or so. If any glue pushes out from the sides of the glued area remove immediately with a damp cloth.

Scriber or small penknife see Tools, pages 55 or 54

Protective gloves see Tools, page 55

Two-part epoxy resin glue see Tools, page 55

Pair of fine tweezers see Tools, page 54,

Cleaning stones

Keeping your precious and semi-precious stone jewelry clean maximizes the beauty of the pieces and ensures that more delicate stones (see box opposite) do not get scratched by surface dirt. Dust, for example, is made up of silicon dioxide, the same mineral component as quartz, a relatively hard stone. For general advice on the storing and care of jewelry, see pages 48–51. The method used to clean gemstones depends on their hardness, porosity, and whether they have been treated with oils or resins. Before you start cleaning, check that the settings are secure and none of the stones are loose. Make any necessary repairs before cleaning, or take the item to a professional jeweler for repair.

Gold ring with opals and diamonds, 1980s

Cleaning a harder gemstone

The following method is suitable for cleaning harder gemstones (see box opposite). These include opal, which is often considered too delicate to be cleaned with soap and water. However, this is not the case with a solid opal. In contrast, inexpensive opal jewelry may consist of thin slices of opal glued to a dark backing (known as a doublet opal). In some cases, a doublet is capped with a glass or plastic dome (known as a triplet opal). If doublet or triplet opals are put in water, moisture can find its way into the glued areas.

1 Rings with double or more claw settings with gaps in between them, as here, are very prone to collecting soap and grime. Place the ring in a bowl of lukewarm water to which you have added a few drops of gentle liquid detergent. Leave the ring to soak for a few minutes to soften the dirt, then brush it gently with a jeweler's brush or a soft-bristled toothbrush. Rinse under a running faucet; make sure the drain hole is covered. Leave the ring to air dry thoroughly, then bring up the shine of the metal with a jeweler's polishing cloth.

Bowl of water

Gentle liquid detergent

Jeweler's brush or soft-bristled toothbrush see Tools, page 53

Jeweler's polishing cloth see Tools, page 53

HARDER GEMSTONES

The composition and hardness of the following gemstones means that they are suitable for cleaning in a bowl of soapy water (see opposite). To check whether they are also suitable for cleaning in an ultrasonic cleaner, go to page 69. The soapy method is suitable only for gemstones that are set in metal, not glued in place. If the stones are glued, clean them as for softer gemstones. You can use a cloth that has been dipped in soapy water first, then wipe with a damp, soft, lint-free cloth to remove any soap. Dry with a soft, lint-free cloth.

Agate	Opal
Amethyst	Onyx
Aquamarine	Quartz
Carnelian	Ruby
Chalcedony	Sapphire
Citrine	Tanzanite
Diamond	Tiger's eye
Garnet	Topaz
Moonstone	Tourmaline

SOFTER GEMSTONES

The composition and hardness of the following gemstones are more delicate, and they need careful cleaning. Do not soak them; simply wipe the stones with a slightly damp, soft, lint-free cloth that has been dipped in tepid water, then dry with a soft, lint-free cloth. Emerald is included here because although emeralds are relatively hard, some are treated with oils or resins to fill any cracks in the stones. The fillers may deteriorate if they are exposed to warm water and soaking. Any stone that has been glued should not be immersed in water.

Emerald
Opals, doublet or triplets (see opposite)
Fluorite
Jade
Lapis lazuli
Marcasite
Turquoise
Malachite

Taxco sterling silver bracelet with green agate, 1960s

Silver ring with coral and turquoise, 1960s

Cleaning softer gemstones set in silver

Delicate stones are affected by chemicals, and should only be cleaned with plain water. But what do you do when your piece of jewelry contains delicate gemstones set in silver? If the silver is very tarnished, my advice is to give the silver a one-time thorough clean, then clean it regularly with a chemical-free polishing cloth to maintain the shine.

1 When cleaning the silver, make every effort not to touch the stone, since silver polish contains substances that can damage delicate stones. You could try masking stones, using a product such as poster putty, but never leave poster putty on a stone for more than 10–20 minutes.

Protective gloves see Tools, page 53

Q-tips see Tools, page 53

Jeweler's silver polishing cloth or silver polish see Tools, page 53

Soft, lint-free cloths

2 Clean the silver with a jeweler's polishing cloth or, if it needs a deeper clean, with liquid silver polish. To apply the liquid silver polish, put on a pair of protective gloves and dip a Q-tip in the liquid. Squeeze the Q-tip of excess liquid, then apply a light film to the silver. Allow to dry. Remove the polish with a soft, lint-free cloth, then wipe with a soft, lint-free damp cloth to remove any excess product. Dry it with a soft cloth. Clean the stones with a soft, lint-free damp cloth or a dampened Q-tip. Dry with a soft, lint-free cloth and leave to air dry thoroughly.

3 Once the silver is tarnish-free and polished, the secret is to clean the silver after every wearing with a jeweler's polishing cloth (a microfiber cloth is also suitable), which does not contain any chemicals. However, the cloth will still remove oils picked up from your skin, lotions, and other products that contribute to the tarnishing process. When you are not wearing the piece, store it in a plastic zip-lock bag with a silica-gel pack, which will help to slow down the tarnishing process.

Cleaning rhinestones

Most rhinestones are made of glass. Many rhinestones also have a metal-coated backing, referred to as foil-backed, which enhances the brilliance of the glass stone. The backing is easy to identify—turn the piece over, and you will see a metallic finish covering the back of the glass stone (see Step 5). Some costume jewelry pieces combine foil-backed and unfoiled glass stones; these should be cleaned as suggested below. The aim is to avoid liquid entering the setting and coming into contact with the metal backing. Water and chemicals coming into contact with the backing may discolor and darken it, as well as dislodge already peeling coating. The metal settings for rhinestone jewelry can be polished with a jeweler's polishing cloth.

Gold-tone pin with red and green rhinestones, 1940s

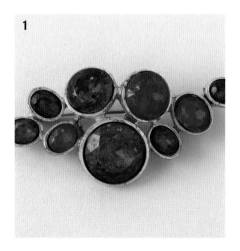

1 There is some question as to the best cleaning solution to use on foil-backed rhinestones. I find window cleaning solution or alcohol works well, but there are proprietary solutions available. Follow the manufacturer's instructions.

2 As you'll be in contact with cleaning solution, wear protective gloves. Use a pointed implement to scrape away gently any deeply embedded dirt between the settings.

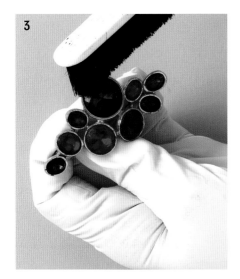

3 Gently brush each glass stone with a jeweler's brush, using a light, sweeping motion, to remove surface dirt. If the item looks clean at this point, polish with a soft, lint-free cloth or a piece of chamois leather to finish.

4 If the item is still dirty, continue to the wet phase. Pour a small amount of window cleaning solution into a container. If you prefer, you could use a spirit with a high alcohol content, such as vodka. Take a Q-tip and dip it into the solution, then squeeze it to remove excess cleaner. The Q-tip should feel barely damp. Wipe each glass stone with the Q-tip.

5 Wipe away any traces of cleaner with a slightly damp, soft, lint-free cloth. Leave the item to dry face down on a sheet of paper towel to avoid moisture running into the back of the piece. When the item is dry, polish with a chamois leather or a jeweler's polishing cloth.

Protective gloves see Tools, page 53

Pointed pin see Tools, page 53

Jeweler's brush see Tools, page 53

Window cleaning solution

Q-tips see Tools, page 53

Soft, lint-free cloth and paper towel

Jeweler's polishing cloth see Tools, page 53

CLEANING OTHER TYPES OF RHINESTONES

Early paste stones Essentially the same composition as modern rhinestones, paste stones were molded or hand cut to resemble precious stones. Eighteenth-century and 19th-century paste jewelry was often foil-backed. If in doubt, take the item to be professionally cleaned.

Unfoiled rhinestones Some rhinestones do not have a foil backing. These may be cleaned as for precious stones if they are set rather than glued; if glued, clean as for foil-backed rhinestones.

Aurora borealis Rhinestones with a metallic, iridescent coating are known as aurora borealis, which can be foil-backed or clear. Clean aurora borealis as for foil-backed rhinestones, but omit Step 2, cleaning with a jeweler's brush. The finish on the stones is delicate and easily scratched.

Swarovski crystal glass A type of leaded crystal glass noted for its luminescent sparkle. Some Swarovski crystal glass stones are foil-backed, others are not. Clean as for the type. They may also be coated in various chemicals to achieve certain finishes. Follow the advice for aurora borealis (see above) for all coated rhinestones.

Acrylic rhinestones These are made from plastic and are foil-backed. You should clean them as for delicate stones, see page 125.

Gold-tone aurora borealis pin, 1960s

Costume jewelry has always drawn on a wide range of materials. Discover more about the other materials commonly used to make jewelry, and how to care for and maintain them. Glass has been used for centuries to make inexpensive beads for necklaces. Plastics are synonymous with costume jewelry, while enamels bring brilliant color to pieces. Ceramics offer interesting faux stones, and animal products include hairwork, horn, and the sea jewels coral and mother-of-pearl. Plant materials encompass amber, jet, and wood. And to close there are cameos that offer miniature works of art.

Other Materials

Glass

Made by heating a mixture of sand and potash, glass has been used since Roman times as a jewelry material both in its own right and to imitate more expensive precious and semi-precious gemstones. Beads (see page 92) and other jewelry elements made from glass can be produced by a number of techniques—wound, lampworked (a type of glasswork developed in Murano, Italy, in the 14th century), drawn, blown, fused, molded, or pressed. Glass jewelry can be translucent or opaque, is found in many colors, and can have a metallic finish. It can also be decorated or cut for effect. You will find further information on glass in jewelry under Rhinestones (see pages 116–19).

Gold-tone green Peking glass pin with rhinestones, 1930s

URANIUM

Glass made by adding uranium oxide to the glass mix prior to melting is known as uranium glass. It was also sometimes referred to as Vaseline glass in the 1920s, because it looked similar to the petroleum jelly produced at that time. The process typically produces a translucent pale yellow-green colored glass, but it can also come in other colors such as green, yellow, amber, pink, and turquoise. There are also opaque and semi-opaque types. Uranium glass was discovered in the early 19th century and it started being mass produced toward the end of the 19th century—for jewelry, usually in the form of beads. It remained popular into the 1920s, but manufacture ceased with the advent of the nuclear bomb, when sales and use of uranium became restricted. Uranium glass is easy to identify as it glows fluorescent green under UV light.

Problems: Uranium is radioactive, but the general consensus is that the amount usually found in jewelry is safe—it is likely to be no more than the radiation found in a wristwatch.

Cleaning and care: Glass can be affected by high temperatures and strong chemical cleaners. If the piece has no glued parts or is strung with synthetic thread, wash in lukewarm water to which you have added a few drops of mild liquid detergent. Use a jeweler's brush to gently clean the surface; use a sweeping movement, never scrub at a piece. Rinse in clean water, then pat dry with a soft, lint-free cloth. Leave to dry thoroughly on a piece of paper

Gold-tone opaline glass pin with rhinestones, 1900s

towel. If the piece has glued parts, clean as for foil-backed rhinestones (see pages 126–7). To clean a glass bead necklace strung with natural thread, see page 105.

OPALINE

Real opaline glass was made in France during the 19th century, and is sometimes referred to as French opaline glass. This slightly translucent opaque glass has a high lead content and comes in a range of milky colors. The term is often used to refer to any glass with an opaque finish.

Problems: Can be scratched if not stored properly.

Cleaning and care: See Uranium, left.

PEKING

True Peking glass was developed in China in the late 17th century and has a one-color glass base overlaid with one or more further layers of contrasting colors that are carved away to reveal the different colors underneath. In jewelry, the term is often used for one-color carved glass in a jade green color, popular during the 1920s.

Wedding cake bead necklace, 1930s

Chevron glass bead necklace, 1920s

Simulated carnelian necklace made from glass, 19th century

Brass bug pin with saphiret glass, 1910s

Gold-tone floral pin with Sappharine stones and rhinestones, 1950s

Problems: Dirt can accumulate in the carved layers.

Cleaning and care: See Uranium, page 130. You may need to use a toothpick wetted in glass cleaning spray to tackle carved areas.

SWAROVSKI
See entry in Rhinestones, page 118.

SAPHIRET
A Czech glass technique dating from the 19th century. Melted real gold was mixed into sapphire-colored glass to create a glass that looks pinky-brown or brick red with a blue reflection on the surface. Later German-made Sappharine stones were made to mimic saphiret, but real gold was not used and the effect is less striking.

Problems: The stones look extremely dull if allowed to get dirty.

Cleaning and care: See Uranium, page 130.

CAMEO GLASS
See entry in Cameos, page 149.

PÂTE DE VERRE
To make pâte de verre ("glass paste"), glass is ground to a powder, colored, placed in a mold and then fired. The result is glass with a gemlike translucency. The process was first developed in ancient Greece and Rome, then revived in the 19th century in France. Some of the well-known French designers who used this technique were René Lalique (1860–1945) and Gabriel Argy-Rousseau (1885–1963). Pâte de verre jewelry was very popular in the Art Nouveau era.

Problems: Store glass jewelry separately from other items; it can be easily scratched.

Cleaning and care: See Uranium, page 130.

DICHROIC
This new type of rainbow glass gem or bead is a side-product of the space program, and has become popular in the 21st century. Thin layers of metal oxides are deposited on a base glass to create a unique layering effect.

Problems: See Pâte de verre, left.

Cleaning and care: See Uranium, page 130.

CHEVRON
Also known as Rosetta or star beads, these glass beads have a V-shaped patterning formed from layers of glass canes. They were popular throughout the 20th century.

Problems: To store, roll a necklace with chevron beads in white acid-free tissue paper so that the beads cannot knock against each other.

Cleaning and care: See Uranium, page 130.

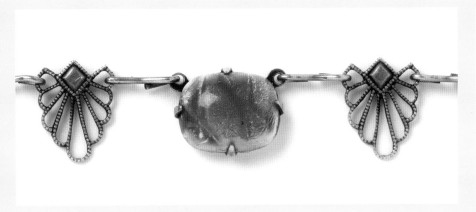

Silver necklace with Murano foiled glass cabochons, 1910s

Pressed glass earrings with rhinestone, 1940s

Gold-tone necklace with Murano foiled glass beads, 1930s

Hammered silver pendant with Czech foiled glass, 1920s

WEDDING CAKE

These glass beads decorated with glass overlays featuring flowers, swirls, and dots are made using the lampwork method. Popular from the 19th century, they are still made today in some glass centers.

Problems: Because the beads have applied decoration, they are more easily damaged than a smooth bead. Store them carefully (see Chevron, opposite) and take care when putting them on so that they don't catch in knitwear.

Cleaning and care: See Uranium, page 130.

CZECH OR BOHEMIAN

The Czech or Bohemian method of glass manufacture, where hot glass is pressed into a heated mold, enabled mass production of faceted glass beads and imitation gemstones from the 19th century, and production has continued to the present day.

Problems: See Pâte de verre, left.

Cleaning and care: See Uranium, page 130.

MURANO

The Venetian island of Murano was an early centre of glassmaking—dating back to the 14th century—where techniques such as aventurine (glass with threads of gold), crystalline (imitates rock crystal), smalto (enameled glass), millefiori (multi-colored glass), and lattimo (milk glass), as well as imitation gemstones were developed. In the early part of the 20th century, it was the main producer of seed beads (see page 93). Most beads today are made individually using the wound lampworking method invented in Murano in the 18th century to meld layers of different colored glass, gold, and silver leaf.

Problems: See Pâte de verre, left.

Cleaning and care: See Uranium, page 130.

Uranium multi-strand glass bead necklace, 1920s

Plastics

We tend to think of plastics as a cheap, modern substitute for more expensive gemstones or animal materials, but they were first used in jewelry in the Victorian period and for much of the 20th century were prized as materials in their own right. The earliest used, gutta percha, is a naturally occurring polymer, but this was superseded by chemically modified natural materials such as vulcanite, Galalith, and celluloid. These plastics were enthusiastically taken up by costume jewelry makers including Coco Chanel in the period between the two world wars. The first truly synthetic plastic, Bakelite, was patented in 1909 and became a valued material for jewelry, particularly in the late 1920s and 1930s. After World War II thermoplastics such as Lucite gained favor in decorative jewelry, especially in the "pop" moonglow jewelry of the 1950s and 1960s.

Elephant's head pin in Galalith with ivorine tusk, 1920s

GUTTA PERCHA

This natural polymer was known to the native people of the Malayan peninsula for centuries before it was brought to the West in the 1840s. The sap of the *Palaquium gutta* tree, when allowed to dry and coagulate in the sun, forms a latex which can be heated and molded in the same way as rubber, creating a durable material with many applications. It is dark in color and hard without being brittle, so became popular as a substitute for woods such as ebony, and as an alternative to jet in mourning jewelry in the 19th century. Distinguishing gutta percha from ebony and jet can be difficult, and it can easily be mistaken for vulcanite (see below). Testing with a hot pin is often suggested for this and all kinds of plastics, but will permanently mark or even destroy an item, so is not recommended.

Problems: Can discolor and deteriorate if exposed to sunlight for long periods; store in a dark place. Splits and cracks need specialist attention.

Cleaning and care: Clean with a jeweler's brush or wipe with a soft cloth. Gutta percha can be washed in warm water, but beware as it can be confused with vulcanite, which needs to be kept dry. Avoid chemical cleaners, and store away from perfumes and cosmetics—solvents may react with plastics of all sorts.

VULCANITE

A mixture of natural rubber and 30–40 percent sulfur in a process later known as vulcanization, vulcanite was discovered by Charles Goodyear in

Shield-shaped gutta percha pendant, 19th century

Engraved vulcanite locket, 19th century

1839 and patented as Ebonite in 1851. Hard, black, and shiny, it was intended originally as a substitute for ebony, but was also used as an alternative to jet (see page 146), particularly for mourning jewelry. It can also be colored or painted, or inlaid with other materials, and molded into almost any shape, making it a popular material with jewelry makers in the 19th century. It can sometimes be identified by a faint sulfurous, rubbery smell especially when scratched or heated, but a less damaging test is to rub it with a cloth: Unlike jet, ebony, or gutta percha, vulcanite builds up static electricity and will attract hair and dust.

Problems: Vulcanite is a brittle material, particularly as it ages, so handle with care. Splits and cracks require specialist repair. Moisture can discolor the surface and take away the shine, as can sunlight, so store in a dark, dry place.

Cleaning and care: Clean with a jeweler's brush or wipe with a soft cloth. Can be washed, but in cold or at most lukewarm water—hot water may make it turn green or brown—and must be dried thoroughly to avoid dulling the shine. Can be buffed to a shine, but avoid cleaning products and polishes unless specifically for vulcanite.

From top left, clockwise: Etched bangle in transparent "apple juice" Bakelite with central floral motif, 1940s; "Josephine Baker" cuff of brass and red Bakelite, 1930s; Striped pin of amber, red, green, and black Bakelite, 1930s; Grapes and leaves pin of amber and green Bakelite, 1930s; Modern collectible pin with transparent "apple juice" Bakelite center of swimming fish with a red etched surround; Pin in transparent "apple juice" Bakelite with floral motif, 1940s.

Green Bakelite bangle with telltale "marbling" discoloration, a sign of Bakelite "sickness," 1930s

Etched celluloid bangles with simple leaf and flower motif, 1920s

Early plastic bead necklaces, 1920s

GALALITH

Made by combining casein (milk protein) and formaldehyde, Galalith was patented in Germany in 1904, and originally developed to make "whiteboards" for schools. Unlike other thermosetting plastics such as vulcanite, Celluloid, and Bakelite, it cannot be molded, and was produced in sheets which were then cut into shapes. However, it can be embossed and drilled, and can also be dyed in bright colors as an alternative to gemstones, although in its original white it was often used as an ivory substitute. In the 1920s it was used by costume jewelry makers such as Coco Chanel, often in combination with chromium; Galalith jewelry became distinctive for its simplicity and clarity of design, notably in the "brick tile chains" by Jakob Bengel of the 1920s and 1930s. Milk shortages stopped production during World War II, and Galalith never regained its former popularity with the advent of thermoplastics.

Problems: Very early Galalith is now beginning to show signs of deterioration, such as surface yellowing or darkening, accompanied by a smell of sour milk. Store separately (or discard) if this is happening to prevent gases affecting other plastic items.

Cleaning and care: Galalith can be washed in warm soapy water, and is resistant to hot water and detergents, but certain solvents and acids can damage the surface. Store in the dark, away from extremes of temperature and humidity.

CELLULOID

The first celluloid was developed in the 1850s and manufactured in Britain as Parkesine. In the US, the Hyatt brothers patented a similar material made from nitrocellulose (nitric acid and starch or wood fibers, known as guncotton) and camphor as Celluloid. This was used as a substitute for ivory, tortoiseshell, and horn, and was variously known as Xylonite, French ivory, and tortine. In jewelry making, it had its heyday between 1900 and 1930, when it was replaced by Bakelite, but enjoyed something of a revival with the invention of Rhodoid (based on cellulose acetate) in France in 1936. Celluloid can be identified by a characteristic camphor smell when rubbed with a soft cloth (cellulose acetate gives off a vinegary smell). Testing for this smell in hot water, however, may irreparably harm the piece—and as Celluloid is highly flammable, on no account use the "hot pin" test.

Problems: Celluloid is fragile, brittle, and flammable, especially as it ages. Splits and cracks need specialist repair. As it deteriorates, Celluloid goes dull, discolors, and becomes smelly, and may even begin to disintegrate—a process known as "sickness." Storing away from perfumes and cosmetics in a cool, dry, and well-ventilated place (not an airtight box or plastic bag) will help to slow the progress of the sickness, but it cannot be reversed, or even halted. Gases from the deterioration can also infect other plastic items, so "sick" Celluloid should be stored separately, or discarded.

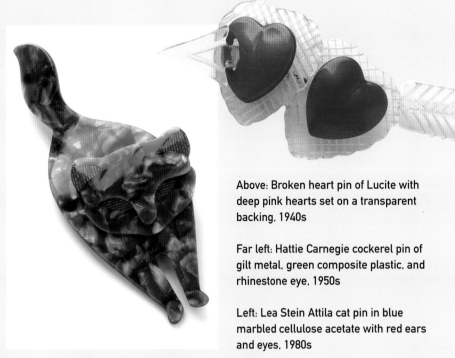

Above: Broken heart pin of Lucite with deep pink hearts set on a transparent backing, 1940s

Far left: Hattie Carnegie cockerel pin of gilt metal, green composite plastic, and rhinestone eye, 1950s

Left: Lea Stein Attila cat pin in blue marbled cellulose acetate with red ears and eyes, 1980s

Cleaning and care: Only clean with a jeweler's brush or wipe with a soft cloth. Do not wash.

BAKELITE

The first truly synthetic plastic, Bakelite was developed and patented by Dr. Leo H. Baekeland in 1909. It is cast as a resin made from phenol (carbolic acid) and formaldehyde, and can be laminated, carved, or machined, inlaid and dyed in many different colors. The patent was taken over by the US Catalin Corporation in 1927, who introduced a transparent version of the material and a greater range of colors, including marbling. Bakelite or Catalin (also known elsewhere as Prystal, Marblette, and Durez) became a favorite in costume jewelry from around this time until the 1950s. However, it was not a cheap substitute for other materials because pieces had to be individually cast, cut, and polished. Bakelite can be identified by its weight (it is heavier than most other plastics) and the distinctive "clack" when pieces are tapped together (other plastics make more of a "click"). When heated by rubbing with a soft cloth or thumb, it gives off a carbolic smell (do not immerse it in hot water for this test).

Problems: Like all plastics, it can deteriorate over time, especially if exposed to extremes of temperature and humidity. Colors tend to darken with age. Store as for Celluloid (opposite), since it can suffer from a similar contagious "sickness", when it gives off a very strong carbolic smell.

Cleaning and care: Brush with a jeweler's brush and wipe with a soft, lint-free cloth. Can be washed in warm water, but dry thoroughly. Avoid chemical cleaners and polishes. Avoid abrasives (and polishing too vigorously) as you may rub away surface Bakelite and get down to a wood flour or carbon filler base.

LUCITE

Originally developed in the 1930s as a light, shatterproof alternative to glass, polymethyl methacrylate (PMMA) was the first of the modern thermoplastics, which differ from the earlier thermosetting plastics in that they can be melted by heat. Marketed in Germany as Plexiglas and in the UK as Perspex, this clear plastic was later sold for various uses under names including Altuglas and Optix, but came to be known as acrylic or simply poly. A form of PMMA, which could be dyed almost any color, transparent or opaque, was produced by DuPont in 1937 under the trade name Lucite, and it began to appear in jewelry in the early 1940s. It is a very versatile material which can be molded, cast, carved, laminated, and polished to a high gloss shine. Lucite became fashionable in the 1950s and especially in the "pop" period of the 1960s. Transparent acrylics sometimes have objects such as flowers or shells set in them, or glitter cast into them (sometimes known as "confetti Lucite"). Lucite and other acrylics can be distinguished from Bakelite by their brighter colors and glossier finish, and the absence of any odor when rubbed.

Problems: Lucite and other acrylics can be quite easily scratched. Older Lucite can also develop cracks and become brittle from age or exposure to heat. Avoid all abrasives and harsh chemicals.

Cleaning and care: Avoid extremes of temperature (especially cleaning in hot water) as this can cause cracks and crazing. Clean with a soft, dry cloth, or wash in lukewarm water with a little soap, rinse, and dry thoroughly.

MODERN PLASTICS

The period from the 1940s onward is sometimes referred to as the "poly" age by materials scientists, because of the profusion of new plastics including polymethyl methacrylate (see Lucite), polyvinyl chloride (PVC), polyethylene (Polythene), polyurethane, polyamide (Nylon), polyacrylonitrile (Courtelle, Orlon), polycarbonate, polyester, and so on. Some of the manmade fibers, particularly nylon, have proved useful for stringing, but many of the new materials have yet to find a place in jewelry making.

Problems: Many of the modern plastics have not been in use long enough to know what the problems of aging will be. It's possible they will deteriorate in ways similar to older plastics, especially in high temperature or humidity, and in reactions to chemical cleaners and perfumes/cosmetics. Also some are prone to scratching.

Cleaning and care: As for Lucite (see above).

Enamels

Sometimes used in imitation of gemstones, but also as a colorful, high-gloss decorative finish, enamels have been used in jewelry making since the time of the ancient Egyptians 3,500 years ago. Various methods evolved over the ages and in different cultures, but all enameling is based on the process of melting either powdered colored glass or a mixture of colorless glass and colorants onto the surface of metal objects. These techniques were perfected in the Middle Ages with particularly fine enamel work produced in Limoges, France, and later by Renaissance makers such as Benvenuto Cellini. Enamel jewelry reached its peak in the Art Deco period and the exquisite decorative work of the Russian House of Fabergé.

David Andersen guilloché enamel butterfly pin, 1950s

CLOISONNÉ

Sometimes known as "cell enameling," cloisonné enamels are made by forming designs on a metal foundation with wire or thin metal strips, making compartments in which powdered enamel is placed. When melted in a furnace, the enamels are kept separate by the wires, which are held in place with adhesive or solder. In this way, a number of different colored enamels can be applied in various shapes at one time. The separating wires are then filed flat so that they lie flush with the surface of the enamel. The technique was one of the first methods of decorative enameling and is used widely in the Middle East and Asia. Although largely superseded by the champlevé technique (see below) in Europe in the Middle Ages, it is also a standard method of producing items of costume jewelry today.

Problems: Surfaces may become chipped or scratched with careless handling and storage. Individual pieces of enamel may come loose or be missing. Repairs need specialist attention.

Cleaning and care: Wipe with a slightly damp, soft, lint-free cloth and allow to dry. Store separately wrapped in acid-free tissue paper.

CHAMPLEVÉ

An alternative method to cloisonné (see above) for creating compartments in the base metal to be enameled is champlevé. In this technique, the foundation piece is carved or etched with "pits" to contain the powdered enamel. The

Limoges enamel pin, 19th century

Plique-à-jour pin, 19th century

process was used in Roman and Celtic jewelry, and reached its peak in the enamel work on copper produced in Limoges in the 12th and 13th centuries, but fell out of favor until a revival of the technique among Art Deco jewelry makers. A related technique, basse-taille (French for "low relief"), uses transparent enamels fused onto a foundation carved or machined with a relief design, which has been used for pins, pendants, and other items. A similar three-dimensional effect is achieved by grisaille: a dark blue or back background enamel is applied to the foundation, and the design is then painted on in successive layers of monochrome translucent enamels.

Problems: Surfaces can get chipped or scratched. Repairs need specialist attention.

Cleaning and care: See Cloisonné, left.

PLIQUE À JOUR

A process developed in the 15th century in which enamels are melted into a wire framework, but not laid on a foundation. Light can then shine through the translucent enamels, giving a stained glass-like appearance. Various methods have been used to create plique-à-jour jewelry, but generally the work is made with a thin copper foil or mica backing which is either dissolved in acid or peeled off after firing. The technique is usually reserved for fine jewelry, using gold or silver cloisonné wire to separate the cells. Plique à jour was popular during the Renaissance, but then not much used until a 20th-century revival.

Arts and Crafts enamel pendant, 1910s

Bernard Instone enamel necklace, 1910s

Cloisonné bead necklace, 1950s

David Andersen ronde-bosse pin, 1950s

Enamel Scottie and Westie dogs pin, 1940s

Problems: Can be very delicate. Pieces of enamel can work loose and fall out of the metal framework. Repairs need specialist attention.

Cleaning and care: See Cloisonné, opposite.

RONDE-BOSSE
Also known as "encrusted enamel," ronde-bosse is a method of enameling three-dimensional figures rather than the flat or curved surface of foundation metal. The design is first cast in solid metal or formed from a network of wire and the surface then roughened to provide a key for the enamel. Unlike other enameling techniques, ronde-bosse is usually on a base of gold, or occasionally silver. As there are no compartments to hold powdered glass, the enamel is mixed with flux and applied as a paste covering the metal, before firing. First developed in 14th-century France, ronde-bosse was much used by the House of Fabergé in the 19th and early 20th centuries.

Problems: Surfaces may become chipped or scratched, and delicate pieces may crack or break. Repairs need specialist attention.

Cleaning and care: See Cloisonné, opposite.

GUILLOCHÉ
A technique of engraving rather than enameling, but often covered with a decorative coat of translucent enamel. The foundation material for guilloché enamels is mechanically engraved on a lathe with an intricate pattern of interlocking and interweaving spirographic lines, similar to those seen on bank notes. This pattern is visible through the colored enamel overlay. Some of the finest examples of guilloché work can be seen on Fabergé eggs, but it is often found on pocket watches and dressing table accessories, as well as in jewelry such as pendants, necklaces, pins or brooches, and rings.

Problems: Surfaces can get chipped or scratched. Individual pieces of enamel may come loose or be missing. Repairs need specialist attention.

Cleaning and care: See Cloisonné, opposite.

Ceramics

The process of baking clay to make pottery has been known about since prehistoric times. Ceramic pots are among some of the earliest archeological finds, but pottery has also been used for making decorative items including jewelry, from hand-shaped beads through decorated medallions to three-dimensional flowers. As techniques of molding, decorating, and glazing became more sophisticated, ceramic items became almost as highly prized as gemstones, and pottery makers such as Wedgwood, Aynsley, and Ruskin devoted a portion of their production to jewelry items. Today, ceramics remain a popular material with makers of costume jewelry.

Porcelain floral pin, 1950s

EARTHENWARE AND STONEWARE

The most common ceramic material, earthenware, is familiar to us all from its use for everyday tableware. Generally white or off-white in color, it can be molded into shapes suitable for jewelry (beads or medallions, for example), and colored, painted, or decorated before glazing. Red clays such as terra cotta are sometimes left unglazed, especially in "ethnic" jewelry. Stoneware is stronger and more resilient, and is made from a finer, gray-brown clay fired at a higher temperature.

Problems: Easily chipped or broken. Unglazed items can become ingrained with dirt and grease, and easily absorb moisture.

Cleaning and care: Clean unglazed items with a brush only. Wipe glazed pieces with a soft, lint-free damp cloth and leave to dry thoroughly. Store items separately wrapped in white acid-free tissue paper.

PORCELAIN

Made from clay with a high proportion of kaolin, porcelain has a characteristic white color and is prized for its fineness. The best-known porcelain came from Limoges in France, but it was also produced from the 18th century onward in Britain, the US, and elsewhere. It is fired at higher temperatures than earthenware and stoneware, and is covered with a transparent glaze, but can also be decorated by painting or the application of a transfer print before glazing. In jewelry, porcelain is used in the form of medallions or plaques (usually decorated with floral designs or portraits) mounted in metal for necklaces, brooches, or rings, but some manufacturers also produced flowers in the round for pins.

Problems: Easily chipped or broken. The glaze may become cracked. Repairs need expert attention.

Cleaning and care: Wipe with a damp, soft, lint-free cloth and leave the item to dry thoroughly. Delicate and intricate pieces should be cleaned with a soft brush or Q-tip. Store pieces separately wrapped in white acid-free tissue paper.

BONE CHINA

In the 18th century, a particularly fine form of porcelain made from kaolin, feldspathic material, and animal bone ash was developed by the English potter Josiah Spode (1733–97). This bone china is not only stronger and more resistant to chipping than porcelain, but is also exceptionally white and translucent. Spode adopted bone china for the finest tableware, and was soon followed by other makers of fine china. Among them was another English potter, John Aynsley (1752–1829), whose grandson John Aynsley II (1823–1907) opened a factory in Stoke-on-Trent, England, to make the very best bone china, using 50 percent bone ash. As well as the traditional tableware, Aynsley produced bone china jewelry, most notably three-dimensional flower pieces which became known as "florals." In the 1950s and 1960s, floral pins and earrings made from either bone china or porcelain, sometimes presented in sets, were very popular.

Problems: Glaze may become cracked. Intricate florals can chip or break if carelessly handled. Repairs need expert attention.

Cleaning and care: See Porcelain, above.

Ruskin cabochon silver earrings, 1900s

WEDGWOOD JASPERWARE

The distinctive blue cameos created by the English potter Josiah Wedgwood (1730–1795, see also page 149) are formed from very fine white stoneware molded onto a base colored with jasper (a form of quartz that comes in yellow, brown, green, or red) and metal oxides, with a distinctive unglazed matte finish. The color most associated with this jasperware is a pale blue now known as Wedgwood Blue, but Wedgwood have also made cameo pieces with sage green, yellow, or dark blue bases, and even produced a black stoneware colored with basalt (a type of volcanic rock). As well as appearing on items of fine pottery, cameos made of Wedgwood jasperware were made into plaques which were mounted in gold, silver, or steel for all sorts of jewelry, including pins, pendants, rings, and necklaces.

Glazed earthenware pendant, 1960s

Swedish bone china hand-painted butterfly pin, 1914

Bone china pin with transfer print, 1960s

Wedgwood jasperware blue and white cameo pin, 19th century

Problems: Easily chipped or broken. Age and handling may cause the matte surface to become ingrained with dirt and grease. Repairs need expert attention.

Cleaning and care: See Porcelain, opposite.

RUSKIN POTTERY

In 1898, Edward Richard Taylor (d. 1912) founded the Birmingham Tile and Pottery Works, in Smethwick near Birmingham, England, together with his son William Howson Taylor (1876–1935). Later, Howson Taylor renamed the pottery the Ruskin Pottery, after the founding father of the Arts and Crafts movement, John Ruskin, whom he admired greatly. Howson Taylor developed an exceptionally fine glaze, which involved a number of firings, and which was used to make

cabochons (small round medallions). These often had beautifully marbled or delicately speckled effects, in colors that included turquoise, mid-tone blues, and reds. The cabochons were mounted in silver or pewter as a less expensive alternative to gemstones for jewelry. These were marketed as "enamels" or "plaques." They became very popular in the early part of the 20th century, particularly with Arts and Crafts jewelers, and were commonly known as "Ruskins." Other makers tried unsuccessfully to copy the style, but the secret of the Ruskin glaze was never shared and died with the closing of the firm in 1933.

Problems: Glaze may become cracked or chipped. Plaques may come loose from their mounts. Repairs need expert attention.

Cleaning and care: See Porcelain, opposite.

DELFT JEWELRY

The Dutch city of Delft gave its name to a style of tin-glazed earthenware, usually with blue underglaze decorations depicting windmills, Dutch landscapes, or flowers, in imitation Chinese porcelain during the 17th century. Makers across the Netherlands adopted the style, and some began producing small round or oval medallions for mounting in jewelry such as pins, pendants, and rings. The comparatively coarse earthenware base is glazed with a tin-based white glaze known as faience, then decorated and reglazed with a clear lead-based glaze. The medallions are generally set in silver mounts, often with intricate filigree designs.

Problems: See Bone China, opposite.

Cleaning and care: See Porcelain, opposite.

Animal materials

According to research on archaeological finds at Skhul in Israel, tiny shells were the earliest materials used in jewelry. Cultures throughout history have crafted organic materials into adornments, including bone, tusk, hide, claw, and hoof (see also Plant Materials, pages 146–7). By the 19th century, exotic jewelry made from wild animals such as tigers' claws, ivory, and tortoiseshell were much in demand. These items and many other wild animal materials are now banned for use in jewelry (see page 145). Jewelry made from animal materials was also popular during and between the two world wars, when metals and gemstones were scarce.

Swedish human hairwork pin, 19th century

BONE

The skeletons of vertebrate animals consist of bone, a hard material primarily made up of calcium phosphate and collagen fiber. It ranges in color from white or yellowish cream to dark brown, and the color can darken with age. To check that a piece is made from bone as opposed to ivory (see page 145) look for the following: brown patches of discoloration (as seen in the bone bracelet opposite); under magnification, there should be no visible grain, which is present in ivory, and you should be able to see tiny dot marks (the remains of channels for blood vessels). Jewelry made from bone was popular in the Art Deco period and during the world wars, when regular materials were unavailable. It was also used as a substitute for ivory.

Problems: Bone is fragile; handle with care. If it chips or breaks, seek specialist advice.

Cleaning and care: To clean bone, follow the advice for cleaning semi-precious stones, the water and detergent method (see page 124). Do not clean bone in an ultrasonic cleaner or steam clean it. Store bone in a cool, dry place.

HORN

A hard, pointed protuberance on some animals, consisting mainly of keratin, a protein, which is also found in nails, claws, hooves, and hair. Horn pieces range in color from a light translucent yellow brown to dark brown. Items are sometimes embellished with paint, stones, and metalwork. Jewelry made from horn was particularly popular in the 19th century and in the early part of the 20th century.

Moth pin made from horn, 1900s

Problems: Horn scratches easily, and can become brittle with age. If it develops cracks and chips, seek specialist help.

Cleaning and care: As for bone (see left), but do not brush horn as this may scratch the surface. Rub it with a soft, lint-free cloth first, then progress to the wet cleaning treatment if necessary.

HAIR AND FUR

Like horn, hair and fur are mainly made up of keratin. In the 19th century, fashioning human hair into jewelry as mourning pieces and keepsakes was extremely popular, particularly during the Civil War. Fur jewelry can be found dating from the 1920s up to the 1950s, when items made from mink were in vogue. Fur for jewelry was mainly sourced from rabbit and mink.

Problems: Various insects, including clothes moths, can attack hair and fur. If stored carelessly, hair and fur items may be irreparably misshapen.

Cleaning and care: Do not attempt to clean hair or fur jewelry at home. Seek the advice of a jeweler or fur specialist. Keep hair and fur items away from light and heat, and store loosely wrapped in acid-free tissue paper in their own boxes. Never store fur in plastic; it needs some air circulation to stop the leather from drying out. If a fur item gets wet, shake it gently to remove excess water and leave it to dry at room temperature.

LEATHER AND SUEDE

Made from the outer skins of animals, leather is formed through a chemical process known as tanning. Typically, the skins of cattle are used to

Playing card expansion bracelet of painted bone, c.1914

Painted butterfly wing pendant with silver surround and glass cover, 1920s

make leather, but items may also be found using snakeskin and other reptile skins. Suede is made from the inner skins of animals, usually lamb, and has a distinctive soft, pliable quality. In the Art Deco period the tanned and dyed skins of sharks and rays, known as shagreen, were used to make jewelry. Shagreen has a unique bumpy texture and was often dyed green, but examples can be found in other colors, including red. Leather jewelry was a feature of the 1960s and 1970s, taking inspiration from ethnic cultures including that of Native Americans.

Problems: Because it is soft and pliable, leather is easily scratched or scuffed. To remove scratches, try rubbing the affected area with a slightly damp cloth. Leather is prone to cracking and color loss if it is not cared for. Seek specialist help if your item is peeling or splitting.

Cleaning and care: To clean leather and suede, wipe it with a slightly damp soft cloth. Gently buff dry with a soft cloth. If the surface is marked, use a proprietary leather cleaner. If leather or suede gets wet, blot with paper towel and allow it to dry at room temperature. To remove a dried-in stain on suede, lightly brush it with a soft-bristled toothbrush. Store leather and suede items away from sunlight. Do not store them in plastic bags (see Hair and Fur opposite).

INSECTS

Real insects—scarabs, beetles, butterflies, and moths—all feature in costume jewelry. In the Art Deco period, real scarabs were used to make earrings, pins, and bracelets. The wings of butterflies and moths, including the South American Morpho butterfly with its peacock-like

colors, were also popular in this period and up to the 1950s. These were set behind glass, often in a silver surround. Scenes were sometimes painted over the wing. Real insects were also set in clear resin and later plastic (see Torque pendant, page 30).

Problems: Butterfly and moth wings are prone to attack by various insects. They can also fade and discolor if exposed to strong sunlight.

Cleaning and care: Clean scarab jewelry with a slightly damp, soft, lint-free cloth, using a very light touch. Dry with a soft, lint-free cloth. Make sure it is completely dry before putting it away. Butterfly and moth wings are very fragile, so clean their settings with care. Use a slightly damp, soft, lint-free cloth to clean the glass; dry immediately with a soft, lint-free cloth.

Clockwise from top: Silver pendant with mother-of-pearl cabochon, 1900s; Bracelet of cowrie shells with filigree-capped glass beads, 1950s; Branch coral necklace, 1920s; Coral bead necklace, 19th century

CORAL

Made from the branch-like skeletal remains of a tiny sea polyp, coral is found in the tropical seas around the Equator. The type used in jewelry, red coral, comes in a range of colors, from pale pink to the prized deep red coral. From ancient times, coral was considered to have special properties that protected the wearer from evil spirits. It was a very popular gemstone in the 19th century, used as beads or en cabochon. As a result of over-harvesting and pollution, many coral reefs are now protected.

Problems: Like all marine-based stones, coral is porous; do not expose to chemicals. Store as for pearls (see page 94).

Cleaning and care: Clean as for pearls, see page 104, using a pearl cleaning kit, or as for softer gemstones, see page 125.

MOTHER OF PEARL

Produced in exactly the same way as pearls (see page 94), mother of pearl is the nacreous lining of mollusks such as abalone, oysters, and freshwater mussels. It is prized for its iridescent qualities, and comes in a range of colors, from white to combinations of lustrous purples, blues, and greens. Mother of pearl is also sometimes dyed. It was used widely in Art Nouveau and Arts and Crafts jewelry (see pages 10–11 and 12–13). The US was once one of the largest exporters of mother-of-pearl buttons, a trade that only ceased with the advent of modern plastics.

Problems: As for Coral, left. It is more brittle than coral, and is prone to cracking. Always store mother-of-pearl jewelry away from heat and light.

Cleaning and care: As for Coral, left.

SHELLS

Made of layers of conchiolin (a type of protein), calcite (a carbonate mineral), and calcium carbonate (chalk), shells are the hardened outer skeletons of mollusks, including snails, clams, and oysters. It is believed they may have been one of the earliest materials used for personal decoration. Two species—*Nassarius* (small whelks) and *Cypraea* (cowries)—are often found in shell jewelry. In the 18th and 19th centuries, shell was used to make cameos (see page 149). As tourism gathered momentum in the 1950s, shell jewelry gained popularity as souvenir jewelry, and featured in back-to-nature jewelry in the 1960s and 1970s.

Problems: Thinner shells can crack or break if carelessly handled.

Cleaning and care: Clean with plain water and a soft, lint-free cloth.

Endangered species

Real tortoiseshell fish pin, 1920s

Plastic imitation tortoiseshell bangle with rhinestones, 1970s

Carved real ivory bangle, 1920s

RESTRICTED MATERIALS

In the past, a number of animal materials were used in jewelry that are now banned from use in the trade. The two most notable are tortoiseshell and ivory, but others such as tiger's claws and teeth are also banned.

Tortoiseshell: Jewelry made from tortoiseshell comes from the shell of the hawksbill turtle. The shell is made from keratin, the same material as hair, fingernails, etc. It was popular in 19th-century jewelry, particularly used in piqué jewelry where the shell is inlaid with delicate designs in silver or gold. In the 1960s and 1970s tortoiseshell sunglasses and hair combs were fashionable, and overfishing resulted in the ban of tortoiseshell by CITES in 1973.

Ivory: This is sourced from animal tusk, a type of tooth made of dentine. The color can range from white to yellowish-white and even light browns. To identify ivory, under magnification look not only for lines that run along the length of the ivory, but also for V-shaped lines (known as Schreger lines) on the surface. This indicates that it is genuine ivory. Carved ivory was widely used in jewelry in the 19th century, and continued to be popular into the 1970s, but overhunting led to ivory from African and Asian elephants being banned by CITES in 1989.

REGULATIONS FOR ANTIQUE PIECES

The Convention on International Trade in Endangered Species (CITES) was set up in 1973 to protect animals, flora, and fauna from being over-exploited by trade. It is an international agreement, with member countries abiding by its rules and regulations. CITES divides at-risk species into three categories. Species that are at risk of extinction appear on CITES Appendix 1 list, which makes it illegal for countries to trade in these species. Species included on this list are the African and Asian elephant, tigers, and the hawksbill turtle. Animals that appear on CITES Appendix II list are strictly regulated. The Appendix III list covers animals that are not endangered but their trade is controlled.

Trade in antique jewelry made from species on the CITES banned or controlled lists are subject to various regulations, and these may vary from country to country. Laws may also change. In some countries, it is usually acceptable to buy and sell antique jewelry of this kind if you have documentation to prove that it is antique—i.e. over 100 years old. You may also be able to import and export such items as long as you have the right documentation (see Resources, page 185, for more details). However, if the item is in its natural state—for example, an actual tiger's tooth, or a piece of ivory that has not been decorated in any way—it is likely to be banned, even if it is an antique. Always check with the relevant authority if you are planning to buy or sell antique jewelry made from species that appear on any of the CITES lists.

CARE OF ANTIQUE PIECES

To clean ivory or tortoiseshell, wipe with a soft, lint-free cloth that is slightly damp, then dry with a clean soft, lint-free cloth. Store in cool, dry conditions, away from heat or light.

IMITATION MATERIALS

Ivory has been imitated since the appearance of early plastics. Ivorine is an early example (see page 134), and other plastics followed. Vegetable ivory is a plant-based material that looks similar to ivory. Tortoiseshell is also often imitated in plastic—the more artistic versions offer an attractive alternative to the real thing, with realistic mottling in rich browns and deep creamy yellows.

Tiger's tooth pendant, 19th century

Plant materials

Materials derived from plants such as wood, seeds, and nuts have been used in decorative jewelry since before the discovery of metals, and when polished have also served as alternatives to gemstones. Wood of all kinds is a versatile material that can be carved, dyed, and painted, and the huge variety of seeds, nuts, and beans form a source of natural beads. The fossilized remains of trees, in the form of jet or so-called petrified wood, and fossilized rosin (the solid resin from pine trees) in the form of amber are even more durable materials, now classed as gemstones and highly prized by collectors.

Carved bogwood pin, 18th century

AMBER

This natural rosin is the fossilized remains of pine tree rosin deposited some 45 million years ago in the Baltic region. Amber was mined and used in jewelry by the Ancient Greeks and Celts and Romans. In the early 20th century, the Arts and Crafts movement favored amber and made great use of it in cameos, mosaics, and other decorative pieces. Amber comes in varying colors, but it is the honey shade that is most often used for jewelry. It can also be colorless, milky white, red, dark blue, and green. There is a market in fake amber, produced by heating and molding colored plastics. There are several ways to check the authenticity of a piece. Real amber has electromagnetic qualities, so rubbing it against wool should attract dust. Rubbing real amber also emits a slightly rosinous fragrance, unlike fake amber. Also, amber glows a fluorescent color when held under ultraviolet light.

Problems: As amber is a relatively soft substance, store it away from other jewels and metals to prevent damage. Keep it out of direct sunlight and avoid contact with perfumes and hair spray, which can damage it.

Cleaning and care: Clean it with slightly warm, soapy water and terrycloth, and then polish with a soft, lint-free cloth and a drop of olive oil.

JET

A semi-precious gemstone formed from fossilized timber. Wood, generally of *Araucaria araucana* or monkey puzzle tree, which has fallen into water and then been buried becomes hard and black under extreme pressure in a process similar to that which produces coal. There are two varieties of jet (also known as lignite): hard jet, formed by

compression in salt water, and soft jet, formed in fresh water. Jet is mined in several locations around the world, but the most prized comes from Whitby in Yorkshire, UK. Because it can be cut and polished to a high shine, it became popular for jewelry, and its black or very dark brown color made it ideal for 19th-century mourning jewelry. Necklaces of long strings of jet beads were also very fashionable in the 1920s. Various materials have been used as fake jet, including anthracite, black glass, ebony, and Ebonite, and it is often difficult to distinguish from the real thing. Real jet, however, does not feel cold to the touch, and leaves a brown mark when rubbed on paper or rough ceramic—but telling it apart from Ebonite requires an expert eye.

Problems: Jet is fragile and can scratch and chip easily. Store wrapped in acid-free tissue paper to avoid knocking and rubbing against other jewelry. Breakages need specialist repair.

Cleaning and care: Wash gently in warm soapy water and remove stubborn dirt with a damp Q-tip, then allow to air dry. The shine can be revived by wiping with baby oil, but avoid other cleaners and abrasives.

WOOD

Many different types of wood have been used in jewelry making, sometimes as a substitute for a more expensive material, but more often for its own distinctive qualities. Because wood can be easily carved or machined and polished, it has been used to make beads, bangles, and rings, as well as decorative pendants to hang from necklaces. Hardwoods, such as olive and rosewood, are especially prized for their color and figure (grain pattern), while ebony

Aarikka silver ring with wood bezel, 1960s

was a favorite for 19th-century mourning jewelry as a substitute for jet. Wood can also be dyed, painted, or lacquered, making it a versatile material for jewelry making. Particularly collectable are bogwood jewelry items made from oak preserved in the bogs of Scotland and Ireland, and so-called petrified wood (actually the mineral replacement of timber in the process of fossilization) found in some Native American jewelry.

Problems: Wood can split and crack and color may fade if exposed to sunlight. Store out of light, and away from extremes of temperature and humidity. Broken items may be repairable at home, but generally require specialist attention, particularly if small parts are missing. Larger pieces are also prone to surface scratching.

Seed necklace, 1960s

Silver and raw amber necklace, 1920s; Clear amber earrings, 1970s

Carved jet earrings, 19th century

Cleaning and care: Clean with a jeweler's brush or soft, lint-free cloth. If necessary, wipe with a damp cloth and dry thoroughly, but avoid immersing in water. Abrasives and chemical cleaners may damage any surface polish or paint.

SEEDS AND NUTS

Seeds and nuts, or at least seed cases and nut shells, have been used as natural beads in cultures throughout the world for millennia, but were only gradually adopted by costume jewelers in the West during the 20th century. Their popularity has grown, however, since the 1960s with the increased popularity of "ethnic" and "New Age" fashions. There is a huge number of different seeds that can be dried and used as beads, ranging in size from the small acai berries

to large sea beans, and although most are shades of brown, they can be found in white and cream and even (such as the rosary pea or crab's eye, *Abrus precatorius*) bright red and black. Some of the larger and sturdier nutshells, notably coconut and coquilla nuts, can be carved and inlaid.

Problems: Some seeds and nuts are fragile, especially when exposed to extremes of temperature and humidity. Broken seeds and nuts can be glued, but it is often not worth the repair. Store as Wood, see opposite.

Cleaning and care: Clean with a jeweler's brush or soft, lint-free cloth. If necessary, wipe with a damp cloth and dry thoroughly, but avoid immersing in water. Abrasives and chemical cleaners may damage polished surfaces.

Chinese carved nut necklace, 1920s

Cameos

Not just fascinating pieces of jewelry, but also exquisite works of art, cameos are highly collectable. A cameo is a piece of jewelry in which an image, usually a portrait, has been carved in relief out of a gemstone, shell, or other material. With layered-colored stones and shells, the cameo is carved in such a way that when the upper layer is carved, a second color emerges that contrasts with the relief. The finished cameo is then set into a gold, silver, or metal frame. Cameos adorned helmets, swords and rings in Ancient Greece and Rome, and were often used as seals. They were widely worn in Renaissance Europe, but enjoyed their greatest popularity during the 19th century.

Coral cameo pin with silver and marcasite surround, 18th century

POTTERY CAMEOS

Some cameos are made of molded porcelain. Some of the most distinctive were first produced by the English pottery manufacturer, Josiah Wedgwood (1730–95), who perfected a technique of producing cameos with black basalt and jasper. Leading artists of the time produced stunning designs, usually of Classical Greek or Roman models, which were made of white porcelain bisque against a jasperware background. These were mounted on cut steel, framed in gold, and used as pins, medallions, and pendants. White on blue jasperware-backed cameos were popular during the Art Nouveau period, and are still produced today.

Problems: Age and handling may cause the cameo to become dirty.

Cleaning and care: Brushing the cameo gently with a sable brush will remove any dust that may have collected.

ANIMAL SOURCES

Shells have been used for cameos since at least the 15th century. The most commonly used are conch shells, particularly carnelian and Sardonyx shells, cowry shells, mollusks (mother of pearl), coral, and abalone. Layers of the shell are carefully carved away to produce an exquisite relief of one color set against a contrasting background. The Victorians were particularly fond of shell cameos, and their popularity continued throughout the 19th century and beyond. Imitation shell cameos are made today by injecting plastic into a mold. It is easy to tell the difference. Plastic cameos are warm to the touch; a genuine shell cameo will feel cool.

Silver ring with onyx cameo, 19th century

Gold ring with lava cameo, 19th century

Problems: Faded colors and cracking.

Cleaning and care: Moisturize your shell cameos twice a year with baby oil. Apply oil with a finger or soft cotton, leave overnight, and wipe off the oil with a soft, lint-free cloth.

PLANT SOURCES

Wood and jet have both been used for carving cameos. Produced from fossilized coal, jet was widely used for black cameos worn during mourning. When Prince Albert died in 1861, Queen Victoria went into permanent mourning. Black cameos were produced especially for her, and other widows followed her lead, stimulating the Victorian jet industry in Whitby, England. Motifs on the cameos were highly sentimental, and included Greek goddesses, bunches of grapes, young boys, and idealized women. Cameos were worn as pendants attached to black ribbon chokers, on bracelets, earrings, and pins. As time passed, jet cameos became popular fashion items in their own right. See also page 146 for more information on jet and wood.

Problems: Scratches; seek advice from a professional jeweler.

Cleaning and care: Wrap jet cameos in white acid-free tissue paper and keep separate from other jewelry (see also page 146).

STONE CAMEOS

Beautiful cameos have been carved from various semi-precious stones, particularly onyx and agate and other stones where two contrasting colors

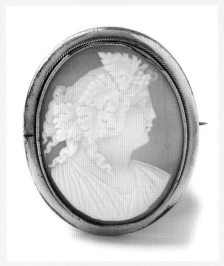

Shell cameo pin set in gold, late 18th century

Plastic cameo pin, 1950s

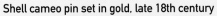

Wedgwood jasperware white on blue cameo pendant (left) and pin (right), 1950s

MOTIFS

Throughout their long history, cameos have been adorned with various recurring motifs, including:

- Gods and goddesses such as Zeus, Leda, and Venus
- The "ideal" woman, reflecting the style of the period
- Personalized images, made to order for a loved one
- Flowers and fruit
- Famous personalities, such as American president George Washington (1732–99) and renowned actress Sarah Bernhardt (1844–1923).

DATING CAMEOS

It is difficult to date a cameo and involves years of research. The type of cameo itself may also provide clues: shell cameos may be 19th century, or later; lava cameos were popular during the 19th century. The clue to dating may also lie in the motif, which can indicate when it was carved. For instance:

- Cameo habilles became fashionable in the late 19th century
- A long Roman nose on a figure suggests pre-1850
- An upturned nose on a figure suggests post-1850
- Upswept hairstyles indicate late 19th century
- Short curls indicate 20th century.

meet. Layered agate produces particularly strong contrasts. From the 19th century onward, other stones such as sapphire, garnet, quartz, turquoise, and topaz were also used. Around this time as well, portraits were carved on cameos that were themselves wearing tiny pieces of jewelry, such as minute diamond earrings, or minuscule silver or gold chains. Known as cameos habilles (dressed cameos), they are highly prized. Cameos have also been carved from lava, the molten rock expelled by a volcano, which were very fashionable during the 19th century.

Problems: Damage to the stone, particularly in the case of lava, which is soft and easily damaged. Professional advice should be sought.

Cleaning and care: Clean with a soft-bristled brush only. Store away from other jewelry.

PLASTICS

From the 1930s, with the rise of synthetic materials, many cameos were made from plastics such as Bakelite, Celluloid, vulcanite, and Lucite (see Plastics, pages 134–7). Most were made in molds, although some cameos, particularly those made from Bakelite, were carved. Most resembled more traditional shell and stone cameos, and featured the same designs or motifs, such as idealized women, on the cameo. Plastic cameos were popular during the 1940s and 1950s, being far less expensive than other cameos, and are once again enjoying some popularity today.

Problems: Discoloration.

Cleaning and care: As for Plastics, see pages 134–7.

GLASS CAMEOS

During the 19th century, extraordinarily beautiful glass cameos were produced by layering different colored glass, fusing or binding them together with glue, then carving a design through the layers. René Lalique and Gabriel Argy-Rousseau are two major designers associated with the period. Glass cameos became fashionable once more during the 1960s and are still produced today. Checking for signs of molding helps to distinguish vintage glass cameos from those made of stone, shell, or plastic.

Problems: Cracks, chips or other damage. Seek advice from a professional jeweler.

Cleaning and care: Store separately from other jewelry; clean with a soft-bristled brush or mild soap and warm water.

Take your skills to the next level with jewel school. Find out about the tools and materials you will need to master a range of increasingly challenging repairs—from dented lockets and broken or missing chain links, to converting clip-on earrings to post and clutch for pierced ears. Also included in this chapter is soldering—from simple repairs such as closing a jump ring to retipping a claw setting. Then test your skills with more advanced projects on how to make a ring larger followed by how to make one smaller. The final project—repairing a box clasp—calls on your ability to measure and cut accurately, working small scale.

Jewel School

Advanced toolkit

For the projects that follow, the tools covered in this section will enable you to restore dented metal, make rivets and links, and repair cup chains. You will also learn how to solder simple repairs such as closing chain links and repairing jump rings and progress to more advanced projects such as making a ring larger and smaller. The last project—making a new snap, or tongue, for a box clasp, see pages 178–81—requires skill and confidence in handling your tools.

Pushover setting tool

Metal pin

In addition to your toolkit, you will also need a flat surface on which to work. For the type of projects featured in this chapter, I recommend that you have a dedicated area set up for working. It needs to have a good light source, and for soldering it is essential that there is good ventilation too.

Practice makes perfect
Before you attempt to repair a special piece from your jewelry box, practice using your tools first. Work out the best way to hold them; discover how each tool behaves when you use it for the job it was designed to do—whether cutting, bending wire, or soldering.

Try your skills on items that you don't mind getting damaged if things go wrong. You may even want to consider buying some inexpensive items from a thrift store to practice on. Follow the pictures and instructions carefully in the step-by-step repair projects, particularly those that involve soldering. Take each repair job slowly. Do not rush them.

PUSHOVER SETTING TOOL
A tool used for pushing claws back into position (see page 120) and for pushing thin metal sheeting, for example pushing dents out of a locket (see page 157). It has a rounded handle and is set with a hardened metal shaft. The one shown above is handmade (see page 52).

Going to jewel school
If you want to make solder repairs in particular, I recommend that you attend a beginner's jewelry-making class. There are many good short and part-time courses available. A course will teach you the basics of jewelry making, all of which is invaluable when it comes to making repairs. You will learn all about your tools, and how to use them effectively and safely. A basic jewelry course should also cover professional polishing, which is another very useful skill.

WORKING SAFELY
- Do not use the kitchen table to work on if there is any risk that chemicals will come into contact with food preparation surfaces. It is preferable to have a dedicated bench space for repair work that involves soldering.

- Always read the manufacturer's instructions before using a tool or a product, and follow their safety guidelines.

- Always wear a face mask and safety goggles when soldering; when making safety pickle (see page 155), wear protective gloves and a face mask.

- If there is any risk of flying objects, wear safety goggles. This is particularly important if you are removing small stones, or cutting small bits of wire.

- Keep your tools and all soldering equipment, including your torch and safety pickle cleaning salts, in a safe place and out of reach of children.

DEGREE GAUGE
Also called a dixième gauge, a degree gauge has pincers at the top of the gauge which are placed around the item to be measured: The gauge arm below points to the corresponding measurement on the gauge. Invaluable for measuring wires when replacing a link (see pages 162–3) or retipping a claw (see pages 170–1).

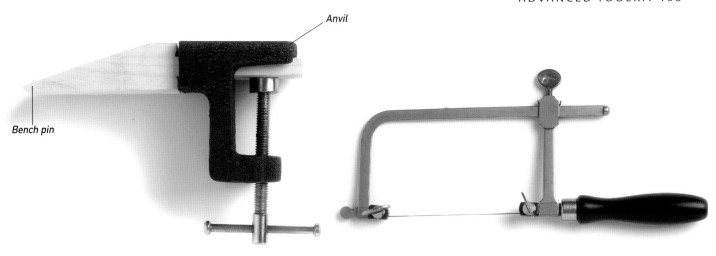

Anvil

Bench pin

JEWELER'S BENCH PIN AND ANVIL

This is an essential piece of equipment for the projects that follow. The bench pin attaches to the worktop with an adjustable screw. The metal platform, or anvil, is suitable for soldering work, and the wooden "pin" is invaluable as a work prop, particularly for holding the hand steady when using pliers or sawing during delicate tasks. As you look through the steps in the projects, study how I use the pin for different tasks—you will soon see how useful the pin is.

JEWELER'S SAW

The saw comes in two parts: (1) a frame, and (2) a separate saw blade which is attached by screws to the frame. A range of blades are available, but I find generally that a size 2.0 blade works for most jobs. The finer the blade, the more teeth it has to the inch; a size 2.0 blade is a fine blade. To maintain it, when the blade starts to "stick" and doesn't saw as well as before, rub beeswax along the blade. This will help it to saw smoothly again and prolong the life of the blade.

BENCH VISE

A tool used for holding items in place. Made from hardened steel, the vise is screwed in place on the work bench. The jaws are opened and closed with a screw mechanism which is attached to a pin lever.

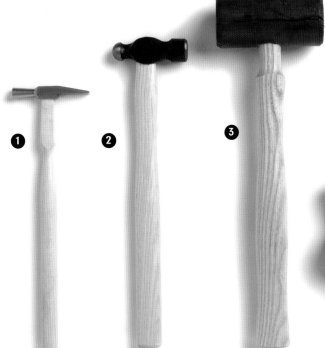

HAMMERS

Used for flattening, straightening, shaping, and indenting.

1 Fine toffee hammer: Ideal for delicate work, such as creating beveled heads on a rivet (see page 158).

2 Ball peen hammer: A very useful all-round hammer.

3 Rawhide mallet: Made from wood, the head is covered in rawhide. The leather ensures that the hammer doesn't mark metal when working with it. It is used for jobs such as shaping rings on a triblet (see page 177).

SPRING DIVIDERS

A tool used for marking measurements on metal surfaces. Made from steel, dividers can also be used to mark out a circle.

FILES

Used for smoothing rough edges on metal and for reshaping work. Files are made from hardened metal with finely ridged surfaces and come with a detachable handle. Three useful file shapes for jewelry making are: **1** Flat, **2** Half-round, and **3** Three-square. These come in different sizes, from large to fine; the narrow files in the packet (right) are needle files used for more delicate work.

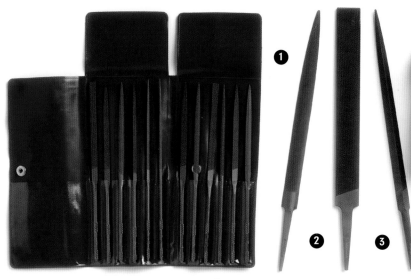

RING GAUGE

A gauge used to establish a ring size. A ring gauge consists of a series of metal rings in different sizes attached to a hoop; each ring is in a standard ring sizing.

DRAWPLATE AND TONGS

Made from hardened steel, a drawplate has a series of holes that gradually go down in size. The drawplate is used to reduce the size of wires—the drawplate is placed in a bench vise, a wire is placed in a hole that is the next size down from its current size, and drawn through the hole (see page 172) using a pair of draw tongs. Draw tongs have a large rounded head and long handles to give a firm grip on the metal.

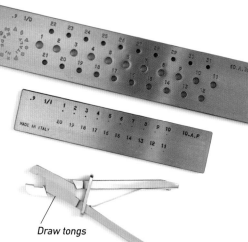

Draw tongs

EMERY STICKS AND PAPERS

Equipment used to sand and smooth metal surfaces. Emery sticks are made of wood and have emery paper bonded to the surface. They come in different shapes, usually round, flat, and three-square, for sanding metal surfaces with different shapes. Sheets of emery paper—similar to sandpaper, but designed to be used on metal—are coated in ground emery, a very hard rock, which acts as an abrasive. These come in different grades, from very fine to rough. To economize, you can wrap a piece of emery paper around the stick when the bonded emery has worn out. Wrap it around as tightly as possible, and secure with sticky tape.

Emery papers

Flat buff stick

Round buff stick

Marks denote standard ring sizes

RING STICK

Also referred to as a mandrel, a ring stick is used to establish the size of a ring. The ring stick is marked at regular intervals with grooves that circle the stick; these denote standard ring sizes. Note that different countries have different sizing systems. Some sticks, as here, show for example US and UK ring sizings on the same stick.

TRIBLET

A tool used for forming, as in forming a ring shape (see page 177). Triblets are made from hardened steel and come in different shapes, including round, square, and even octagonal and hexagonal.

Soldering

This technique involves using heat and solder to attach one metal to another. To solder effectively, make sure that the areas to be soldered together are completely clean—any tarnish or grease on surfaces will make soldering impossible. The areas to be soldered should also be flush, with no gaps. The solder (see below) is used to join, not to fill gaps (see also page 166). Before soldering, read through the descriptions of the various equipment and materials listed below. Also read the safety boxes on pages 152 and 167.

HAND TORCH AND SOLDERING BLOCKS

Hand torch: For soldering at home, a self-igniting hand torch that has an adjustable flame is suitable. It runs on butane lighter fuel. You can use it for the soldering projects shown in this book. I use a jeweler's professional torch which works on gas and oxygen, and is shown in the step sequences that follow. Please handle your torch with respect at all times. When operating it, be aware that the tip is very hot. Always turn off your torch immediately you stop soldering—never leave the flame alight while the torch is not being used.

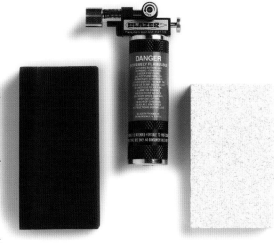

Soldering block: I sometimes use the metal anvil on my bench pin for soldering, but generally it is advisable to use a soldering block. These come as a charcoal block (top left) or a replacement asbestos block (top right; note, there is no asbestos in this block).

OTHER EQUIPMENT FOR SOLDERING

You will also need the following equipment:
Flux: Borax, a mineral, is used as a flux. It cleans the surface of the metal, which helps the solder (see below) to flow. It has some heat-conducting properties, drawing heat from the flame of the torch to the metal; and it also helps to remove oxides and flame marks on metal surfaces that occur during soldering. For working with non-fluxed solder, you will need a borax cone and a dish. Put a small amount of water in the dish and grind some borax into it to form a flux paste. You can also buy ready-made borax in paste form.

Brush: Use an artist's brush to apply the flux to the jewelry.

Solder: This is a metal alloy (a compound made up of two or more metals) that contains a high proportion of the metal to be soldered. Solder comes in the form of sheets, strips, wires, or a paste and there are different types for different metals. For working with silver, I prefer to use prefluxed silver solder paste, which comes ready-made in a syringe, and is easy to use. For gold, I use sheets of gold solder generally and apply the flux separately. Solder comes in easy, medium, and hard—for repairs that have only one joint, easy solder is usually suitable. For repairs that have more than one joint, start with medium or hard solder.

Safety goggles and face mask: It is strongly recommended that you wear safety goggles and a face mask when soldering.

Straight-bladed shears: These are handy for cutting sheet solder.

Pin: I find a fine metal pin very useful for transferring prefluxed solder paste to the jewelry to be soldered (see page 152).

Stainless steel tweezers: A tool for holding the item steady while soldering.

Brass tweezers: Used to remove jewelry from the safety pickle (see box right).

SAFETY PICKLE CLEANING SALTS

Safety pickle is used to remove oxides from metal after soldering. It also removes any residual flux on the metal. Safety pickle is made from sodium bisulfate (sodium hydrogen sulfate), a chemical that comes in the form of a white powder.

Making pickle: When making safety pickle, wear safety goggles, a face mask, and PVC gloves. Always work in a well-ventilated room. To make the pickle, add the powder to hot water—never the other way around—and stir with a wooden spoon until the granules dissolve. Follow the manufacturer's instructions on quantities. Ideally, keep the pickle solution at between 86°F (30°C) and 122°F (50°C). Professional jewelers keep pickle on a hotplate to keep it warm, but if you are soldering one item, there is no need. Make up the pickling solution while the soldered jewelry is cooling down and use it straight away. Never put hot metal into the warm pickle; it can release a chemical vapor which is hazardous to inhale.

Removing jewelry from the pickle: To remove jewelry from the safety pickle, use brass or copper tweezers. Never use steel implements. The steel causes a chemical reaction in the pickle which will copperplate silver.

Disposal of pickle solution: Contact your county authority for guidance.

Safety guidelines: Sodium bisulfate is mildly corrosive to skin, eyes, or to inhale when it is wet. If it splashes onto your skin, wash it off immediately with soap and water. If you get safety pickle into your eyes, wash them with lots of water. If you accidentally swallow pickle, rinse your mouth out with water and drink lots of water. If in doubt, seek medical help.

Intermediate projects level 1

The following projects require a higher level of skill than those covered in previous chapters. Some, such as the locket repairs on this page and opposite, may look simple, but they require a deft hand together with a light touch. As always, be patient and take your time. Don't rush these jobs.

Repairing a locket catch

A locket is a pendant consisting of a small metal case with a hinge on one side and a catch mechanism on the other, designed to hold a picture, a lock of hair, or other memento. Because it can be opened and closed, the catch on a locket is prone to damage. Locket catches vary in design, but a common type is the push-in bayonet clasp. This consists of a small metal tab on the interior rim that slots into a hollow clasp on the opposite side.

Gold locket with etched star motif, 1960s

1 The metal tab on this locket has been pushed out of shape and can no longer slip into the interior hollow clasp on the opposite side of the locket.

Duckbill pliers see Tools, page 54

2 Open the locket and try to work out which way the metal tab would naturally fit to close. Once you have established this, use a pair of duckbill pliers to adjust the tab gently to its proper position. Do not force the tab or you may break it. Test the catch every time you make an adjustment to check the fit. When the catch clicks into place, the job is finished.

Repairing a dent in a locket

Vintage lockets were often made from thin sheets of metal and then engraved, embossed, or chased. Their thin metal casing means that lockets are very prone to damage and denting. They may also have a few dings (very small dents), but these are usually seen as signs of authenticity and part of the charm of an old locket.

Gold engraved locket, 1920s

REPAIRING DENTS WITH THE SOLDER METHOD

To repair very delicate, damaged pieces where it is not possible to push out the dent as shown, you can repair the locket from the front. To do this, remove any internal parts then solder (see pages 155, 166–7) a flat-faced piece of wire onto the front of the locket, in the center of the dented area. Hold the outside of the locket with one hand and in the other use a pair of pliers to carefully and lightly pull out the dent until the locket face regains a smooth surface. Remove the flat-faced piece of wire by lightly heating it with a low flame, then place the locket in warm pickle (see page 155).

1 This locket is a typical example of a vintage locket with a large dent in the center. Before starting the repair, open the locket and remove any internal parts, usually a picture or a lock of hair. This will enable you to see the damage more clearly and protect the removed parts of the locket. Some lockets have a bezel (an inner metal rim that holds a picture in place), others have a removable internal frame that holds a transparent cover (originals were made of glass, but these are often replaced by a cover of clear plastic when the glass is lost). Remove these, taking care not to push on the outside of the locket, since this could cause further denting. If the locket has a holding frame, as here, use a small penknife to lift the holding frame slowly away from the locket. Remove the clear cover and contents.

2 Turn the locket so that the inside of the dent is facing toward you, flat on the work surface. Use a pushover tool to press lightly and evenly from the sides to the center of the dented area. Repeat this as often as necessary. Check the front of the locket regularly to see how the repair is going, and stop as soon as you have achieved a more even surface. Bear in mind that the locket is delicate and should not be overworked.

Small penknife see Tools, page 54
Pushover tool see Tools, page 152

Replacing a rivet

Fastener pins are sometimes held in the hinge with a rivet (for information on non-rivet joints, see page 88). This thin metal bolt passes through the holes in the fastener pin and hinge and holds them together. The rivet can become loose over time, and the fastener pin falls out. You cannot buy ready-made rivets, so you will have to make one from scratch.

Sterling silver globe pin with enamel details and marcasites, 1970s

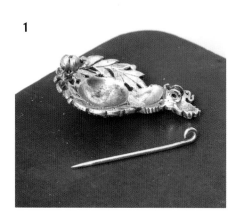

1 If you have to replace the fastener pin as well as the rivet, make sure the fastener pin is the right size for the hinge. The length should be approximately 2–3 mm beyond the holding catch. Fastener pins can be bought ready-made from most findings stores.

2 For the rivet, use a wire that is slightly wider in diameter than the holes in the hinge. Generally, 1 mm to 1.2 mm wire will fit (if you need to customize the size of the wire, see page 172). Cut a length of 1 in (2.5 cm) silver wire with side snips. File one end with a three-square file or needle file to a slight point, turning the wire every so often so that it is graduated. This will enable the rivet to pass through the holes of the hinge and fastener pin. Place the eye of the fastener pin in the hinge and pass the rivet through the holes as shown.

3 Lift the fastener pin up and down to check that there is not too much side movement, or play. If you are satisfied that the rivet is tight, push it through from the left to leave only 3-4 mm of the straight end clear of the hinge. Place the pin face down on the anvil and cut off the tapered end with a jeweler's saw; here, I have used a 2.0 saw blade. Be very careful not to cut into the pin at this point. You can also use side snips to cut off the excess wire, then file the end flat before making the rivet secure (see step 4).

4 To secure the ends of the rivet, they need to be rounded out to form beveled heads. Hold the pin in one hand and use a toffee hammer in the other to tap around the edges of one end of the wire, using a side-to-side motion. The action is a gentle tapping, not a hard hammering motion. The metal will start to spread out to form a beveled head. Work evenly around the end of the wire. When one end is finished, work the other end. The rivet is secure and the job completed.

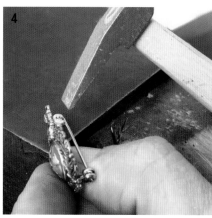

Jeweler's bench pin see Tools, page 153
Silver wire see page 172
Side snips see Tools, page 54
Three-square file see Tools, page 154
Jeweler's saw see Tools, page 153
Toffee hammer see Tools, page 153

Shortening a bracelet

Bracelets of chain links (also referred to as jump rings) can be made shorter by removing one or more links. It is more difficult to make a chain-link bracelet larger because you have to match the design of the existing links, but in some cases this is possible (see for example pages 162–3).

Sterling silver identity bracelet, 1970s

1

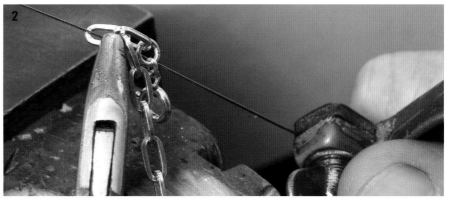

2

1 First of all, check that the jump ring that holds the bolt ring clasp in place is open, as here. Open the jump ring using a pair of duckbill pliers (see page 78) to release the bolt ring clasp. If the link is soldered, cut it open using a jeweler's saw as in Step 2. Make sure that you cut through the original joint. This is very important, since any joint is a weak spot. If you cut elsewhere on the link and solder there, the original joint may fall apart when resoldering.

2 This bracelet is to be shortened by two links, which forms the design sequence for this chain (see box right). Check where the joint is (the joint that was originally soldered), here on the second link along from the spring ring clasp, and cut through it with a jeweler's saw. To saw it safely, hold the link to be cut with a pair of round-nosed pliers in one hand. Position the saw blade inside the link—take off the blade, slide it through the link, then attach it again to the saw frame. Saw the joint carefully until it is cut through.

3 Rejoin the jump ring that is attached to the spring ring clasp to the bracelet using a pair of duckbill pliers (see page 78). The repair is complete.

3

Jeweler's bench pin see Tools, page 153

Two duckbill pliers see Tools, page 54

Jeweler's saw see Tools, page 153

Round-nosed pliers see Tools, page 54

SHORTENING CHAINS

There are two important factors to consider when shortening a chain on a bracelet or necklace:

- Always shorten the chain on the longest side if it has one. Not all pieces will have a longer side, but here for example, the identity bracelet is longer on the side where the spring ring clasp is fastened.
- If the chain is made up of a sequence of links that form a distinct pattern that is repeated (see for example a Figaro chain, page 77), always reduce the chain by one complete sequence. Here the sequence is two links, so I have reduced it by two links. Shortening a chain in the middle of a sequence can result in: (1) the chain no longer sitting properly when done up, and (2) the clasp not sitting properly and twisting the link to which it is attached; this can result in the link snapping eventually.

Converting clip-ons to post and clutch

From the start of the 20th century to the early 1970s, most earring findings were either screw-on types or, after their invention in the 1930s, clip-ons (see page 83). The drawback of earrings that attach to the surface of the ear is that they can pinch the ear lobes, even after adjusting the fittings and attaching comfort pads (see page 84). Screw- or clip-on earrings can also come away from the ear easily and the earring can be lost as a result. Fortunately, most screw- or clip-on earrings can be converted to pierced ear fittings.

Sterling silver earrings with glass stones, 1940s

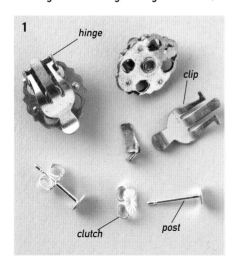

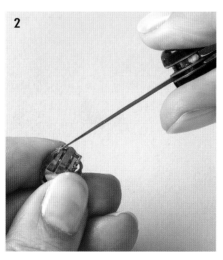

1 This project may seem complicated, but with a little more experience and practice it is very achievable. I have taken apart one of the clip-on findings so that you can see the parts that need to be removed. For this project, the clip-ons are being replaced with post-and-clutch findings (see page 83).

2 First, remove the earclip from the hinge. Use a fine penknife to ease the hinge apart until you can release the metal legs from the holes in the hinge.

3

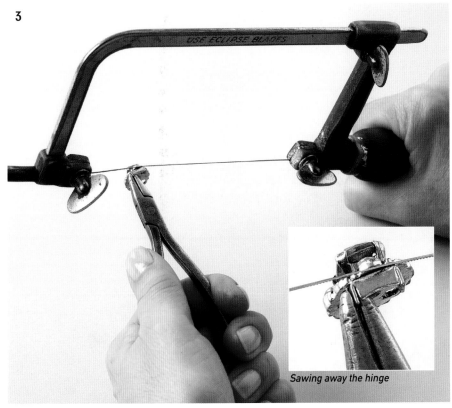

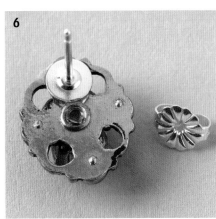

Sawing away the hinge

5

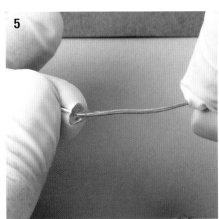

6

3 Hold the upright part of the hinge with a pair of needle-nosed pliers. With a gentle motion, use a jeweler's saw to cut through the metal hinge between the back of the earring and the hinge. Work slowly and be very careful not to saw into the earring itself. Take your time. Once the hinge has been removed, file away any sharp edges that remain with a three-square file and lightly buff with a buff stick and emery.

4 Decide where you want the post to sit on the back of the earring. If you are converting earrings for yourself, hold one earring up to your ear to see where it sits best on your earlobe. This will give you a guide as to where to position the post. Quite often, positioning the post in the center of the earring means that the earring falls forward when affixed to the ear. Here, I have placed the post toward the top of the earring to avoid this problem.

5 Wearing protective gloves, take up a small amount of glue on the end of a spare piece of wire and apply the glue to the cup end of the earring post.

6 Glue in place, then attach the post to the second earring. When gluing the posts, you can use a pair of tweezers to apply pressure to the post and earring. The tweezers can be left in place until the glue is dry. When the glue is dry, give the earrings a polish with a jeweler's polishing cloth to finish.

FINDINGS THAT CAN AND CANNOT BE CONVERTED

Most button and stud-type earrings with non-pierced findings (see pages 82–3) are suitable for conversion to pierced findings. However, not all styles of earrings (see pages 34–37) with non-pierced findings are suitable to be converted to pierced findings. This is because they are either large and designed to hug the ear closely—when a very large disk-shaped earring is set on the earlobe, a pierced finding tends to pull away from the ear—or the earrings are very heavy, which can drag down the earlobe and be uncomfortable. There is also a risk that they could eventually damage the pierced hole in the earlobe. The following non-pierced styles are usually not suitable for conversion: Large dome earrings, large cluster earrings, heavy chandelier earrings, heavy dangle earrings, heavy door knocker earrings. However, some chandelier and dangle earrings, if they are made of sufficiently light materials, may be suitable for conversion to pierced ear findings.

Post-and-clutch findings see Earring findings, page 83

Small penknife see Tools, page 54

Needle-nosed pliers see Tools, page 54

Jeweler's saw see Tools, page 153

Three-square file see Tools, page 154

Buff stick and emery see Tools, page 154

Two-part epoxy resin glue see Tools, page 55

Protective gloves see Tools, page 55

Tweezers see Tools, page 54

Jeweler's polishing cloth see Tools, page 53

Making a replacement link

Many necklaces and bracelets are made up of or include distinctively shaped links, or jump rings, that cannot be found ready-made in a findings store. They may be unsoldered or soldered (see page 76), depending on the quality of the work—soldered links indicate a higher-quality piece of jewelry. Unsoldered links can work open and fall off. If you lose a custom-made link, you will need to make a replacement.

Japanned brass bracelet with multi-metal inlay, 1940s

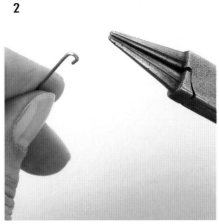

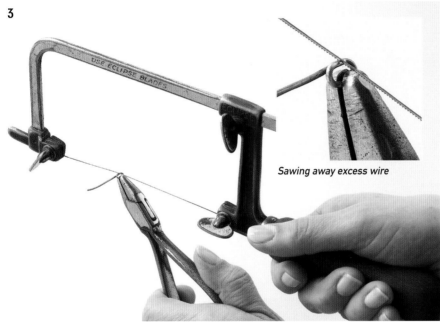

Sawing away excess wire

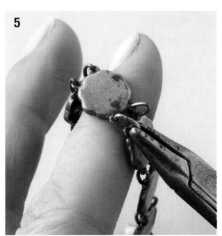

1 Using a degree gauge, measure the wire on one of the existing links to establish the size of the replacement wire—here, made from brass. This will usually be 0.8 mm to 1 mm in diameter. It is very important that the gauge of the new wire is the same as that used for the original links. Wire of different gauges is sold in findings stores. If you cannot buy the exact thickness of wire, you will have to make your own using a drawplate (see page 172).

2 Use side snips to cut a length of wire—about 2 in (5 cm) should be sufficient. Use a pair of round-nosed pliers to curve the wire to form a half circle. Keep checking that the shape of the new link matches the shape of the links on the piece of jewelry. Turn the wire around and form the rest of the wire to make a complete circle or, as here, an oval shape.

3 Hold the base of the new link firmly with a pair of duckbill pliers. With your other hand, use a jewelry saw to cut away the excess wire. Hold the new link firmly and be very careful not to let the saw frame slip. You'll find after a few practice tries that you can saw confidently and accurately.

4 Make sure that the new link is sufficiently open to place it in position on the item. Hold it with a pair of duckbill pliers and slip the link in place.

5 Take a pair of duckbill pliers in either hand and close the link (see page 78). The repair is completed. It is always worth checking all the other links to make sure that none of the others need reclosing or replacing.

Degree gauge see Tools, page 152
Wire
Side snips see Tools, page 54
Round-nosed pliers see Tools, page 54
Two duckbill pliers see Tools, page 54
Jeweler's saw see Tools, page 153

Repairing a rhinestone cup chain

Rivière rhinestone necklaces (see page 31) and line bracelets (see page 43) are often constructed using a cup chain design. Each rhinestone is set in a cup with four claws. Each cup has a T-shaped tab that inserts into its neighboring cup, and so on, forming a semi-flexible chain. Depending on the quality of metal used, the tab can snap off and/or the claws can work loose and stones fall out and are lost. The manufacture of cup chains has remained the same since the 1920s, so the following repair covers a wide period of necklaces.

1

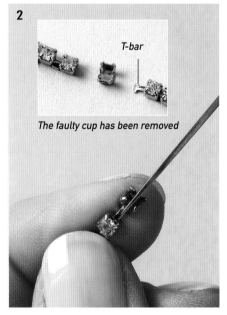

2

T-bar

The faulty cup has been removed

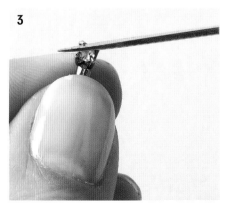

3

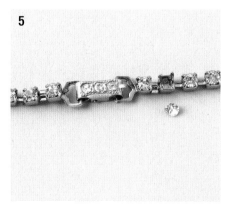

5

1 The aim of this repair is to remove the cup with the missing T-bar and rhinestone and relink the necklace, making the necklace shorter by one cup.

2 Begin the repair by removing the empty cup. To do this, you will need to release its T-bar, which is held within a split setting in the neighboring cup. Use a fine penknife to widen the split in the setting—you need enough space to be able to turn the T-bar on its side and slide it out from between the setting. If there is a rhinestone still in place in the broken cup, you will need to remove it first in order to access the T-bar, which lies underneath the stone. See Step 3 for directions on how to remove a rhinestone from its claw setting. Discard the faulty cup.

3 You now have a good cup with a T-bar on one side, and a good cup to receive the T-bar on the other. To relink the necklace, first remove the rhinestone in the cup that is to receive the T-bar. Use a fine penknife to ease up the first claw carefully, and work around the cup, lifting each claw in turn. Remove the rhinestone and set it aside in a safe place.

4 Check that the cups on both sides of the broken section are in good order and not about to break or the stones fall out.

5 To rejoin the necklace, use a fine penknife to widen the split in the setting facing the T-bar. Slide the T-bar into the split setting sideways, then slowly turn it so that the T-bar sits flat in the base of the cup. Gently close the joints with a pair of duckbill pliers or parallel-action pliers, being careful not to damage the other links. Once closed, reset the missing rhinestone using a pushover setting tool (see page 120). The repair is complete.

Small penknife see Tools, page 54

Duckbill pliers or parallel-action pliers see Tools, page 54

Pushover setting tool see Tools, page 152

Silver-tone rivière necklace with rhinestones, 1960s

Intermediate projects level 2

The following projects require more advanced jewelry repair skills, in particular soldering. You will first learn how to solder a jump ring to close it, then proceed to more advanced projects, such as building up a worn ring. Before you start any soldering, please read the guidelines on page 152, 155, and the safety advice opposite. You will also learn how to customize wires for a wide range of projects.

Soldering a jump ring

The simple jump ring (see page 76) is an essential jewelry component. While unsoldered jump rings are easier to put on and take off, soldered jump rings are more secure and give a more polished appearance to the finished piece of jewelry. I use an oxy-propane torch for my work, but for soldering jump rings a small butane torch will work just as well. Before you start, make sure that you have everything to hand. If you are a beginner, I recommend that you practice soldering on spare jump rings before attempting to repair a real piece of jewelry.

Gold harp charm, 1960s

1 Make sure that the jump ring is clean and that the ends of the jump ring fit neatly together. Solder is a joining medium, not a filling one, so It is important that the ends of the ring sit flush with each other.

2 Attach the jump ring to the charm using the two-plier technique (see page 78). If the charm has a stone in it, read the advice on soldering and stones on page 171. As this is a gold item, the solder should match the karat of the repair. Here, I have used gold sheet solder. Cut off a small piece of solder with a pair of side snips and place it beside you on the bench. With a fine paint brush, apply a generous amount of flux to the open ends of the jump ring. Hold the charm with tweezers by its attached ring. Apply more flux to your paint brush, and use this to pick up the piece of solder. Place on the joint.

3 Make sure that the joint is positioned facing outward, as far away as possible from the rest of the charm. You want to heat the ring, not the charm. Try to hold the tweezers as far away from the jump ring as possible. When soldering, the tweezers will attract the heat, dispersing its energy and making it difficult to solder.

4

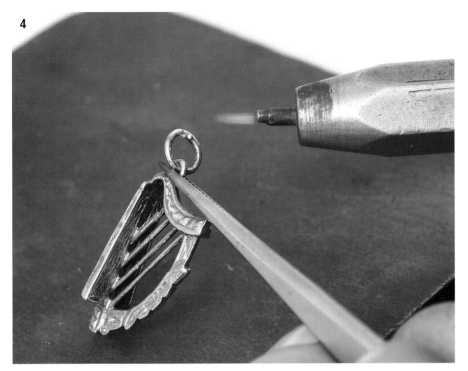

5 You will see that the jump ring has darkened. This is caused by the heat oxidizing the surface of the metal. The pickling solution will de-oxidize the metal and remove any residual flux at the same time. Allow the charm to cool, then drop it into the warm pickling solution using a pair of brass tweezers or a piece of brass or silver wire curved into a hook. Do not use steel tweezers; if they come into contact with the solution, the steel will react with the pickle and will copperplate any item placed in it. Leave the charm in the pickle for 15 seconds or more until you can see gold metal again and the flux has broken down.

6 Remove the charm from the pickle using brass tweezers. Rinse under a running faucet—make sure the sink hole is covered—then dry. Finally, polish with a jeweler's polishing cloth.

4 Put on a face mask and safety goggles. Turn on the solder flame and bring it to a low flame. Hold the flame about 1 in (2.5 cm) away from the joint. The aim is not to heat the solder, but the two sides of metal it is joining. Solder flows to the hottest part or parts, so you need to heat both sides of the joint evenly. Move the flame evenly from side to side so that the solder flows toward both ends of the jump ring. Note that the hottest part of the flame lies just beyond the blue part of the flame. The solder will start to melt and become liquid. This may take anything from 30 seconds to a minute. As soon as the solder starts to run, or flow, stop.

SOLDERING AND SAFETY

Before you start soldering, read through the following safety guidelines. Anything that involves working with a very hot flame is potentially hazardous, and you need to be dressed appropriately and properly prepared.

1 Make sure that the room you are working in is well ventilated and have a fire extinguisher close to hand.

2 Always read the manufacturer's instructions and safety precautions for the items you'll be using. This is especially important when it comes to the soldering torch. It needs to be assembled properly, and you need to understand how to turn on and turn off the gas (and/or oxygen) safely.

3 If you are working with oxygen and gas, keep the oxygen bottle away from any grease or oil—oxygen and oil combined together are combustible.

4 Wear a face mask while soldering. When flux (see page 155) is exposed to high heat, it smokes and this can irritate the airways. Always wear safety goggles. Wash your hands after you have finished soldering.

5 Make sure that your arms, legs, and body are covered, and wear shoes that cover the whole of your feet. If you have long hair, tie it back. Remove any bracelets or rings; do not wear dangly earrings, long necklaces, or scarves when soldering.

6 Practice using the soldering torch until you are confident that you can handle this piece of equipment safely.

Jeweler's bench pin see Tools, page 154

Two pairs of fine round-nosed pliers see Tools, page 54

Gold sheet solder see Tools, page 155

Side snips see Tools, page 54

Fine paint brush see Tools, page 155

Flux see Tools, page 155

Tweezers see Tools, page 54

Face mask and safety goggles see Tools, page 155

Hand torch and soldering block see Tools, page 155

Pickling solution see Tools, page 155

Brass tweezers see Tools, page 155

Protective gloves see Tools, page 55

Jeweler's polishing cloth see Tools, page 53

Soldering a worn jump ring

Although it is possible to buy replacement jump rings from a findings store, they will not necessarily match the other jump rings in your costume jewelry, here a silver charm bracelet. Depending on how worn the jump ring is, it is possible to reshape and solder the worn jump ring to give it a new lease of life. Please read the guidelines on pages 152, 155, and 167 before you start soldering. Before you begin, make sure you have everything to hand.

Sterling silver charm bracelet, 1970s

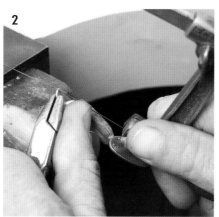

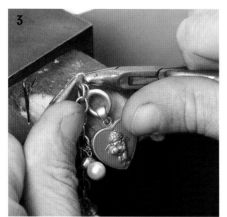

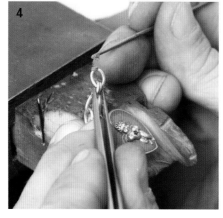

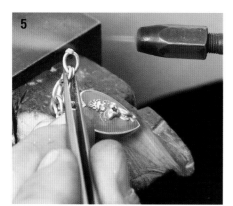

Jeweler's bench pin see Tools, page 153

Two round-nosed pliers see Tools, page 54

Jeweler's saw see Tools, page 153

Tweezers see Tools, page 54

Soldering equipment: face mask, safety goggles, hand torch, soldering block, easy prefluxed silver solder paste, pin, pickling solution, brass tweezers, protective gloves, see Tools, page 155

1 As the jump ring for repair is relatively large, the easiest way to repair it is to cut out the worn area, rejoin the ends, and solder them together.

2 Hold the jump ring upright with a pair of round-nosed pliers, the worn part of the ring facing upward. Use a jeweler's saw to carefully cut through the damaged section. You may find one cut through the jump ring is sufficient to remove the worn area. Sometimes, a second cut is required.

3 Use two round-nosed pliers to close the jump ring. Make sure that the two ends of the jump ring are flush with each other.

4 Squeeze out a tiny amount of easy prefluxed silver solder paste. Hold the jump ring with a pair of tweezers positioned as shown. The aim is to keep the area to be soldered as far away from the rest of the bracelet as possible. Use the end of a fine pin to place a small dab of solder onto the joint.

5 Put on a face mask and safety goggles. Solder the joint as before (see page 167). Work with a low flame, moving it from side to side so that you heat either side of the joint as evenly as possible. As soon as the solder starts to flow—this happens very quickly and suddenly—stop. Allow the bracelet to cool, then put the soldered area in the warm pickling solution using brass tweezers and hold it there for 5–10 seconds. Pearls and other absorbent gemstones should not be put in pickle.

6 Put on a pair of protective gloves. Remove the charm from the pickle using brass tweezers and rinse under a running faucet. Dry with a clean cloth.

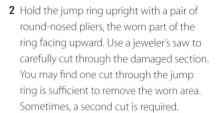

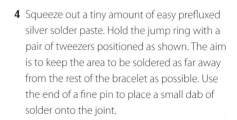

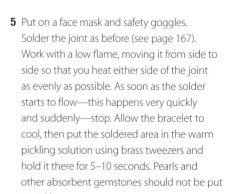

Repairing a broken chain

This is the final jump ring repair in this sequence. All necklace chain repairs are different because of their different styles and construction. On more decorative chains, such as this Georg Jensen silver chain, there's more at stake when soldering. This is a fine piece of jewelry that requires skillful soldering to restore it to its pristine form. Please read the guidelines on pages 152, 155, and 167 before you start soldering. Make sure that you have everything to hand before you begin.

Sterling silver Georg Jensen chain
with pendant, 1980s

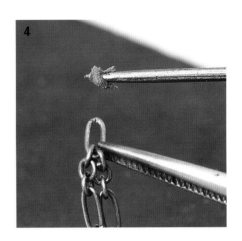

1 Even soldered links can come apart over time. Here, the solder has worked loose and the chain has come undone. With more elaborate chains, if a link is missing in a sequence, cut away the next link to it, or however many links are necessary in order to keep the pattern in the chain symmetrical.

2 Hold the open link with a pair of tweezers and use your other hand to slip the jump ring back in place on the chain.

3 As the chain is made of fine links, it is possible to rejoin the link by holding it with a pair of tweezers (or pliers if the chain is heavier) and pushing the link together with your finger or a fine-pointed tool, such as a scriber.

4 Squeeze out a tiny amount of prefluxed silver solder paste and apply it to the link. Easy solder is fine for this job. I find that working with ready-fluxed silver paste solder is very helpful. After a little practice, it's easy to work out how much solder you require, it stays in place, and doesn't fall off while you are working with it. Use a fine pin to place a small dab of solder over the joint.

5 Put on a face mask and safety goggles. Position your tweezers as far away from the area to be soldered as possible. Solder as before (see step 5 opposite). Work with a low flame, moving it from side to side so that you heat either side of the joint as evenly as possible. As soon as the solder starts to flow, stop.

6 Because the patina on this piece is part of its charm, it does not necessarily need to be put into pickle. Only pickle (see Steps 5 and 6 opposite) if the soldered area has a crust of hardened borax on it that cannot be removed manually. Simply give it a wipe with a jeweler's polishing cloth to bring back a soft gleam to the silver.

Jeweler's bench pin see Tools, page 153

Tweezers see Tools, page 54

Soldering equipment: face mask, safety goggles, hand torch, soldering block, prefluxed silver solder paste, pin see Tools, page 155

Optional: pickling solution, brass tweezers, protective gloves see Tools, page 155

Jeweler's polishing cloth see Tools, page 53

Retipping a claw

Claw, or prong, settings for stones are very common (see page 47). Although claws can vary in design, a well-made claw should be smooth with no sharp areas, sit flat on the crown of the stone, and retain more or less the same metal thickness throughout. Although any claw can break, less well-made claws (see Step 1) are much more prone to this problem. Please read the guidelines on pages 152, 155, and the safety guidelines on page 167 before you start soldering. Make sure that you have everything to hand before you begin.

Sterling silver ring with cubic zirconia, 1980s

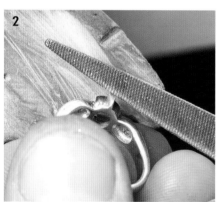

1 Wear and tear can result in the tip of any claw breaking off, but poor design and manufacture casting problems can also contribute to the problem. The area of the claw that folds to hold the stone in place is particularly vulnerable. If the bent part is significantly thinner in relation to the rest of the claw, this creates a fault line that is liable to catch and weaken. First, remove the stone (see box opposite). I have left the two small cubic zirconia in place as they can take the heat from soldering (see box opposite).

2 Hold the ring at an angle . Using a three-quarter file, file at a long, flat angle on the area of the claw to be retipped. This provides a clean, flat surface on which to solder the new claw tip.

3 Measure the diameter of the existing claw with a degree gauge. For retipping, you need a piece of replacement wire slightly larger than the size of the existing claw. For example, if the wire measures 1 mm, use a 1.1 mm wire. This allows you to file the new claw down to the correct thickness, matching the other claw or claws. Cut a length of replacement wire about 2 in (5 cm) long— this allows you to grip the wire with tweezers and hold it steady while soldering. File the end of the wire with a large three-square file to make an angled edge so that the claw will solder into the correct position.

4 Put on a face mask and safety goggles. Position the ring on the iron anvil or a soldering block—here, I have customized a pair of old spring tweezers by cutting the ends off so that they hold the back of the ring steady. Use a fine pin to place a small dab of easy prefluxed silver solder paste over the joint. Hold the replacement wire in position with a pair of tweezers. Solder the joint as before. Work with a low flame, moving it from side to side so that you heat the claw and the replacement wire. As soon as the solder starts to flow—this happens very quickly and suddenly—stop.

5

6

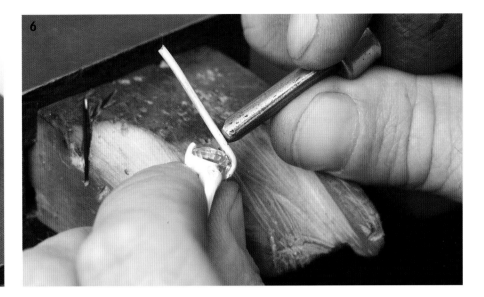

5 Leave the ring to cool down slowly. Never plunge a hot ring in cold water to cool it down quickly. Any stones will break or crack. As soon as the ring has cooled down, put it in the warm pickling solution using a pair of brass tweezers and leave it there for 5–10 seconds. Put on protective gloves, remove with brass tweezers, and rinse the ring under a running faucet.

6 Check that the claw has been soldered correctly before moving on to the next stage. If it has, put the stone into position in the ring. To reset the stone, you may need to file away some of the inside of the new claw using a round needle file to allow it to be pushed over the stone safely. Hold the ring in one hand and use a pushover setting tool to push the claw into position.

7

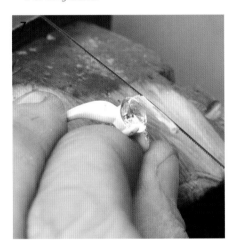

8

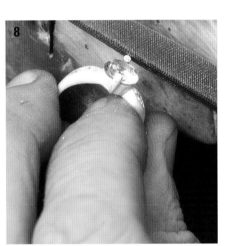

7 Holding the ring firmly, use a jeweler's saw to cut away the excess claw. Be very careful when sawing not to injure yourself.

8 Using a fine three-square needle file, file to round off the new claw, then polish the ring to finish the job.

SOLDERING AND STONES

It is always advisable to remove stones from a setting before soldering a repair. Heat can scorch or even crack a stone. Diamonds, sapphires, and rubies can take the heat from soldering, and should not be affected, but if you have a good-quality ruby or sapphire it is always advisable to remove the stone or stones if possible. If you leave a diamond, sapphire, or ruby in place, never plunge the hot ring in cold water, but let the ring cool down naturally. Most other stones—see precious stones (pages 108–109), semi-precious stones (pages 110–15), and rhinestones (pages 116–19)—will be harmed by the heat from soldering. To remove a stone from a claw setting with thin metal claws, see page 164. To remove a stone from a claw setting with thicker claws, as here, use a scriber (see Tools, page 54). Place the scriber against the claw, not the stone, and very gently push the claw away from the stone. Work slowly and gently around the ring until the stone is released.

Jeweler's bench pin see Tools, page 155

Three-square file see Tools, page 154

Degree gauge see Tools, page 152

Replacement wire for claw

Spring tweezers and tweezers see Tools, page 54

Pin see Tools, page 155

Soldering equipment: mask, safety goggles, silver solder with flux, hand torch, soldering block, pickling solution, brass tweezers, protective gloves see Tools, page 155

Round needle file see Tools, page 54

Pushover setting tool see Tools, page 152

Jeweler's saw see Tools, page 153

Fine three-square needle file see Tools, page 154

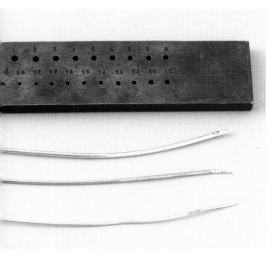

Customizing wires

Wire for jewelry-making is sold in standard sizes. A drawplate allows you to customize the size of a wire for a particular job—a wire is drawn through smaller and smaller holes in the drawplate until the required size is achieved. A drawplate is also handy if you have run out of a standard wire size but you have other sizes to hand on your bench—it is far quicker to make up the required wire size yourself than go down to the findings store for it or order it online.

Steel drawplate with graduated holes

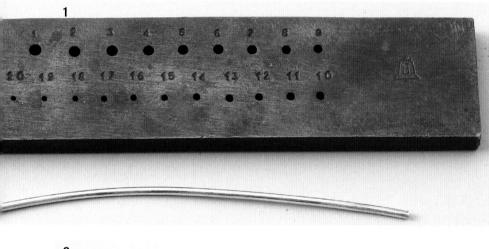

1 Start by filing one end of the wire to be reduced in size using a three-square file. Rub beeswax or a 3-in-1 oil over the wire.

2 Place the drawplate in a bench vise. Push the filed end of the wire through a hole the next size down to the wire. Pull it through using a pair of draw tongs. Depending on the size required, continue working through smaller and smaller holes.

3 After passing the wire through 2–4 holes, it will become hard. If at this point you need to reduce the size of the wire further, you will need to anneal (soften) it. To do this, lay the wire on a heat-resistant block and slowly warm it evenly along its length with the torch. When the wire reaches a cherry-red glow, turn off the torch and leave the wire to cool naturally—if you drop the wire into water to cool it quickly, it will harden again. Refile the end of the wire, and continue as before.

Wire

Three-square file see Tools, page 154

Beeswax or 3-in-1 oil

Drawplate see Tools, page 154

Bench vise see Tools, page 153

Draw tongs see Tools, page 154

Attaching a C-catch

Before the advent of the rollover catch, which was invented in around 1910, the C-catch was widely used to secure the fastener pin to the back of a brooch. It is often an indication that the pin is either antique (over 100 years old) or vintage (usually defined as less than 100 years old). C-catches can break away from old pins, but it is possible to solder a new C-catch in place. Please read the guidelines on pages 152, 155, and 167 before you start soldering.

Cut steel arrow pin, 18th century

1

2

4

1 To make the new catch, take a piece of 0.9 mm or 1 mm silver wire and use a pair of round-nosed pliers to turn one end into a simple curved shape as shown.

2 As this pin is made of steel, you can use silver paste solder, soft paste solder (which contains lead), or low-grade gold paste solder (all of which contain flux). Place a small amount of solder paste on the catch pin and on the base of the pin.

3 Put on a face mask and safety goggles. Turn on the torch and lightly warm the back of the pin where the C-catch will sit until the solder starts to run. Apply the catch and solder until it is fixed, then stop.

4 Allow the pin to cool. Cut off the excess wire at an angle with a jeweler's saw. Lightly file the sawed end with a fine three-square needle file to smooth away any sharp areas.

5 Using brass tweezers, place the pin in warm pickling solution for a few seconds. Put on protective gloves and remove the pin from the pickle. Rinse under a running faucet, then dry. (Discard the pickling solution. The steel brooch will have contaminated the pickle, and will copperplate any subsequent silver items.)

Jeweler's bench pin see Tools, page 153

Silver wire

Tools: Round-nosed pliers see page 54, jeweler's saw see page 153, fine three-square needle file see page 154

Soldering equipment: face mask, safety goggles, hand torch, soldering block, solder with flux, pin, pickling solution, brass tweezers, protective gloves see Tools, page 155

Advanced projects

The following projects—making a ring larger and making a ring smaller, and making a replacement snap—require a high level of skill. The last project in particular calls on accuracy and precision, As ever, be patient and take your time. Do not rush these jobs. Please read the safety guidelines on pages 152, 155, and 167 before soldering.

Making a ring larger

Jewelers can stretch a ring mechanically if the ring needs to be enlarged by only a small amount, usually half to one full size larger maximum. If the ring needs to go larger than this, it will need to have an extra piece of metal inserted into the ring.

White-gold ring with sapphires and diamonds, 1980s

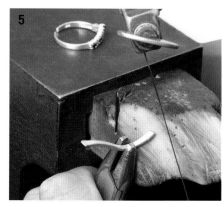

1 First of all establish the size the ring needs to be. Take a ring you can comfortably wear and measure it on a ring stick. The measurement is taken from the part of the ring that touches the ring stick. Alternatively, use a ring gauge to establish the size. Then measure the ring you want to make larger on the ring stick—here it is 5½ (the equivalent to a British K½). To prepare for Step 4, use a degree gauge to measure the width of the ring shank at the back. You will need a strip of metal—here white gold—that is slightly wider and thicker than the existing shank.

2 Check the back of the ring to see if you can locate where the ring was originally soldered together. This indicates the place where you should saw through the ring. If you cannot see a line, go to Step 3. Note: if there is a hallmark, cut to one side of it (see also Step 3, page 176).

3 Turn on the torch to a very low flame and gently warm the back of the ring. The previous joint will show up as a line. Cut the ring with a jeweler's saw as shown in Step 2, page 159. To restore the shape of the ring, place it on a triblet and push it up the taper until it reaches the correct size. Remove the ring, turn it around, and repeat to keep the ring shape even.

4 Place the end of the metal strip flush with one cut side of the ring, then move it from side to side. A mark or line will appear on the wire, indicating the place to cut it.

5 Cut the metal strip with a jeweler's saw and file it with a three-square file to make the wire a snug fit.

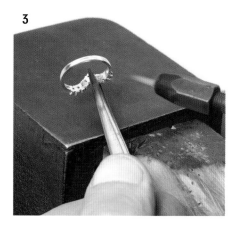

6

7

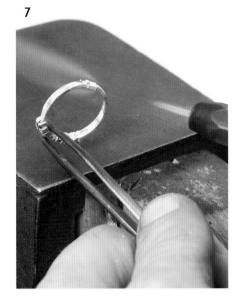

Move the position of the ring to work both sides of the wire

6 Hold the ring with a pair of tweezers at a point as far away from the site to be soldered as possible—this is particularly important if there are stones in the ring. Apply a small dab of easy prefluxed gold solder paste to the areas to be joined. Note: Because I work extremely quickly and accurately when soldering, I don't always remove stones from a ring. Here, for example, I have left in the diamonds and sapphires, which can stand up to the heat from soldering. However, for students I recommend, if at all possible, to remove all the stones before soldering.

7 Put on a face mask and a pair of safety goggles. Work with a low flame, moving it from side to side so that you heat the shank and the replacement strip of metal. Reposition the ring so you work both ends of the metal strip. As soon as the solder starts to flow—this happens very quickly and suddenly—stop.

8 Leave the ring to cool down slowly. Never plunge a hot ring into cold water to cool it down quickly. Any stones will break or crack. As soon as the ring has cooled down, put it in the warm pickling solution using a pair of brass tweezers and leave it there for 5–10 seconds. Wearing protective gloves, remove the ring from the pickle using brass tweezers. Rinse under a running faucet, then dry.

9 Using a half-round file, file away any excess metal from the inside of the ring. Be careful not to remove too much metal. Put the ring on a triblet and tap around it with a rawhide mallet to restore its shape. Then recheck the size on the ring stick. If the size is correct, use a large three-square file to file away the rest of the excess metal on the outside of the ring.

10 Buff the inside of the ring with a round emery stick. Use a flat emery stick to smooth the sides and top. Polish the ring to complete the job.

Ring stick or ring gauge see Tools, page 154

Degree gauge see Tools, page 152

Metal strip of white gold

Jeweler's bench pin see Tools, page 153

Jeweler's saw see Tools, page 153

Triblet see Tools, page 154

Three-square file see Tools, page 154

Tweezers see Tools, page 54

Soldering equipment: face mask, safety goggles, easy prefluxed gold solder paste, pin, hand torch, soldering block, pickling solution, brass tweezers, protective gloves see Tools, page 155

Half-round file see Tools, page 154

Rawhide mallet see Tools, page 153

Round and flat emery sticks see Tools, page 154

8

9

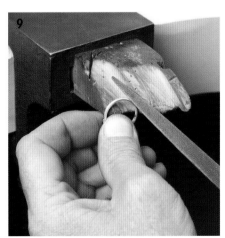

10

Making a ring smaller

To make a ring permanently smaller, you must remove part of the shank (the undecorated part of the band), reshape the ring, and solder it back together. If you want a temporary solution, use a ring guard. This is a narrow strip of metal with small metal tabs, or teeth, on all four corners. The guard is placed inside the ring and the tabs secured in place on the shank with a pair of pliers. Alternatively, a jeweler can solder sizing beads—small gold balls—to the inside of your ring. Please read the safety guidelines on pages 152, 155, and 167 before soldering.

Modern silver Baroque-style ring

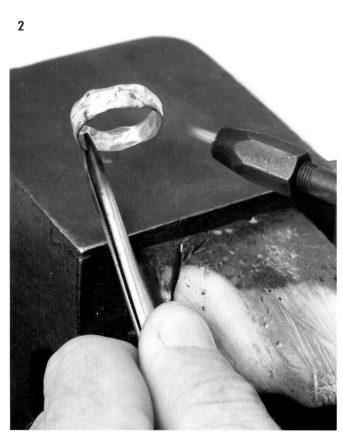

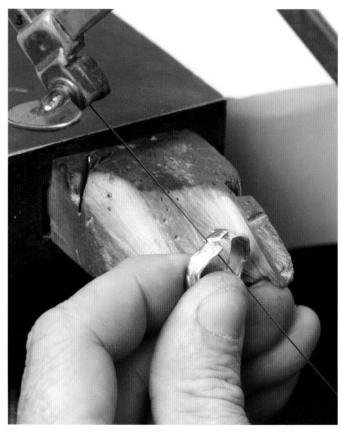

1 First of all establish the size the ring needs to be. Take a ring you can wear comfortably and measure it on a ring stick. The measurement is taken from the part of the ring that touches the ring stick. Alternatively, use a ring gauge to establish the size. Then take the ring you want to reduce in size and measure it on the ring stick to establish how much it needs to be reduced by. This ring is to be reduced by three sizes. Each finger size is approximately 1 mm, so here approximately 3 mm needs to be removed. For students, I would suggest

reducing the ring by slightly less than the desired size; you can always cut out more of the ring if necessary, reducing the risk of getting the size wrong.

2 Check the back of the ring to see if you can locate the joint where the ring was originally soldered together. This is the only place you should saw through the ring. If you cannot see a line, turn on the torch to a very low flame and gently warm the back of the ring. The previous joint will show up as a line.

3 Mark the ring with spring dividers to show where to make your two cuts. However, if there is a hallmark or maker's mark where you plan to cut, work to either side of it—removing a hallmark can decrease the value of a piece significantly. Carefully cut through the first mark you made with a jeweler's saw, then cut through the second to remove the excess amount of shank. These are minute measurements, so work slowly and carefully. Do not rush this job.

4

5

6

4 The ring has been cut through and is ready to resize. Using a pair of half-round pliers, pull each side of the shank together to close the gap. Check the finger size again on the ring stick. Make sure that the ring is as round a shape as possible.

5 Put on a face mask and safety goggles. Hold the ring with a pair of tweezers at a point as far away from the site to be soldered as possible—this is particularly important if there are stones in the ring. Apply a small dab of easy prefluxed silver solder paste to the areas to be joined. Work with a low flame, moving it from side to side so you are heating the shank, not the solder. As soon as the solder starts to flow—this happens very quickly and suddenly—stop.

6 Leave the ring to cool down slowly. Never plunge a hot ring into cold water to cool it down quickly. Any stones will break or crack.

As soon as the ring has cooled down, put it in the warm pickling solution using a pair of brass tweezers and leave it there for 5–10 seconds. Wearing protective gloves, remove the ring from the pickle using brass tweezers. Rinse under a running faucet, then dry.

7 Remove any excess solder on the inside of the ring using a half-round file on the inside of the ring. Use a fine three-square file on the outside of the ring to remove any excess solder along the edges of the shank.

8 Place the ring on a steel triblet, then gently tap the soldered area with a rawhide mallet.

9 Using a flat emery stick, buff off any remaining solder on the outside of the ring. Buff the inside of the ring using a round emery stick. Finally, polish the ring to complete the job.

Ring stick and gauge see Tools, page 154

Jeweler's bench pin see Tools, page 153

Spring dividers, page 153

Jeweler's saw see Tools, page 153

Half-round pliers see Tools, page 54

Tweezers see Tools, page 54

Soldering equipment: face mask, safety goggles, easy prefluxed silver solder paste, pin, hand torch, soldering block, pickling solution, brass tweezers, protective gloves see Tools, page 155

Half-round file see Tools, page 154

Fine three-square file see Tools, page 154

Triblet see Tools, page 154

Rawhide mallet see Tools, page 153

Flat and round emery sticks, page 154

Polishing cloth see Tools, page 53

7

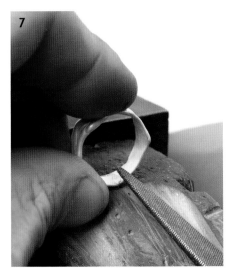

8

9

Making a replacement snap

Certain styles of jewelry have an integral clasp and it is not possible to replace them with a new one if part of the clasp breaks. Here, the snap on a box clasp (see page 74) has broken off. The housing is integrated into the bracelet, so it is not possible to replace the entire clasp. Before undertaking this repair, it would be advisable to look at some old box clasps and examine them carefully in order to understand their construction.

Silver-tone bracelet with rhinestones, 1960s

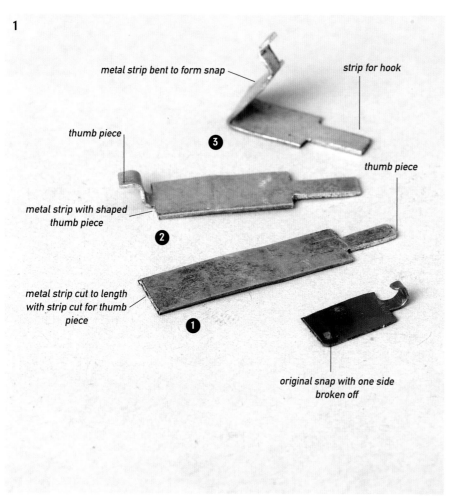

1

metal strip bent to form snap

strip for hook

thumb piece

③

thumb piece

metal strip with shaped thumb piece

②

metal strip cut to length with strip cut for thumb piece

①

original snap with one side broken off

1 The aim of this project is to make from one sheet of silver a double-sided snap that inserts into the housing on the bracelet, with a thumb piece, or trigger, on top and a hooked catch to attach the snap to the bracelet. Shown here are three of the stages in the process: (1) shows the metal cut to length with a strip for the thumb piece cut out; (2) shows the metal with the thumb piece formed, and (3) shows the snap doubled over. The hook that will attach the snap to the bracelet still needs to be formed.

2

2   Measure the width of the original snap, then measure its length and double this measurement (the snap is folded over in order to create a spring action when inserted in the housing). Add extra for the thumb piece, or trigger, and the hook that attaches the snap to the bracelet. This gives the total length of metal to be cut. Mark these measurements on the metal strip with spring dividers but don't cut it to length yet. It is much easier to cut out the thumb piece on a longer strip of metal, and then cut it down (see Step 9). If you don't have the original snap, measure the housing and make the snap very fractionally smaller than the housing.

3   To make the thumb piece, mark two parallel lines on the metal as shown; these two outer strips will be cut away to leave a length of metal for the thumb piece.

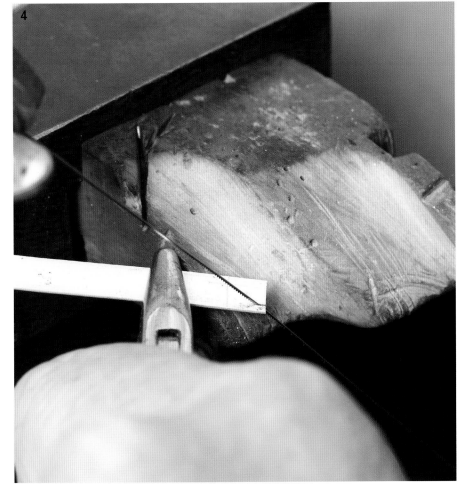

4   Hold the metal strip with half-round pliers. Using a jeweler's saw, carefully cut down the two lines to form the outline of the thumb piece. It is important that these two lines are parallel, so take your time when cutting away the two strips.

Jeweler's bench pin see Tools, page 153

Ruler

Strip of sheet silver

Spring dividers see Tools, page 153

Jeweler's saw see Tools, page 153

Half-round pliers see Tools, page 54

Needle-nosed pliers see Tools, page 54

Fine duckbill pliers see Tools, page 54

Round-nosed pliers see Tools, page 54

Fine three-square needle file see Tools, page 154

5 Carefully cut away the excess strips. The thumb piece is now revealed.

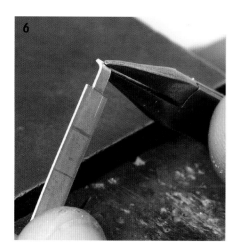

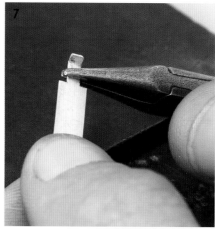

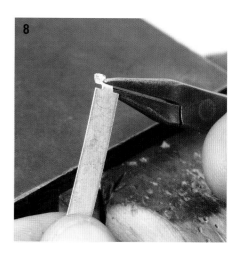

6 Using a pair of needle-nosed pliers, start to form the thumb piece by slowly bending the tip of the strip at a right angle.

7 Turn the metal over and place the pliers 1 mm in from the base of the thumb piece. For the catch to work, it needs to fit within the existing box with a gap of approximately 1 mm from the end.

8 Bend the thumb piece to a second right angle. The thumb piece is fully formed.

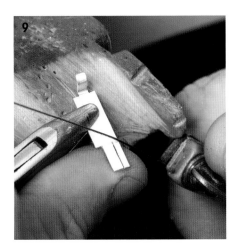

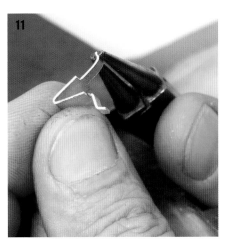

9 Cut the metal strip to length (see Step 2). Before you start sawing, double check your measurements. Using spring dividers, mark the length and width of the hook. Cut the excess metal away as before (see Steps 4 and 5).

10 The sides of the snap should not be equal. The side that holds the hook should be 1 mm longer. Mark this, then use a pair of fine duckbill pliers to slowly and carefully bend the tongue into shape.

11 Using a pair of round-nosed pliers, turn the strip cut for the hook into a tube shape. As you work, stop every so often and check that the hook will fit onto the bracelet.

12 Check that the snap fits into the housing and make any slight adjustments if necessary by lightly filing with a fine three-square needle file. Place the hook on the bracelet and secure it by tightening the tube with a pair of needle-nosed pliers. The job is complete.

Whether you would like to start collecting vintage costume jewelry or you want to get started on repairs, details of selected outlets for tools, findings, and stringing materials are listed here. These include outlets sourced from the internet that offer a specialist service, such as selling vintage beads and findings. When it comes to buying tools, I recommend you visit the store if you can. Knowledgeable staff can advise you if you have any queries. If you get the chance to visit a findings store, seize it. These Aladdin's caves of clasps and fastenings, threads, and beads are a source of discovery and inspiration.

Resources

Resources

JEWELRY TOOL AND FINDINGS SUPPLIERS

Note: The website www.guidetobeadwork.com provides exhaustive listings for bead stores in every state; most bead stores also stock findings and tools for stringing.

Online stores

Abeadstore.com
www.abeadstore.com
Email: info@beadedimpressions.com
Tel: 1–800–532–8480 or 1–303–442–1933
An online store that stocks a wide range of findings. They also stock beads and beading and jewelry-making supplies. Also offers beading project ideas and tutorials.

Bead-O-Matic
229 Crawford Street
Toronto, ON M6J 2V5
Canada
www.bead-o-matic.com
Tel: 416–910–7244
Online store selling findings and jewelry cord; also offers a wide selection of beads

B'sue Boutiques
www.bsueboutiques.com
Online store selling findings, beads, and rhinestones, and a range of jewelry tools.

Esslinger and Company
www.esslinger.com
Tel: 651–452–7180
Online store selling a wide range of jewelry tools, as well as gemstones, beads, and findings.

Fire Mountain Gems and Beads
www.firemountaingems.com
Email: Questions@firemtn.com
Tel: Customer Service 1–800–423–2319
Online store with a wide range of findings, tools for stringing, as well as beads. Also offers a jewelry-maker's library.

Jan's Jewelry Supplies
C K Marketing Inc.
3629 NW 10th Street
Oklahoma City, OK 73107
www.jansjewels.com
Email: jan@jansjewels.com
Tel: 405–600–3043
Online store that offers a wide range of

jewelry-making supplies including findings; tools, including soldering equipment; new and vintage beads and rhinestones. The warehouse is open to the public on certain days; check website for details.

National Jewelry Suppliers
www.nationaljewelerssupplies.com
Email: store@nationaljewelerssupplies.com
Tel: 888–657–8665
Offers a wide range of jewelers' tools, equipment, and supplies.

Rio Grande Jewelry Supplies
www.riogrande.com
Tel: 1–800–545–6566
Online store that stocks a wide range of jewelry-making tools, including tools for soldering, findings, beads, and stringing supplies. Also offers a learning center with instructions on a wide range of jewelry-making skills.

New York

Metalliferous
34 West 46th Street
New York
NY 10036
metalliferous.com
Email: info@metalliferous.com
Tel: 212–944–0909
Stocks tools, including soldering equipment, findings, beads, vintage pieces, and stringing materials. There is also an online store.

Myron Toback Inc
25 West 47th Street
New York
NY 10036
myrontoback.com
Email: info@myrontoback.com
Tel: 212–398–8300/800–223–755
Stocks tools, including soldering equipment, findings, beads, and stringing materials.

Elvee/Rosenberg Inc.
11 West 37 Street
New York
NY 10018-6235
www.elveerosenberg.com
Email: info@elveerosenberg.com
Tel: 212–575–0767
Stocks beads, including vintage beads, and tools for stringing beads.

Denver

The Naja Inc.
6810 N Broadway Unit J
Denver, CO 80221
www.najatools.com
Email: naja@najatools.com
Tel: 303–426–6284/888–340–6252
Stocks jewelers' equipment, tools, and supplies. There is also an online store. Next door to the store is the Denver School of Metal Arts on metalsmithing with classes, short workshops, and intensives.

Los Angeles

A & A Jewelry Supply
319 West 6th Street, Los Angeles, CA 90014
aajewelry.com
Tel: 213–627–8004/1–888–888–8770
Stock includes jewelry tools and equipment, findings, and jewelry boxes. There is also an online store. The website also offers a list of jewelry-making courses across the nation.

Bella Findings House
607 S. Hill St. Arcade #6
Los Angeles CA, 90014
www.designatbella.com
Email: bellausa@yahoo.com
Tel: 213–629–4840
and
427 W. 7th Street
Los Angeles, CA 90014
www.bellafindings.com
Tel: 213–489–4252
Offers a wide range of beads, findings, as well as tools and equipment for stringing.

Chicago

Let's Get Stranded
3604 W Irving Park Road
Chicago, IL 60618
letsgetstranded.com
Email: info@letsgetstranded.com
Tel: 312–588–4044
Stocks stringing tools and equipment, plus a wide range of beads. Check website for opening times.

Houston

Sunnylook Design
2727 Fondren Road
Houston, TX 7703
www.sunnylookdesign.com
Email: sunnylook2@yahoo.com
Tel: 903–729–449
Stocks an interesting range of findings, also new and vintage beads.

Jemco Jeweler's Supply
9000 S.W. Freeway, Suite #300
Houston, TX 77074
www.jemcousa.com
Tel: 713–541–4242
Email: jemco@jemcousa.com
One-stop jewelry supply store. There is also an
online store.

Philadelphia
Pamma Tools
809 Sansom Street
Philadelphia PA 19107
www.pammatools.com
Email: sales@pammatools.com
Tel: 215–928–6004
Sells jewelry tools and equipment.

VINTAGE FINDINGS AND BEADS
A Grain of Sand
www.agrainofsand.com
Email: Suzanne@agrainofsand.com
Tel: 704–660–3125
Online store offering new and vintage findings,
also beads and gemstones; also offers tools and
equipment for stringing.

The Beadin' Path
5 Main Street, Freeport, ME 04032
www.beadinpath.com
Tel: 207–865–4785
Shop and online store selling new and vintage
beads, also vintage findings, and tools and
equipment for stringing. The shop offers
beading classes.

Costume Jewelry Supplies
www.costumejewelrysupplies.com
Email: costumejewelrysupplies.com@hughes.net
Tel: 434–836–0099
Online store offering jewelry-making supplies,
including new and vintage beads, rhinestones,
gemstones, and new and vintage findings. Also
stocks a selection of tools.

Earthly Adornments
www.earthlyadornments.com
sales@earthlyadornments.com
Tel: 707–823–8978
Online store which stocks vintage and antique
jewelry and beads; also stocks vintage findings.

I Found Gallery
4578 Main Street, Vancouver BC
ifoundgallery.com
Email: ifoundgallery@gmail.com
Tel: 604–876–2218
Extensive collection of authentic vintage
findings in Canada. There is also an online store.

Jewelex Collection Inc NY USA
www.jewelex.com
Tel: 516–771–9473
Online store offering vintage beads and
findings, including vintage clasps.

M K Beads
422 SW 2nd Terrace Ste 210
Cape Coral, FL 33991
www.mkbeads.com
Email: sales@mkbeads.com
Tel: 1–239–634–2232
Shop and online store selling vintage and
contemporary beads and stones, and findings.

Pudgy Beads
www.pudgybeads.com
Email: pudgybeads@pudgybeads.com
Online store for vintage Czech, West German, and
Japanese glass beads. They also sell vintage clasps,

Splendor in the Glass
www.splendorintheglass.net
Email: ellen@splendorintheglass.net
Tel: 407–333–9780
Online store offering vintage and antique beads,
stones, and pendants.

Vintage Beads Laramie Studios
www.vintagebeadslaramiestudios.com
Email: elspeth@laramiestudios.com
Online store that stocks vintage beads, chains,
findings, and more.

USEFUL WEBSITES
The Ganoskin project
www.ganoskin.com
An invaluable resource, including in-depth
articles on jewelry manufacturing methods and
techniques by industry experts.

Collecting Costume Jewelry
www.collectingcj.com
Covers a wide range of jewelry designers and
manufacturers, with close-ups photographs of
designers' and manufacturers' marks.

Collectors Weekly
www.collectorsweekly.com/
A resource for people who love antique and
vintage stuff, including in-depth articles and
information on prices.

FURTHER READING ON COSTUME JEWELRY
Shields, Jody, with photographs by Max Vadukul
and others, *All That Glitters*; Rizzoli International
Publications, Inc., New York, 1987
Miller, Judith, *Costume Jewelry*; Dorling
Kindersley, New York, 2003
Mascetti, Daniela and Triossi, Amanda, *Earrings
from Antiquity to the Present*; Thames & Hudson
Ltd, London, 1990
Mascetti, Daniela and Triossi, Amanda, *The
Necklace from Antiquity to the Present*; Thames &
Hudson Ltd, London, 1997
Carroll, Julia C., *Collecting Costume Jewelry 101:
The Basics of Starting, Building and Upgrading,
2nd edition*; Collector Books, A Division of
Schroeder Publishing Co., Inc.
Bell, G.G., C. Jeanenne, *Answers to Questions
about Old Jewelry 1840-1950: Identification and
Value Guide, 7th edition*; Krause Publications, Iola

VINTAGE JEWELRY AND ENDANGERED SPECIES
As the laws on the domestic sale as well as
import and export of antique and vintage
jewelry made from endangered and at-risk
species changes from time to time, check with
the US Fish and Wildlife Service for current
guidelines: www.fws.gov. For information on
the United States Endangered Species Act (ESA)
go to: www.fws.gov/laws/lawsdigest/esact.html.
and follow the link to a pdf of the Act.

Index

Acknowledgments

AUTHOR'S ACKNOWLEDGMENTS

The author would like to thank the following for their contributions to this book: A. L. Mortimore, P. & B. Harrison, Keith Gordon, Sharon Green, Owen Weston, Caroline Maguire, Stuart Farnham, Jason Stevenson, Circa 1900, Dreamtime, Dorit Schnieber. Special thanks to Lynette of Dreamtime for all her help and the use of large amounts of her stock for the making of this book. A special thanks to Jennifer Latham for all the work and effort that she put into making this book. She was a pleasure to work with. Finally, to my wife, Claudia, for all her help and support.

OTHER ACKNOWLEDGMENTS

Fil Rouge Press would like to thank Paul Bricknell for the photography; David Jones for the design; Ann Kramer and Marcus Weeks for additional material; Diana Vowles for proofreading; jeweler Mandana Oskoui for modeling—visit mandanaoskoui.com; Circa 1900 for the loan of several pieces of jewelry for photography—visit www.circa1900.org; H. S. Walsh & Sons Ltd for the loan of tools and equipment featured on pages 52–55 and 152–5—visit www.hswalsh.com.

Special thanks to Lynette Gray of Dreamtime, 13 Pierrepont Row, Camden Passage, Islington, London N1, Tel: 07804 261 082, for generously lending many of the pieces photographed in this book, and for her expert advice.

ABOUT THE AUTHOR

David McLoughlin grew up in London. After leaving school in 1977, he became an apprentice diamond mounter with P. & B. Harrison Ltd for five years. He stayed with the company for a further seven years, learning not only basic jewelry repairs and alterations, but also working on commissions and designs. It was here that he learnt and came to appreciate the beauty of fine antique jewelry. He was taught how to make stunning Georgian and Victorian reproduction pieces, including settings, designs, and the original methods used to obtain special finished work. Many thanks to A. L. Mortimer for his patience, and the skills and tricks that David stills uses today. After a stint working in mass-production jewelry, a new side of the industry, he decided to go freelance. David has run two small shops in Camden Passage, Islington, London, and he is currently working very happily in a shared workshop at Craft Central in Clerkenwell, London, both designing and repairing jewelry. To find out more visit his website at www.davidmcloughlinjewellery.com

Opposite: Gold-tone earrings and pin set with rhinestones and mink, 1950s

Tree Craft
*35 Rustic Wood Projects
That Bring the Outdoors In*
By Chris Lubkemann

Beautify your home with rustic accents made from twigs and branches. More than 35 eco-chic projects for a coat rack, curtain rods, candle holders, desk sets, picture frames, a table, chess set, and more.

ISBN: 978-1-56523-455-0
$19.95 · 128 Pages

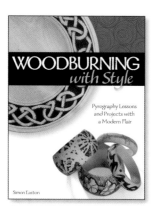

Woodburning with Style
*Pyrography Lessons and
Projects with a Modern Flair*
By Simon Easton

This beautifully photographed, hands-on instructional guide to the art of pyrography will take you on a journey of skill-building exercises that begin at the basics and finish with stylish, gift-worthy projects.

ISBN: 978-1-56523-443-7
$24.95 · 208 Pages

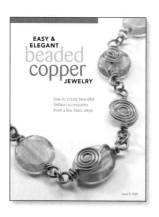

Easy & Elegant Beaded Copper Jewelry
*How to Create Beautiful Fashion
Accessories from
a Few Basic Steps*
By Lora S. Irish

Make your own affordable and stylish copper jewelry with a few simple tools, some wire, and beads.

ISBN: 978-1-56523-514-4
$24.95 · 256 Pages

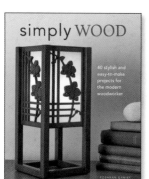

Simply Wood
*40 Stylish and Easy-to-Make
Projects for the Modern
Woodworker*
By Roshaan Ganief

Breathe new life into your scroll saw projects with unique, modern designs that will add beauty and flair to your home decor.

ISBN: 978-1-56523-440-6
$19.95 · 200 Pages

Illustrated Guide to Sewing Home Furnishings
*Expert Techniques for Creating
Custom Shades, Drapes,
Slipcovers, and More*
By the Editors at Skills Institute Press

With the expert sewing techniques shared in this book, anyone can create home-made soft furnishings with a designer's flair.

ISBN: 978-1-56523-510-6
$19.95 · 144 Pages

Learn the classic techniques that have been employed by seamstresses and designers for years. This series covers everything you need to know about choosing fabric, taking measurements, altering patterns, fitting, design, and more.

Illustrated Guide to Sewing: Couture Techniques
The Home Sewing Guide to Creating Designer Looks
By the Editors at Skills Institute Press

ISBN: 978-1-56523-534-2
$24.95 · 200 Pages

Illustrated Guide to Sewing: Tailoring
A Complete Course on Making a Professional Suit
By the Editors at Skills Institute Press

ISBN: 978-1-56523-511-3
$24.95 · 288 Pages

Illustrated Guide to Sewing: Garment Construction
A Complete Course on Making Clothing for Fit and Fashion
By the Editors at Skills Institute Press

ISBN: 978-1-56523-509-0
$19.95 · 176 Pages